Post-Conviction Relief: Second Last Chance

Kelly Patrick Riggs

FREEBIRD
PUBLISHERS

Freebird Publishers
www.FreebirdPublishers.com

Freebird Publishers

Box 541, North Dighton, MA 02764
Info@FreebirdPublishers.com
www.FreebirdPublishers.com

Copyright © 2020
Post-Conviction Relief: Second Last Chance
By Kelly Patrick Riggs

All Freebird Publishers titles, imprints and distributed lines are available at special quantity discounts for bulk purchases for sales promotions, premiums, fundraising educational or institutional use.

ISBN-13: 978-1-952159-21-3

Printed in the United States of America

FRIENDS FROM WITHIN

With a nickname like Mad Dog, you can imagine how hard it is to make friends. My facial expression is the kind only a mother could love.

Kelly (I thought that was his last name; Most only give their last name when asked; it's a Jailhouse thing) was no different from the rest.

I met Kelly in a 14-man dayroom when he became my bunkie. Like all of the guys in the dayroom, Kelly also tip-toed around me and gave me a lot of space – until he spilled his coffee on my bed. Kelly didn't really know me, and my nickname being Mad Dog, he automatically thought life as he knew it was over. Kelly nervously apologized and waited for what he thought he knew was going to happen.

I know an accident when I see one, and I understand that things happen. I asked Kelly to help me clean it up, and he also helped me change my sheets (I always keep extra stuff). In all eyes (seemed like the whole room was holding their breath), the crisis was over.

We began talking more and I found out that Kelly is OCD. He started calling me a hoarder (who doesn't have extra stuff?) because I had 6 pair of shoes and Kelly made it his business to make sure the shoes were straight under the bed (*now* that's OCD).

Kelly asked about my case (I've been locked up 25+ years and asking about anyone's case – you never do) and for some reason I felt compelled to respond to his request. Kelly looked at my case and said he could – and wanted to – help me.

I was surprised (suspicious), and I waited for the other shoe to drop, but it never happened.

Kelly never asked me for a dime or a penny to help me with my case. I don't have very much money, except what I make in UNICOR. Kelly could've had every penny for what he's done for me.

Kelly Patrick Riggs (yeah, I know your whole name) is the real deal when it comes to friendship. I'm very glad I met him and proud to call him a friend. My name is Michael DeAngelo Davis, you can call me Mad Dog – everyone else does.

Always,

Michael (Mad Dog) Davis

FOREWORD

My name is Donovan Mercer. I'm pleased that I was invited to write the foreword for this new book, written by Kelly Patrick Riggs.

My first experience with the American Criminal Justice System began with my federal indictment. As you can imagine, my being actually innocent and knowing nothing about the law brought me a great deal of confusion. I was in total disbelief when I discovered that a law-abiding American citizen with an air-tight alibi defense could be prosecuted. But my horrors were confirmed when I was indicted, tried, convicted, and on my way to serve a prison sentence of 265 months (over 20 years). I suffer all this for a crime that occurred while I was miles away, at work as an employee for the State of Oklahoma.

While I was on my way to federal prison, the deputy U.S. Marshal who drove the bus asked us (the prisoners on the bus) if we knew the difference between us and him. He answered his own question, "ya'll got caught."

One would think that the judicial system would operate on the principles of truth and justice. That concept, however, is undermined when investigators and prosecutors conspire to lie and deceive the courts to obtain convictions. This condition ensures that we fail to find justice no matter what we do in a criminal case. Out of fear, most people in federal custody would rather roll over and play dead than fight the federal government to stop these injustices. Even as I was going through my direct appeal, I was confused and had no clue what was really going on or what they were doing to my life behind the scenes.

I was sent to the Federal Correctional Institution in Seagoville, Texas after my direct appeal. Within the first few days after my arrival, I made a few friends. While talking to one of my new friends about my case, he opened his locker and handed me a book written by Mr. Riggs himself. That book was my first meaningful exposure to the federal procedures and how courts conduct the procedures in real life. With that first book, I learned about a law called 28 U.S.C. §2255, along with the basics of how to prepare and file a personalized §2255 motion of my own. I learned that to obtain relief under §2255, defendants must show that they were denied a constitutional right during their trial process. I learned that they must also show why they did not raise the claim in their direct appeal and that the denial of the right had to have an effect that was detrimental to them in some way. This is what is called the "cause and prejudice" test.

I followed Mr. Riggs's instruction and prepared my own §2255 motion, which I filed in the U.S. District Court. To my surprise, and just as Mr. Riggs predicted, the district court declined review of my §2255 motion, claiming that "because the issues raised were not raised on direct appeal they [the claims] were procedurally barred from review."

Ultimately, it took not one but two petitions to the Tenth Circuit Court of Appeals to finally be granted a Certificate of Appealability.

Even after I was granted a C.O.A., and the district court ordered to resolve some obvious issues with the evidence, I was not surprised to be denied by the district court based on a great deal of additional false testimony.

Of course, I filed my third notice of appeal. Based on my own appeal brief, the Tenth Circuit Court of Appeals appointed counsel to represent me in my latest appellate case.

By this time, I had little to no confidence in the reliability of the Federal Criminal Justice System. Because of my lost faith in justice, I tried to figure out my next step. During all this, and by great happenstance, Mr. Riggs showed up where I was, on the yard at the Federal Correctional Institution in Seagoville, Texas.

I met Mr. Riggs, and our shared zeal for the law drew us together into a quick friendship. I shared with him my desire to try to stay in the fight, but he quickly advised me to wait before filing anything in the courts. After Mr. Riggs reviewed my whole case file, he explained that the system was finally beginning to work correctly.

A couple of weeks later, I learned that Mr. Riggs was finally prevailing in his own situation and was soon to be released. I then asked him what my next step would be if I were to lose once again. He quickly told me to start studying the rules and decisions that governed relief from judgment under Federal Rules of Civil Procedure, Rule 60(b). Once I finished writing my own 60(b) motion, I asked Mr. Riggs to review it before I sent it off. After all the term "path of least resistance" means when we mistakenly use the wrong Rule or wording that the court can twist out of context and deny the motion as an unauthorized second or successive §2255.

Mr. Riggs agreed to read my motion and give his input. He explained that he was writing a book on the subject and it would give him some good practice. I was grateful for his help, but a few days later Mr. Riggs caught me on the yard and said, "You have a good claim, but your wording turns your motion into a second successive §2255." He went on to say, "Let me fix this for you and use your 60(b) motion as an example in my new book." I can't explain with words how far beyond grateful I was.

The best defense you can have is to educate yourself. Mr. Riggs has a whole series of books to help the layman navigate the courts to obtain justice. Mr. Riggs really does care about truth and justice and he expresses this in his writing. His books are not only beneficial to the layman but educational also – I promise you won't be disappointed.

Don't ever stop fighting for your rights!

– Donavan Mercer

SCOPE AND PURPOSE

This book is written with the freedom of its readers in mind. As most are aware, there is a misguided myth going around claiming that the Post-Conviction Relief Process ends with the denial of a §2255 motion. This myth is simply untrue.

What is unknown to a large number of prisoners, and most legal professionals, is that there exists a number of additional forms of relief that are available. Also, diligent readers will learn that recent changes in law have provided more avenues for relief in the 21st century than ever before. These facts combined lead to a plethora of options that are open to prisoners who intend to seek relief in a federal court.

This book is the sixth in the *Post-Conviction Relief* series and it is dedicated to informing its readers about the forms of relief that are available after the §2255 process has concluded.

TABLE OF CONTENTS

INTRODUCTION

The process of post-conviction relief is much like any other battle. You have, at a minimum, two opposing parties and a field on which to fight. In the criminal justice system this battle is identified by an American citizen who seeks justice, a federal judge who seeks to maintain the finality of the conviction (of a modern-day slave), and the processes of federal law that represents the battlefield. The disturbing part is that the American citizen is out-numbered and out-matched. He is most often untrained in law, fighting against the judge, the prosecutor, and his own criminal defense lawyer who are now, as they always have been working together to perpetuate mass-incarceration.

When I first heard someone say words much like these, I was shocked. I couldn't believe that the government, which I supported for so many years, would use our criminal justice system to funnel tax dollars into privately held companies, and at the expense of someone's liberty. It wasn't until I witnessed blind men convicted of seeing and fishermen sentenced to prison for throwing the small ones back into the ocean, that I opened my eyes. It's only now, as I watch a federal judge try to conceal her own culpability in the murders of DeAndre Washington and Gary (Sambo) Hazelrigg, that I realize how broken our criminal justice system really is.

The foregoing makes it important to share more of the federal procedure with the prisoners of war who seek justice in America.

CHAPTER ONE

REVIEW OF PROCEDURES RELATING TO §2255

Since you are reading this book, I can safely assume that you or someone you know has failed to obtain relief in all proceedings, up to and including the initial §2255 or other first-tier collateral proceedings. Although your options to seek relief have diminished in number, and as a result have become more difficult, that is not to say that relief is impossible to obtain. You are not the first prisoner to fail nor are you at the end of the road. I can assure you that thousands of prisoners have pursued post-conviction relief and failed before you did. Although many motions are rightfully denied, there are an equal or greater number of meaningful and valid claims that are denied based simply on technicalities. This book is all about what you can do about it now. In the chapters that follow, you will learn about a number of alternative proceedings, but first a review of the purpose of 28 U.S.C. §2255.

At its enactment, Congress intended, and the Supreme Court has upheld that §2255 restates, clarifies, and simplifies the procedure in the nature of common law writ of error *Coram Nobis*. *Coram Nobis*, which is codified as an extraordinary writ under 28 U.S.C. §1651, authorized relief to a petitioner, from his or her judgment by the U.S. District Court of conviction, if the petitioner fails to present, at trial, certain evidence that might have aided the petitioner's defense. This does not mean that §2255 has superseded *Coram Nobis*. The difference between the two forms of relief is found in the jurisdictional provision of §2255, "in custody under sentence of a court established by act of Congress ..." 28 U.S.C. §2255(a) (see Appendix). This simply means that if you are in the custody of the Federal Bureau of Prisons and not as a result of a military conviction, then you should file under §2255. If, however, you are not in BOP custody and you are challenging a federal conviction, then you file for relief under *Coram Nobis* §1651.

A good example of this is the Supreme Court decision in *United States v. Morgan*, 346 U.S. 502, 198 L. Ed. 248, 74 S.Ct. 247 (1954). In this case Morgan served a four-year federal sentence. Upon his release from federal custody, he was incarcerated under a state sentence that was made longer because of the prior federal conviction. Morgan then filed an application for a writ of error *Coram Nobis* claiming that he had been denied counsel at his federal trial. The Federal District Court re-characterized Morgan's filing into a motion under §2255 and denied relief. The United States Court of Appeals reversed the District Court's denial and the Supreme Court affirmed the Court of Appeals judgment. The Supreme Court said that §2255 did not cover the entire field of remedies in the nature of *Coram Nobis* in the federal courts.

Congress intended for §2255 to provide an expeditious remedy for correcting erroneous sentences without resorting to invoking the court's authority under a writ of habeas corpus. But the Supreme Court also said, in *United States v. Addonizio*, 442 U.S. 178, 60 L Ed. 2d 805, 99 S.Ct. 2255, that §2255 provides a remedy for federal prisoners within the jurisdiction of the sentencing court that is equally as broad as the remedy provided by a habeas corpus petition filed in the district of confinement. While the remedy under §2255 is in this sense comprehensive, it does not encompass all possible errors in conviction and sentencing. This is true because the scope of an attack under §2255 remains far more limited than the scope of habeas corpus when considering claims that do not raise issues such as a lack of jurisdiction or of constitutional error.

Ordinarily with the §2255 process behind you, you would have no other opportunity to seek relief from your conviction or sentence. But there are some limited circumstances where a prisoner has additional opportunities to seek relief. Keep in mind that in these certain circumstances the standard of review and the level of proof required are different than in the initial §2255 proceeding and are a bit more difficult to achieve. The reason that these processes are more difficult is because of the way prisoners think. Nine out of ten prisoners will forever remember what happened during their trial process and as a result continue to try to seek vindication from those errors. What you must consider above all things is that every step of post-conviction relief has its own burden of proof and its own standard of review. So please disconnect yourself from all other standards and pay attention only to the specific standards set out for each form of relief. Now then let's move forward and discover which of these provisions may provide you with your Second Last Chance.

CHAPTER TWO

MOTION WRITING

I know that I am in great danger of appearing repetitive in writing this chapter, especially to those of you who have followed my writing throughout the *Post-Conviction Relief Series*, but I include motion writing in this book for two reasons: 1) for some of you, this may well be the first book of this series that you have encountered; and 2) your motion writing will be judged a bit more strictly now that you are seeking relief after your first §2255 proceeding.

I believe that the tips in this chapter are essential for submitting effective motions in any court, but also know that there are many more good ideas out there that are not in this book. So, pay attention and use good reasoning if you decide to stray from these essential tips for effective motion writing.

Again, I've said it a thousand times and I'm going to say it again; there is no replacement for the services of competent counsel if such a thing really exists. I have recently proven this theory in a New Mexico case involving a §2255 proceeding, see *Thomas R. Rodella v. United States* in the U.S. District Court, District of New Mexico (2020). In that case I prepared an out-of-time §2255 that included a claim of actual innocence. The court required that I show cause why the motion should not be dismissed, and I did so. My reasoning was accepted by the court and the government was required to respond to Mr. Rodella's grounds for relief. I filed a reply to the government response and then the court put the case on the back burner as they usually do. The fact is that all U.S. District Courts treat pro se petitions differently than those filed by attorneys.

In Rodella's case, I advised him to retain counsel after I set the facts and arguments before the court. Once his counsel filed her notice of appearance with the district court, the court dismissed the Magistrate judge from the case and set Mr. Rodella for an expedited hearing. Bottom line – having counsel in your post-conviction relief case will get you real access to the court. I know that this appears to be cronyism, and I know it appears that way because it is. But let's face facts: If you want expedited access to the courts and you can afford to trigger the pay-to-play courts, hiring counsel is the best way to do that. The post-conviction filings in Mr. Rodella's case are made public in *Ineffective Assistance of Counsel: Overcoming the Inevitable*, made available by Freebird Publishers (Diane@freebirdPublishers.com) if you are incarcerated.

Now then, for the rest of us: Sometimes prisoners don't have the resources to retain the assistance of an attorney, but they still have a good claim and they want to get the court's review in their case. So, you ask yourself how is that done without a lawyer? The answer is to file a pro se motion.

Keep in mind that this book provides specific motions that pertain to certain claims in very precise proceedings. But be mindful of the information in this chapter, because it pertains to every motion listed herein.

Motion writing may seem like a mysterious practice to the average person. That is because our common knowledge of criminal cases comes from movies, paperback books, and television shows, and of course all three sources tend to center around the drama of trial matters, such as opening statements and cross examination. Behind the scenes, however, developing a good practice of motion writing can give you an important advantage in any case.

"Motion" is nothing more than a fancy word for "written request," asking the court to do something. In some more advanced situations, a "motion" can be made verbally. Keep in mind also, that, the term "motion" comes from the idea that you are trying to "move" the court to act in some particular way, like issuing an order.

There are some specific standard motions that the court typically handles, such as a motion to suppress evidence. But a motion could be any request that may come to mind. If you want the court to give you some type of relief like a new trial, vacatur of your sentence, admission of newly discovered evidence et cetera you must file a motion. Most all standard motions are easily identified and understood by the courts because they are set in form, like §2255's, §2254's, §2244's and many others. But this book is going to guide you through a number of proceedings that are not yet standardized, like the many forms of relief provided by the recently enacted First Step Act. Because they are not yet standardized, many of the motions you will find in this book are not set in fill-in-the-blank forms. Because of all this, it is very important that you follow these four tips while you are applying the facts of your case to the motions in this book.

BE ORGANIZED

Keep in mind that the court's personnel – judges, clerks, and staff attorneys – are people also, well most of them anyway. That means that anything you send them in writing needs to be easy to read and understand. What makes a piece of writing easy, is organization. If you would rather read something that has short, clear paragraphs with bold headings for guidance, and that makes good logical sense, then it is likely that the court and its personnel would want to read the same thing.

One of the best ways to present an organized argument in your motion is to start out by outlining your thoughts. Make sure also that you write out your outline, so you have your own personal standard to follow as you write your motion. If you're writing a motion it is likely that you want some sort of relief, but like most of us you have several different reasons why you think the court should grant your request. Be sure then, that you flesh out each reason in your outline. Once your outline is finished, make sure that you follow it, which will keep your memory fresh as you write your motion.

RESEARCH BEFORE YOU START

If you have ever worked with another human being to accomplish any goal in life, you have likely discovered that the best way to influence someone to follow your idea is to provide support with facts and examples. The same is true with your motion – you are trying to get the court to do things your way, so you must support your motion with good reasons for the court to grant your request. You will most likely have to make a good argument sooner or later. To make your argument persuasive, you must have something to help support why your side of the argument is correct.

In other words, before you start writing a motion, especially if it is more intricate than a notice of appeal, you should do a little legal research to find other cases or even written rules and laws that give support to what you are asking the court to do. Let's say for example that you are asking the court to vacate the sentence that was imposed in your criminal case. Then it would make sense for you to first find a case or a statute that indicates that the correct standard is for the court to vacate the sentence that it previously imposed. If possible, it would be ideal for you to find a case where the defendant was similarly situated, as you were on your case, or the sentence and conviction were similar to your own case, and the court in that other case found that the sentence was due to be vacated.

Also keep in mind that similarly situated means that the legal precedents you are relying on are in the same area of law that your criminal case happens to stem from. In other words, don't use a case that was vacated in a Military Court Marshal if you were convicted under federal criminal law in a United States District Court.

MOTION STRUCTURE

So far, you have identified your issue, you have outlined your thoughts, and you have researched your argument. Now it is time to put it all down on paper. This is where the rubber meets the road, so to speak. Writing a motion is not like writing a letter. Yes, you have a lot to say, and getting it out is important, but so is the structure of your presentation.

When reading a motion from a prisoner, the Court's personnel are looking for a reason to deny the motion quickly so they can get on to what they consider to be meaningful motions. And with years of experience of motion writing, I can assure you that the courts treat pro se motions as some infectious, diseased item that must be discarded. I can almost see them holding their breath as they snub their noses while reading. So, let's not give them any help.

Any motion that you write should provide them with what they need – good reason to grant your motion – and it should provide it quickly. What the court needs is:

- Your Issue – this is the question that is relevant and that requires the government to provide a particular counter argument.

- Current Rule – this is the law, the case, or any other established legal standard that is controlling in the jurisdiction that your sentence happens to be out of (i.e. Northern District of Alabama).

- Your Analysis – this is where you compare the facts of your case to the legal rule that you have raised. Keep in mind also that there have been many prisoners who have set the standard. This means that they have had no previous standard to make their point and that they lead the way, see Supreme Court cases of *Johnson v. United States* (2015); *Welch v. United States* (2016); *United States v. Davis et. al.* (2019)

- Your Conclusion – This is where you provide a brief summary of your motion. You ask for a specific court action like review your case as compared to the facts that you've presented, i.e. "Wherefore above premises considered." Next, be specific about your desired result, i.e. "Mr. Martinez moves this court to vacate his sentence." Finally, give the very pointed reason why the court should do so, i.e. "because he is actually innocent." You may make your conclusion clearer by adding very brief but additional information as long as you are sure to supply everything that the court may need to rule on your issue in your favor.

Here is an example of how to express these four elements of motion construction.

- Issue – Was Mr. Martinez's conduct prohibited by the statute of conviction as it was enacted by Congress? Rule – It is a bedrock tenet of the law that in order to be criminal it, must be defined by Congress within the four corners of the statute, see the Supreme Court case of *Viereck v. United States*, 318 U.S. 236 (1942).

- Analysis – In Mr. Martinez's case he was arrested after he and his fiancé moved to Texas in preparation for their wedding, with parental consent. The government accused Mr. Martinez of enticing a minor under the federal prostitution statute, 18 U.S.C. §2422(b) and §2423(a). But, because of the statute's construction, the government had to reword the statute to make it appear applicable, thus expanding the law to include Mr. Martinez's conduct as criminal.

- Conclusion – Because Mr. Martinez's conduct is not prohibited by the statutes as they were enacted by Congress, this court should vacate his sentence because he is actually innocent.

(This example is from an actual case filed in a U.S. District Court and is used as an example in full in Chapter Three).

If you follow this formula for each argument in your motion, you will find that your work is much more precise. Thus, it will be concise, easier to read, and more persuasive. As a last thought on motion construction, keep the insults, mudslinging, and name calling out of your writing. The court doesn't want to hear what you have to say in the first place, so don't compound this problem by offending its friends. It is always best to keep your work limited to the facts and the law, and always avoid personal attacks on the other parties to the case.

PROOFREADING

This is probably the most important part of successful motion drafting. As ironic as this may seem, a judge will gladly deny your motion for a typo. Although in most cases a misplaced comma or period wouldn't matter much, in legal writing it can become critical. This is especially true for a pro se filer whose motion the court is looking to dismiss anyway. I have also been witness to the courts denying a motion because of a misspelled word. The court, of course, claimed that it caused an ambiguity. The next most critical thing to look for is missing critical words, one of my favorites is the word "not." Imagine this, "The statute does *not* prohibit Mr. Martinez's conduct, he is therefore actually innocent." Now if you remove the word "not" you reverse the meaning of the statement.

So, let me say again proofread, proofread, and proofread again. You can even recruit some help as I do in not only my legal writing but in my fiction writing as well.

Remember, that your work is not finished until you have done a thorough proofread. I also suggest that you set your finished work aside for a long period of time, a few hours or a day, whatever it takes. After you have written everything that you think is necessary, take time to clear your head. I even plan for this step three times in my schedule, once after I outline, once after I write my motion out, and once again after I have it typed.

These brief tips should be followed in all legal writing, but also know that there is much more good information out there about legal writing, see also *Post-Conviction Relief: Advancing Your Claim* published by Freebird Publishers.

CHAPTER THREE

OUT-OF-TIME § 2255

Let me begin this chapter by saying that the term "out-of-time §2255" is a monster of my own creation. I use this term to describe §2255 motions that are legally time-barred, but yet also legally authorized to proceed. The statute, in 28 U.S.C. §2255, provides for a very strict one-year limitation, to the consideration of claims brought in a §2255 motion, 28 U.S.C. §2255(f). The statute also goes on to describe two specific sets of circumstances when it authorizes the consideration of claims brought in a second or successive §2255 motion, 28 U.S.C. §2255(h).

Notice that §2255(f)(4) provides an opportunity to file a motion out-of-time, but its consideration is governed by a court-fashioned rule of due diligence. Although the statute specifically uses the words "exercise of due diligence," I consider it a court-fashioned rule because "due diligence" is not defined in §2255 and thus, left up to the courts to determine. This is most important to pro se prisoners because the court determined "due diligence" standard is almost never met by pro se prisoners, in the court's view.

Now moving on to §2255(h), we find two circumstances in which the statute authorizes the filing of a second or successive §2255 motion (second or successive authorization is covered more thoroughly in its own chapter).

In §2255(h)(1), the statute provides authorization to file a second or successive §2255 motion based upon the presentation of "newly discovered evidence that if proven and viewed in light of the evidence as a whole would be sufficient to establish by clear and convincing evidence that no reasonable factfinder would have found the movant guilty of the offense ..." 28 U.S.C. §2255(h)(1).

In a §2255(h)(2), the statute provides authorization to file a second or successive §2255 motion based upon "a new rule of constitutional law, made retroactive to cases on collateral review by the Supreme Court, that was previously unavailable."

Please note that if your claim is based on a new rule of law, as described in §2255(h)(2), and you have never filed a §2255 motion before, you will have no need to seek second or successive authorization. For those who have never filed for §2255 relief before and are relying on a change in law, review is authorized under 28 U.S.C. §2255(f)(3). Thus, your §2255 motion would not be filed out-of-time because it would be a timely-filed claim, 28 U.S.C. §2255(f)(3).

The "out-of-time §2255" motion is specifically reserved for first time filers who can prove "actual innocence." The filing of an out-of-time §2255 that is based on proof of actual innocence, is not subject to "the exercise of due diligence" as most courts believe that §2255(f)(4) requires. This is a gap that was created by the poor draftsmanship of the §2255 statute.

In strictly reading the statute, as many courts do, a first-time movant that could prove that he was actually innocent would be left without any avenue to prove his actual innocence – a clear violation of the Thirteenth Amendment.

When §2255 was passed into law there was no fixed statute of limitations for filing a §2255 motion. But on April 24, 1996, former President Bill Clinton (Slick Willy) signed into law the Antiterrorism and Effective Death Penalty Act. The new law established a very strict statute of limitations – a one-year limit on the filing of all §2255 motions. This limitation applied to both initial and successive §2255 motions.

THE "ACTUAL INNOCENCE" EXCEPTION

For at least fifteen years, after the AEDPA established a hardline statute of limitations, the federal courts struggled to figure out whether AEDPA's statute of limitations was subject to the "actual innocence" exception. The exception had always applied to many of the court-established procedural limitations to habeas corpus review and relief. But the AEDPA was different in two ways: one~ it seemed to have already applied a type of provision for actual innocence into the new law; and two, it was a law handed down by Congress as opposed to a rule established by a court. Ultimately the courts were split on the issue. Some found that an actual innocence exception did in fact exist, and others determined equally that "actual innocence" was a factor that justified equitable tolling.

The circuit split drew the attention of the Supreme Court. In *McQuiggin v. Perkins*, 569 U.S. __, 185 L. Ed. 2d 1019 (2013), the Supreme Court resolved the issue. The Court decided that "actual innocence, if proved, serves as a gateway through which a petitioner may pass whether the impediment is a procedural bar … or, as in this case, expiration of a statute of limitations." The Court further explained that "[a]t the time of AEDPA's enactment, multiple decisions of this Court applied the miscarriage of justice exception to overcome various threshold barriers to relief," and "[i]t is hardly 'unprecedented,' therefore, to conclude that 'Congress intended or could have anticipated [a miscarriage of justice] exception' when it enacted AEDPA."

The Court also reasoned from "Congress's incorporation of a modified version of the miscarriage of justice exception in §§2244(b)(2)(B), and 2254(e)(2)," controlling respectively "second-or-successive petitions and the holding of evidentiary hearings in federal court," to "[t]he … rational inference" that "[i]n a case not governed by those provisions, i.e., a *first* petition for federal habeas relief, the miscarriage of justice exception survived AEDPA's passage intact and unrestricted." After taking a good look at the variety of contexts in which "[w]e have applied the miscarriage of justice exception to overcome various procedural defaults" in an effort to "see[k] to balance the societal interests in finality, comity, and conservation of scarce judicial resources with the individual interest in justice that arises in the extraordinary case," the Court observed that "[s]ensitivity to the injustice of incarcerating an innocent individual should not abate when the impediment is AEDPA's statute of limitations."

As with any other situation in which the procedural limitation is subject to the "actual innocence" exception, the rule announced in *McQuiggin v. Perkins*, allows a habeas corpus petitioner whose petition is late under AEDPA's statutes of limitations to "overcome" the "time bar" by making "a convincing showing that she committed no crime." The standards by which a prisoner can show "actual innocence," or "a convincing showing that she committed no crime," are:

- One – a production of new reliable evidence, meaning evidence that the Court has never considered and that is newly obtained by the prisoner;

- Two – that the prisoner's alleged conduct was not criminal under the law at the time of its commission, see *Bousley v. United States*, 523 U.S. 614 (1998).

The Supreme Court has provided guidance as to what a federal prisoner would have to demonstrate to show the actual innocence that would make a prisoner entitled to relief under §2255.

In *Bousley v. United States*, 523 U.S. 614; 140 L. Ed. 2d 828; 118 S.Ct. 1604 (1998), the Supreme Court remanded a case to allow a federal prisoner – in an out-of-time §2255 – an opportunity to show actual innocence in order to relieve the procedural default caused by the prisoner. The prisoner claimed that his guilty plea was not knowing and intelligent because he was misinformed by the district court as to the nature of the charged offense. The Supreme Court described what the prisoner would have to demonstrate to show actual innocence that would entitle him to review under §2255. The prisoner followed the Supreme Court's direction and showed that the Supreme Court's decision, in *Bailey v. United States*, 516 U.S. 137; 133 L. Ed. 2d 472; 116 S.Ct. 501 (1995), had identified that his conduct, for which he was convicted, was outside of the permissible reach of the federal statute, 18 U.S.C. §924(c)(1).

The Supreme Court said that, with respect to the prisoner's claims, actual innocence meant factual innocence, not mere legal insufficiency, and that the government was not limited to the existing record to rebut any showing that the prisoner might make. The only "new evidence" cited by Bousley was the Court's decision in *Bailey v. United States*, 516 U.S. 137 (1995), which when applied to his facts supported his claim of actual innocence.

The rest of this chapter is an actual claim in an out-of-time §2255, and the subsequent filings. This case is also of very specific interest to anyone who is charged under the residual clauses of 18 U.S.C. §§2422(b) and/or 2423(a) and whose case did not involve prostitution or the production of child pornography.

MOTION UNDER 28 U.S.C. § 2255 TO VACATE, SET ASIDE, OR CORRECT
SENTENCE BY A PERSON IN FEDERAL CUSTODY

United States District Court	District	
Name *(under which you were convicted)*: CHARLES RILEY MARTINEZ		Docket or Case No.: MO-19-CV-242
Place of Confinement: Seagoville, Tx		Prisoner No.: 10930-380
UNITED STATES OF AMERICA	V.	Movant *(include name under which convicted)* MARTINEZ

MOTION

1. (a) Name and location of court which entered the judgment of conviction you are challenging:

   Midland / Odessa

   (b) Criminal docket or case number (if you know): 7:13-CR-65-01

2. (a) Date of the judgment of conviction (if you know): 5-07-2013

   (b) Date of sentencing: **Sept. 20, 2013**

3. Length of sentence: **121 Months**

4. Nature of crime (all counts):

   18 U.S.C. §2422(b), 18 U.S.C. §2423(a)

5. (a) What was your plea? (Check one)

   (1) Not guilty [X]   (2) Guilty [ ]   (3) Nolo contendere (no contest) [ ]

   (b) If you entered a guilty plea to one count or indictment, and a not guilty plea to another count or what did you plead guilty to and what did you plead not guilty to?

   N/A

6. If you went to trial, what kind of trial did you have? (Check one)   Jury [x]   Judge only [ ]

7. Did you testify at a pretrial hearing, trial, or post-trial hearing?   Yes [ ]   No [x]

8. Did you appeal from the judgment of conviction?   Yes [x]   No [ ]

AO 243 (Rev. 01/15)

9. If you did appeal, answer the following:

    (a) Name of court: __Fifth Circuit__

    (b) Docket or case number (if you know): __13-50876__

    (c) Result: __Affirmed__

    (d) Date of result (if you know): __September 10, 2014__

    (e) Citation to the case (if you know): __Unpublished__

    (f) Grounds raised:

    > The Court erred by denying the motion to aquit.

    (g) Did you file a petition for certiorari in the United States Supreme Court?   Yes ☐   No ☒

    If "Yes," answer the following:

    (1) Docket or case number (if you know): __N/A__

    (2) Result: __N/A__

    (3) Date of result (if you know): __N/A__

    (4) Citation to the case (if you know): __N/A__

    (5) Grounds raised:

    > N/A

10. Other than the direct appeals listed above, have you previously filed any other motions, petitions, or applications, concerning this judgment of conviction in any court?
    Yes ☐   No ☒

11. If your answer to Question 10 was "Yes," give the following information:

    (a) (1) Name of court: __N/A__

    (2) Docket or case number (if you know): __N/A__

    (3) Date of filing (if you know): __N/A__

    (4) Nature of the proceeding: __N/A__

    (5) Grounds raised: __N/A__

13

AO 243 (Rev. 01/15)

(6) Did you receive a hearing where evidence was given on your motion, petition, or application?

Yes ☐   No ☒

(7) Result: **N/A**

(8) Date of result (if you know): **N/A**

(b) If you filed any second motion, petition, or application, give the same information:

(1) Name of court: **N/A**

(2) Docket of case number (if you know): **N/A**

(3) Date of filing (if you know): **N/A**

(4) Nature of the proceeding: **N/A**

(5) Grounds raised:

N/A

(6) Did you receive a hearing where evidence was given on your motion, petition, or application?

Yes ☐   No ☒

(7) Result: **N/A**

(8) Date of result (if you know): **N/A**

(c) Did you appeal to a federal appellate court having jurisdiction over the action taken on your motion, petition, or application?

(1) First petition: Yes ☐   No ☒

(2) Second petition: Yes ☐   No ☒

(d) If you did not appeal from the action on any motion, petition, or application, explain briefly why you did not:

N/A

12. For this motion, state every ground on which you claim that you are being held in violation of the Constitution, laws, or treaties of the United States. Attach additional pages if you have more than four grounds. State the facts supporting each ground.

AO 243 (Rev. 01/15)

GROUND ONE: <u>Mr. Martinez was deprived of a fair trial because...</u>

<u>See attached</u>

    (a) Supporting facts (Do not argue or cite law. Just state the specific facts that support your claim.):

Mr. Martinez is serving a sentence in federal prison

because his counsel...   See attached

    (b) Direct Appeal of Ground One:

      (1) If you appealed from the judgment of conviction, did you raise this issue?

         Yes ☐   No ☒

      (2) If you did not raise this issue in your direct appeal, explain why:

      This claim is not cognizable in direct appeal

      <u>Massaro V. U.S., 538 U.S. 500.</u>

    (c) Post-Conviction Proceedings:

      (1) Did you raise this issue in any post-conviction motion, petition, or application?

         Yes ☐   No ☒

      (2) If you answer to Question (c)(1) is "Yes," state:

      Type of motion or petition: N/A

      Name and location of the court where the motion or petition was filed:

               N/A

      Docket or case number (if you know): N/A

      Date of the court's decision: N/A

      Result (attach a copy of the court's opinion or order, if available):

        N/A

      (3) Did you receive a hearing on your motion, petition, or application?

         Yes ☐   No ☐   N/A

      (4) Did you appeal from the denial of your motion, petition, or application?

         Yes ☐   No ☐   N/A

      (5) If your answer to Question (c)(4) is "Yes," did you raise the issue in the appeal?

         Yes ☐   No ☐   N/A

(6) If your answer to Question (c)(4) is "Yes," state:

Name and location of the court where the appeal was filed:

N/A

Docket or case number (if you know): **N/A**

Date of the court's decision: **N/A**

Result (attach a copy of the court's opinion or order, if available):

N/A

(7) If your answer to Question (c)(4) or Question (c)(5) is "No," explain why you did not appeal or raise this issue: Mr. Martinez is a layman who was deprived of an opportunity to raise an ineffective assistance of counsel claim in direct appeal, and he was deprived of counsel to prepare a first tier collateral review motion.

GROUND TWO: Mr. Martinez was deprived of his statutory right to appeal because... See Attached.

(a) Supporting facts (Do not argue or cite law. Just state the specific facts that support your claim.):

Mr. Martinez incorporates by reference the facts in ground one here in ground two. He further... See attached.

(b) **Direct Appeal of Ground Two:**

(1) If you appealed from the judgment of conviction, did you raise this issue?

Yes ☐   No ☒

(2) If you did not raise this issue in your direct appeal, explain why:

This claim is not cognizable in direct appeal.
Massaro V. U.S., 538 U.S. 500.

(c) **Post-Conviction Proceedings:**

(1) Did you raise this issue in any post-conviction motion, petition, or application?

Yes ☐   No ☒

(2)   If you answer to Question (c)(1) is "Yes," state:

Type of motion or petition: _____N/A_____

Name and location of the court where the motion or petition was filed:

N/A
_____

Docket or case number (if you know): _____N/A_____

Date of the court's decision: _____N/A_____

Result (attach a copy of the court's opinion or order, if available):

N/A
_____

(3)   Did you receive a hearing on your motion, petition, or application?

Yes ☐   No ☐   N/A

(4)   Did you appeal from the denial of your motion, petition, or application?

Yes ☐   No ☐   N/A

(5)   If your answer to Question (c)(4) is "Yes," did you raise the issue in the appeal?

Yes ☐   No ☐   N/A

(6)   If your answer to Question (c)(4) is "Yes," state:

Name and location of the court where the appeal was filed:

N/A
_____

Docket or case number (if you know): _____N/A_____

Date of the court's decision: _____N/A_____

Result (attach a copy of the court's opinion or order, if available):

N/A
_____

(7)   If your answer to Question (c)(4) or Question (c)(5) is "No," explain why you did not appeal or raise this
issue: Mr. Martinez is a layman who was deprived of an opportunity
to raise an ineffective assistance of counsel claim in direct
appeal, and he was deprived of counsel to prepare a first tier
collateral review motion.

_____

GROUND THREE: _____N/A_____

_____

(a)   Supporting facts (Do not argue or cite law. Just state the specific facts that support your claim.):

N/A

AO 243 (Rev. 01/15)

(b) Direct Appeal of Ground Three:

    (1) If you appealed from the judgment of conviction, did you raise this issue?

        Yes ☐   No ☐ **N/A**

    (2) If you did not raise this issue in your direct appeal, explain why:

        N/A

(c) Post-Conviction Proceedings:

    (1) Did you raise this issue in any post-conviction motion, petition, or application?

        Yes ☐   No ☐ **N/A**

    (2) If you answer to Question (c)(1) is "Yes," state:

Type of motion or petition: **N/A**

Name and location of the court where the motion or petition was filed:

        N/A

Docket or case number (if you know):   **N/A**

Date of the court's decision: **N/A**

Result (attach a copy of the court's opinion or order, if available):

        N/A

    (3) Did you receive a hearing on your motion, petition, or application?

        Yes ☐   No ☐ **N/A**

    (4) Did you appeal from the denial of your motion, petition, or application?

        Yes ☐   No ☐ **N/A**

    (5) If your answer to Question (c)(4) is "Yes," did you raise the issue in the appeal?

        Yes ☐   No ☐ **N/A**

    (6) If your answer to Question (c)(4) is "Yes," state:

Name and location of the court where the appeal was filed:

        N/A

Docket or case number (if you know):   **N/A**

Date of the court's decision: **N/A**

Result (attach a copy of the court's opinion or order, if available):

        N/A

(7) If your answer to Question (c)(4) or Question (c)(5) is "No," explain why you did not appeal or raise this issue:

    N/A

GROUND FOUR: N/A

(a) Supporting facts (Do not argue or cite law. Just state the specific facts that support your claim.):

    N/A

(b) **Direct Appeal of Ground Four:**

(1) If you appealed from the judgment of conviction, did you raise this issue?

Yes ☐ No ☐ N/A

(2) If you did not raise this issue in your direct appeal, explain why:

    N/A

(c) **Post-Conviction Proceedings:**

(1) Did you raise this issue in any post-conviction motion, petition, or application?

Yes ☐ No ☐ N/A

(2) If you answer to Question (c)(1) is "Yes," state:

Type of motion or petition: N/A

Name and location of the court where the motion or petition was filed:

    N/A

Docket or case number (if you know): N/A

Date of the court's decision: N/A

Result (attach a copy of the court's opinion or order, if available):

    N/A

(3) Did you receive a hearing on your motion, petition, or application?

Yes ☐   No ☐   **N/A**

(4) Did you appeal from the denial of your motion, petition, or application?

Yes ☐   No ☐   **N/A**

(5) If your answer to Question (c)(4) is "Yes," did you raise the issue in the appeal?

Yes ☐   No ☐   **N/A**

(6) If your answer to Question (c)(4) is "Yes," state:

Name and location of the court where the appeal was filed:

N/A

Docket or case number (if you know): **N/A**

Date of the court's decision: **N/A**

Result (attach a copy of the court's opinion or order, if available):

N/A

(7) If your answer to Question (c)(4) or Question (c)(5) is "No," explain why you did not appeal or raise this issue:

N/A

13.   Is there any ground in this motion that you have <u>not</u> previously presented in some federal court? If so, which ground or grounds have not been presented, and state your reasons for not presenting them:

The grounds for this motion are raised here for the
first time, in Martinez's first tier collateral review.

14.   Do you have any motion, petition, or appeal <u>now pending</u> (filed and not decided yet) in any court for the you are challenging?   Yes ☐   No ☒

If "Yes," state the name and location of the court, the docket or case number, the type of proceeding, and the issues raised.

N/A

15. Give the name and address, if known, of each attorney who represented you in the following stages of the you are challenging:

(a) At the preliminary hearing:

Alvaro Martinez

(b) At the arraignment and plea:

Alvaro Martinez

(c) At the trial:

Alvaro Martinez

(d) At sentencing:

Alvaro Martinez

(e) On appeal:

Alvaro Martinez

(f) In any post-conviction proceeding:

Pro Se

(g) On appeal from any ruling against you in a post-conviction proceeding:

N/A

16. Were you sentenced on more than one court of an indictment, or on more than one indictment, in the same court and at the same time?   Yes ☐   No ☒

17. Do you have any future sentence to serve after you complete the sentence for the judgment that you are challenging?   Yes ☐   No ☒

(a) If so, give name and location of court that imposed the other sentence you will serve in the future:

N/A

(b) Give the date the other sentence was imposed: N/A

(c) Give the length of the other sentence: N/A

(d) Have you filed, or do you plan to file, any motion, petition, or application that challenges the judgment or sentence to be served in the future?   Yes ☐   No ☐   N/A

18. TIMELINESS OF MOTION: If your judgment of conviction became final over one year ago, you must explain why the one-year statute of limitations as contained in 28 U.S.C. § 2255 does not bar your motion.*

This motion is timely under the actual innocence exception and the limited exception carried out by the Supreme Court of the United States in Martinez V. Ryan, 566 U.S. 1.

---

* The Antiterrorism and Effective Death Penalty Act of 1996 ("AEDPA") as contained in 28 U.S.C. § 2255, paragraph 6, provides in part that:

A one-year period of limitation shall apply to a motion under this section. The limitation period shall run from the latest of –

(1) the date on which the judgment of conviction became final;

(2) the date on which the impediment to making a motion created by governmental action in violation of the Constitution or laws of the United States is removed, if the movant was prevented from making such a motion by such governmental action;

(3) the date on which the right asserted was initially recognized by the Supreme Court, if that right has been newly recognized by the Supreme Court and made retroactively applicable to cases on collateral review; or

(4) the date on which the facts supporting the claim or claims presented could have been discovered through the exercise of due diligence.

Therefore, movant asks that the Court grant the following relief:

Vacate his sentence.

_____

or any other relief to which movant may be entitled.

_____

Signature of Attorney (if any)

I declare (or certify, verify, or state) under penalty of perjury that the foregoing is true and correct and that this Motion under 28 U.S.C. § 2255 was placed in the prison mailing system on _____ .

(month, date, year)

Executed (signed) on _____ (date)

_____

Signature of Movant

If the person signing is not movant, state relationship to movant and explain why movant is not signing this motion.

Ground One:

Mr. Martinez was deprived of a fair trial because his counsel did not understand the scope of the convicting statute. Thus, counsel's ineffectiveness facilitated the guilty verdict of someone who is actually innocent.

Supporting Facts:

Mr. Martinez is serving a sentence in federal prison because his counsel didn't know the reach of the statute of conviction. The criminal case is based on the government's belief that it has the authority to change the wording of the federal statute. By changing the statute's meaning, the government has effectively criminalized marriage and nullified the laws of the State of Wisconsin. **TO WIT:**

1) Mr. Martinez is a musician who is a Texas resident with a minor bit of celebrity on his social media.

2) Through his social media, Mr. Martinez maintains a fan base and comes in contact with many people.

3) In 2012, Mr. Martinez became acquainted with Ms. Jordan Tilot. They discussed music, poetry, and writing for several days. Later, Mr. Martinez and Ms. Tilot developed a steady friendship.

4) After Ms. Tilot turned 16 years of age, their relationship started to turn a bit more affectionate. Over time, the couple began to love one another.

5) When the idea of actually meeting came up in conversations, Mr. Martinez maintained that he would have to get permission from Ms. Tilot's mother.

6) Mr. Martinez was then introduced to Ms. Wanda Tilot. They corresponded for a while before Ms. Tilot decided to give her permission for Mr. Martinez to visit and meet the family in Green Bay, Wisconsin.

7) Mr. Martinez made a third trip to Wisconsin in July of 2012 so that he and Ms. Tilot's family could solidify wedding arrangements.

8) The couple's new life included Ms. Tilot continuing her education. They had planned for her to enroll in a Texas school after marriage.

9) Prior to their wedding, the couple decided to make a trip to Texas to scout local schools and their requirements.

10) After the couple arrived in Texas, Ms. Tilot was threatened by government agents. Ms. Tilot then came to Texas to pick up her daughter.

11) On January 31, 2013, Mr. Martinez was questioned by federal agents where he signed a Miranda Waiver and spoke freely with agents.

12) Mr. Martinez was later charged with Enticing a Minor to Engage in Prostitution and/or Enticing a Minor to Engage in Sexual Activity for which the minor (any person) could be charged with a criminal offense.

13) Mr. Martinez's counsel was unaware of the conduct that the two criminal statutes prohibited. Thus, he failed to argue at trial that legal marriage and illegal prostitutions are not synonymous under the law.

Mr. Martinez's counsel did not familiarize himself with the convicting statute well enough to realize that the government changed its wording in the charging papers. Nor did he realize that changing the phrase "any person could be charged" to "he could have been charged ..." changed the scope of the conduct that could be charged under the residual clause of the two statutes.

Mr. Martinez is deprived of his liberty under the 13th Amendment for planning to get married, which is conduct that is not criminalized by either statute of conviction. Thus, Mr. Martinez's sentence under 18 U.S.C. §2422 and §2423 should be vacated.

Ground Two:

Mr. Martinez was deprived of his statutory right to appeal because his appellate counsel provided ineffective assistance of counsel.

Supporting Facts:

Mr. Martinez incorporates by reference the facts In ground one here in ground two. He further explains that he was deprived of an opportunity to raise a meaningful claim at appeal because his appellate counsel provided ineffective assistance of counsel.

1) At trial, Mr. Martinez was charged and convicted for conduct that was not criminal under the statutes of conviction.

2) Mr. Martinez's trial counsel was ineffective because he did not understand the scope of the criminal statutes involved. Nor did counsel recognize that the government had changed the wording of the statutes in the charging papers, so that the reach of the statutes could be broadened to criminalize conduct beyond that of Congress's intent.

3) Mr. Martinez was represented at appeal by the same attorney that represented him at trial. Thus, appellate counsel had no way of raising Mr. Martinez's best claim in appeal because of his ignorance of federal law.

4) Mr. Martinez was charged for conduct not criminalized by the statutes of conviction. Thus, Mr. Martinez' best ground for appeal was this obvious structural error. Mr. Martinez' appellate counsel provided ineffective assistance of counsel. Therefore, his sentence should be vacated so that he may file a meaningful appeal with the assistance of competent counsel. See 18 U.S.C. §3006A.

UNITED STATES DISTRICT COURT
WESTERN DISTRICT OF TEXAS
MIDLAND-ODESSA DIVISION

CHARLES RILEY MARTINEZ, Petitioner,	§ § §	
	§	Crim. No. MO-13-CR-065-(1)-DC
v.	§ §	Civil No. MO-19-CV-242
UNITED STATES OF AMERICA, Respondent.	§ § § §	

**GOVERNMENT'S RESPONSE TO MOTION UNDER 28 U.S.C. § 2255 TO VACATE,
SET ASIDE OR CORRECT SENTENCE BY A PERSON IN FEDERAL CUSTODY**

The United States of America, by and through the United States Attorney for the Western District of Texas, and the undersigned Assistant United States Attorney, files this the Government's Response to Petitioner's Motion under 28 U.S.C. § 2255 to Vacate, Set Aside, or Correct Sentence, and states that the Motion should in all things be denied and respectfully shows the Court as follows:

I. PROCEDURAL HISTORY

On February 1, 2013, a criminal complaint was issued against Petitioner. Docket Entry 1, *United States v. Martinez*, MO-13-CR-065-1 (W. D. Tex. 2013). On February 27, 2013, Petitioner was named in a three-count Indictment charging Violations of Title 18, United States Code, Sections 2422 and 2423. *Id.* at Docket Entry 14. On May 7, 2013, Petitioner was found guilty by a jury of Counts 1 and 3 of the Indictment, after the Government abandoned Count 2. *Id.* at Docket Entries 31 & 42. On July 31, 2015, Petitioner was sentenced to 121 months of imprisonment on each count to run concurrently. *Id.* at Docket Entry 46. The Petitioner appealed his sentence, and the 5th Circuit affirmed the conviction on September 10, 2014. *Id.* at Docket Entry 59. On October 9, 2019, Petitioner filed his § 2255 Motion. *Id.* at Docket Entry 78.

Mr. Alvaro Martinez was Petitioner's counsel of record for this case and was appointed on February 6, 2013. *Id.* at Docket Entry 6. Mr. Martinez represented Petitioner for the entirety of his case. See generally *Id.* Petitioner filed his §2255 motion pro se. See *Id.* at Docket Entry 78.

II. ISSUES

In the instant motion, Petitioner raises two grounds for relief stating that his counsel Alvaro Martinez, Jr. was rendered ineffective assistance of counsel at trial, and on Petitioner's appeal. Additionally, throughout Petitioner's motion he makes multiple references to "actual innocence" that Mr. Martinez failed to pursue and/or litigate. Therefore, when construing liberally as required by *Haines v. Kerner*, 404 U.S. 519, 520 (1972), the Government reads the sum of Petitioner's motion as follow: 1) Mr. Martinez rendered ineffective assistance of counsel, and 2) Petitioner is actually innocent of the crimes of conviction.

III. ARGUMENT

a. *Petitioner's motion must be denied as time barred.*

Petitioner's motion must be denied as time barred. In his § 2255 motion, the Petitioner conceded that his motion was filed after the expiration of the one-year period, during which Petitioner could have filed the motion.

The time period for Petitioner to file a motion under § 2255 was within one year after his conviction became final. See 28 U.S.C. § 2255(f)(I). In has been held that 2255 motions' limitation period begins to run when the judgment of conviction becomes final. See *Clay v. United States*, 537 U.S. 522, 524 (2003) ("A motion by a federal prisoner for post-conviction relief under 28 U.S.C. § 2255 is subject to a one-year time limitation that generally runs from 'the date on which the judgment of conviction becomes final.'") (quoting 28 U.S.C. § 2255(f)(I)). A judgment becomes final when the defendant's time for seeking review by the Court expires. *Id.* at 526.

United States v. Gamble, 208 F.3d 536 (5th Cir. 2000) (per curiam). Petitioner did not file a Petition for a Writ of Certiorari within 90 days of the 5th Circuit's Judgment (*see* USCS Supreme Ct. R. 13), therefore Petitioner's conviction became final when the 5th Circuit issued its Judgment/Mandate on September 10, 2014. Since Petitioner had one year in which to file his § 2255 motion, Petitioner had to file his motion on or before September 10, 2015. Based on the record, it appears that Petitioner filed his instant motion October 10, 2019, which is the date the motion was signed and was presumably mailed to the District Clerk's office. "A pro se motion is deemed filed at the time it is delivered to prison officials." *United States v. Patterson*, 211 F .3d 927, 930 (5th Cir. 2000) (citing *Spotville v. Cain*, 149 F.3d 374, 378 (5th Cir.1998)). Thus, Petitioner's motion was signed and dated over four years after the expiration of the deadline of September 10, 2015. Therefore, his motion is untimely and should be denied, unless he is entitled to relief pursuant to "equitable tolling" or he was otherwise unable to discover the issues with an exercise of due diligence.

b. *Petitioner is not entitled to equitable tolling.*

The Government contends that Petitioner is not entitled to relief because he filed his instant motion more than a year after the facts supporting the claims in his § 2255 motion could have been discovered through the exercise of due diligence. The Government also contents that Petitioner is not entitled to relief based on "equitable tolling."

According to 28 U.S.C. § 2255(f)(4), the one-year limitation period shall run from:

> the date on which the facts supporting the claim or claims presented could have been discovered through the exercise of due diligence.

28 U.S.C. § 2255(f)(4).

In his Petition, Petitioner outlines a very specific factual scenario regarding the arrangements he was making with the minor victim's family – factual scenarios that ultimately led to the

Defendant's arrest and subsequent conviction. Based on the Government's review of the issues raised in his § 2255 motion, Petitioner knew of the issues with his attorney *prior to and during the course of the case* (emphasis added), and failed to raise them either on direct appeal or in a timely habeas motion. Accordingly, the Petitioner has failed to demonstrate that he filed his § 2255 Motion within one year of the date on which the facts supporting the claims could have been discovered through due diligence.

The Government contends that Petitioner is not entitled to relief based on "equitable tolling." According to *Holland v. Florida*, 560 U.S. 631,648, 130 S.Ct. 2549, 2562, (2010):

> a "petitioner" is "entitled to equitable tolling" only if he shows "(1) that he has been pursuing his rights diligently, and (2) that some extraordinary circumstance stood in his way" and prevented timely filing.

Id.; quoting *Pace v. DiGuglielmo*, 544 U.S. 408, 418, 125 S.Ct. 1807, (2005). The Government re-urges the arguments discussed above. Petitioner did not timely file his §2255 Motion after the Judgment on his Appeal became final and the one-year period lapsed. Hence, Petitioner did not pursue his rights diligently. Also, as indicated above, Petitioner cannot demonstrate that an "extraordinary circumstance stood in his way and prevented timely filing," his §2255 Motion. Petitioner is not entitled to relief under "equitable tolling."

In his motion Petitioner claims that his petition is timely because of the "actual innocence" exception. Pet. Mot. at 11. Additionally, throughout his argument Petitioner makes multiple references to being innocent of the charge. However, merely making these statements is not enough to reach the actual innocence standard to overcome the limitation period on a § 2255 Motion.

"Actual innocence, if proved, serves as a gateway through which a petitioner may pass whether the impediment is a procedural bar, as it was in *Schlup v. Delo*, 513 U.S. 298, 115 S.Ct. 851, 130 L. Ed.2d 808, and House *v.* Bell, 547 U.S. 518, 126 S.Ct. 2064, 165 L. Ed.2d 1..."

McQuiggin v. Perkins, 569 U.S. 383, 386; 133 S.Ct. 1924, 1928 (2013). In other words, if Petitioner could show that he is actually innocent of the charges, he would be entitled to equitable tolling and his § 2255 motion would not be time barred. However, actual-innocence gateway pleas are rare, and a petitioner does not meet the threshold requirement unless he persuades the district court that, in light of the new evidence, no juror, acting reasonably, would have voted to find him guilty beyond a reasonable doubt." *Id.* When making this assessment the Court shall consider the timing of the petition as a factor bearing on the reliability of the evidence purporting to show actual innocence. *Id.* at 386-387.

In this case, the Court does not even need to reach the "reliability of the evidence" analysis of the defendant's actual innocence claim because the Defendant has brought forth no new evidence in his Petition. As the basis for his motion, the Defendant recites facts from the year 2013 and prior outlining his "relationship" with the minor victim in this case and his desire to marry her. None of the facts are newly discovered evidence, nor are they facts that remotely show Defendant is innocent of his crimes of conviction. Therefore, Petitioner is not entitled to equitable tolling of the one-year limitation, and the Court should deny Petitioner's motion in full.

IV. CONCLUSION

The Government submits that it does not need to address the merits of Petitioner's claims as his § 2255 Motion to Vacate is time-barred. Additionally, Petitioner is not entitled to equitable tolling and Petitioner's Motion under 28 U.S.C. § 2255 to Vacate, Set Aside, or Correct Sentence, should be denied.

In the event, this Honorable Court determines that the Government should address Petitioner's motion on the merits, then the Government respectfully requests that upon such a determination, the Government be allowed thirty days from the Court's ruling to respond to Petitioner's § 2255

motion on the merits.

Respectfully submitted,

JOHN F. BASH
UNITED STATES ATTORNEY

BY: /s/ Shane A. Chriesman
SHANE A. CHRIESMAN
Assistant United States Attorney
Texas Bar No. 24082818
400 W. Illinois Ave., Suite 1200
Midland, TX 79701

CERTIFICATE OF SERVICE

Thereby certify that a true and correct copy of the foregoing document was delivered via USPS, to

Petitioner Charles Riley Martinez, Reg. No. 10930-380, FCI Seagoville, PO Box 9000, Seagoville,

TX 75159, on January 10, 2020.

/s/ Shane A. Chriesman
SHANE A. CHRIESMAN
Assistant United States Attorney

UNITED STATES DISTRICT COURT
WESTERN DISTRICT OF TEXAS
MIDLAND-ODESSA DIVISION

CHARLES RILEY MARTINEZ, Petitioner, v. UNITED STATES OF AMERICA, Respondent.	§ § § § § § § § §	Crim. No. MO-13-CR-65-(1)-DC Civil No. MO-19-CV-242

MARTINEZ'S MOTION FOR ENLARGEMENT OF TIME
TO FILE HIS REPLY

Mr. Martinez recently filed an instant motion under 28 U.S.C. §2255. The government filed its response on January 10, 2020, and Mr. Martinez was served with a copy on January 15, 2020. Mr. Martinez moves this court to grant him until February 15, 2020 to reply to the government's motion.

Mr. Martinez does not make this motion for the purpose of delay nor will the government be prejudiced by the granting of it. Moreover, Mr. Martinez believes that good cause exists because of the following:

1) Although this court ordered the government to respond to Mr. Martinez's grounds for relief complete with an affidavit from defense counsel, the government chose not to do so. In the alternative the government filed the equivalent of a motion to dismiss. Mr. Martinez is a layman at law, and he had prepared to argue the merits of his claims, but now is required to perform additional research to respond to the government's motion.

2) Mr. Martinez is a federal prisoner and as such he is not equally situated with counsel for the government. In the more restricted environment Mr. Martinez has little time and access to legal resources and must also compete with nearly 2,000 other prisoners who wish to use the 14 computer terminals supplied by the prison.

3) Mr. Martinez received the government's motion less than 48 hours before a long holiday weekend during which time the legal library will be closed. Thus, Mr. Martinez will not even have access to a computer terminal until January 21, 2020.

Wherefore, above premises considered, Mr. Martinez moves this court to grant this motion in the nature of fairness and equity.

Respectfully submitted on January 21, 2020, by:

Charles Riley Martinez, pro se
Reg. # 10930-380
Federal Correctional Institution
P.O. Box 9000
Seagoville, TX 75159

CERTIFICATE OF SERVICE

I hereby certify that on January 21, 2020, I served a true and correct copy of this motion on the attorney for the government, 400 W. Illinois Ave., Suite 1200, Midland, TX 79701. Delivery of the motion was completed by placing it in the legal mailing system as made available to inmates via U.S. mail, properly addressed, and first-class postage prepaid.

Respectfully submitted on January 21, 2020, by:

Charles Riley Martinez, pro se
Reg. #10930-380
U.S. District Court

Western District of Texas

THIS IS AN OFFICIAL NOTICE FROM THE COURT

The following transaction was entered by the court at 8:08 AM CST on 1/28/2020:

Case Name: USA v. Martinez
Case Number: 7:13-cr-00065-DC (1)

Docket Text:
Text Order GRANTING DOC. # [81] Motion for Extension of Time to File Response/Reply as to Charles Riley Martinez (1), up to and including Monday, February 17, 2020. Entered by Judge David Counts. (This is a text-only entry generated by the court. There is no document associated with this entry.) (tlm)

> This is a text-only entry generated by the court.
> There is no document associated with this entry.

UNITED STATES DISTRICT COURT
WESTERN DISTRICT OF TEXAS
MIDLAND-ODESSA DIVISION

CHARLES R. MARTINEZ	§	
	§	
	§	Crim. No. MO-13-CR-65-(1)-DC
v.	§	Civil No. MO-19-CV-242
	§	
UNITED STATES OF AMERICA	§	
	§	
	§	
	§	

MR. MARTINEZ'S REPLY TO GOVERNMENT'S RESPONSE

Mr. Martinez filed an instant motion under 28 U.S.C. §2255 and recently received the United States Government's (hereinafter government) response thereto, he now files his reply in opposition to the government's theory.

DISCUSSION

Mr. Martinez's motion raised two grounds – both of which concerned his counsel Alvaro Martinez's (hereinafter counsel) ineffectiveness that resulted in Mr. Martinez being found guilty (by jury) of count one, a violation of 18 U.S.C. §2422 and of count three, a violation of 18 U.S.C. §2423, crimes which Mr. Martinez was actually innocent of.

Grounds one and two are as follows:

1) **"Mr. Martinez was deprived of a fair trial because his counsel, did not understand the scope of the convicting statute. Thus, counsel," s ineffectiveness facilitated the guilty verdict of someone who is actually innocent."**
2) **"Mr. Martinez was deprived of his statutory right to appeal because his appellate counsel provided ineffective assistance of counsel."**

The government opposes Mr. Martinez's motion, but agrees that "… if Petitioner could show that he is actually innocent of the charges, he would be entitled to equitable tolling and his §2255 motion would not be time barred." See "Government's Response …," page 5, ¶ 1.

Thus, because of the government's agreement, the only actual issue before the court at this juncture in the proceeding is whether Mr. Martinez can show proof of his actual innocence to overcome his procedural default.

In its response, the government raised only two issues that Mr. Martinez must address. These follow:

a. Petitioner's motion must be denied as time barred.

The timeliness of Mr. Martinez's motion is not in dispute. His motion is time-barred pursuant to §2255 (f)(1). This is the "procedural default" which Mr. Martinez must overcome prior to having his §2255 motion considered on the merits.

This bar on federal habeas (and §2255) relief can be overcome if the movant can demonstrate "cause" for the default and "prejudice" suffered as a result, (*Strickland v. Washington*, 466 U.S. 668 (1984" or the movant can demonstrate that failure to consider his claim would result in a "fundamental miscarriage of justice." See *Edwards v. Carpenter*, 529 U.S. 446, 451 (1991) and *Coleman v. Thompson*, 501 U.S. 722, 750 (1991)).

The "fundamental miscarriage of justice" test applies narrowly in certain instances when a constitutional violation probably has caused the conviction of one innocent of the crime. *McCleskey v. Zant*, 499 U.S. 467, 494 (1991).

Thus, although the government is factually correct in alleging that Mr. Martinez's §2255 motion is untimely, his procedural default is excused under the "actual innocence" exception ("actual innocence" and "fundamental miscarriage of justice" are used interchangeable by various courts).

"'In appropriate cases' the principles of comity and finality that inform concepts of cause and prejudice 'must yield' to the imperative of correcting a 'fundamentally unjust incarceration.' [citing *Engle v. Isaak*, 456 U.S. 107, 135 (1982)]. We remain confident that, for the most part, 'victims of a fundamental miscarriage of justice will meet the cause-and-prejudice standard.' But we do not pretend that this will always be true. Accordingly, we think that in an extraordinary case, where a constitutional violation has probably resulted in conviction of one who is actually innocent a federal habeas court may grant the writ even in the absence of a showing of cause for the procedural default." *Murray v. Carrier*, 477 U.S. 478, 495-6 (1986).

Mr. Martinez contends that his is an "appropriate case" for the application of this exception.

b) Petitioner is not entitled to equitable tolling.

The second issue raised in the government's response is "that Petitioner is not entitled to relief because he filed his instant motion more than a year after the facts supporting the claims in his §2255 motion could have been discovered through the exercise of due diligence. The government also contends that Petitioner is not entitled to relief based on 'equitable tolling.'" See "Government's Response ...," page 3, ¶ 2.

The government's second argument for denial of Mr. Martinez's §2255 makes reference to a number of legal principles that are governed by things such as "due diligence," "equitable tolling," "extraordinary circumstances," "actual innocence," and "new evidence." Notwithstanding the government's impressive vocabulary, it seems to rely only on Mr. Martinez's failure to present "newly discovered evidence" to support his "actual innocence." In an ordinary case, the government would be correct. But in Mr. Martinez's case he relies only on federal statutes to prove that his conduct is not prohibited by law and the government is well aware that a movant is prohibited from citing or arguing law in a 28 U.S.C. §2255 motion. Thus, the government intends to hide the law from the court as grounds to support its position that the court "does not need to address the merit of petitioner's claims ..." claims that rest fully on the proper application of federal statutes enacted by Congress. See Government's Response, page 5, ¶ 3.

Mr. Martinez contends:

First, regarding new evidence – it appears as if the government is arguing that the presentation of new evidence is somehow a prerequisite to the bringing of a claim under §2255. Mr. Martinez would posit the following in opposition to that argument:

1) Nowhere in §2255 is "new evidence" mentioned, *except* §2255(h) (1) which deals: with "second or successive" motions and is to be read in conjunction with 28 U.S.C. §2244. This is Mr. Martinez's initial §2255 motion and thus is subject to neither §2255 (h) (1) nor §2244.

2) "New evidence" is indeed discussed in the context of many actual innocence/miscarriage of justice decisions – See *Schlup v. Delo*, 513 U.S. 298, 329 (1994) – [A] petitioner does not meet the threshold requirement unless he persuades the district court that, in light of new evidence, no juror acting reasonably, would have voted to find him guilty." Accord, *Mc.Quiggin v. Perkins*" 569 U.S. __, 185 L. Ed. 2d 1019 at 1028 (2013). Both *Schlup* and *Mc.Quiggin*, Mr. Martinez would point out were second or successive motions, and in both cases, movants were proffering new evidence in support of their claims; thus, the Supreme Court naturally framed its pronouncements in terms of evaluating the new evidence. This does not make "new evidence" however, a predicate to pursuing an actual innocence claim as is shown in *Bousley v. United States*, 523 U.S. 614 (1998) in which Bousley filed his collateral claim attacking the validity of his guilty plea under an out-of-time first §2255 filing and was granted relief. The only "new evidence" cited by Bousley was the court's decision in *Bailey v. United States*, 516 U.S. 127 (1995), which when applied to his facts supported his claim of actual innocence.

Mr. Martinez in effect is offering "new evidence" similar to Bousley's in the form of his reliance on the statutes, actually enacted by Congress as opposed to the deviations that the government provided, to the court and the jury, at his trial. What the government is now trying to hide from the court is that Lt reworded the residual clause of 18 U.S.C. §§2422(b) and 2423(a), thus expanding the reach of the statute to criminalize the conduct Mr. Martinez was lawfully engaged in.

The government goes on to argue that "the court does not even need to reach the 'reliability of the evidence' analysis of the defendant's actual innocence claim because the defendant has brought forth no new evidence in his petition." Government's Response, page 5, ¶ 2, citing *McQuiggin v. Perkins*, 569 U.S. 383, 386-387; 133 S.Ct. 1924, 1928 (2013). Again, *McQuiggin* is based on the analysis of a second or successive petition and readily distinguishable from Mr. Martinez's first §2255 motion. Additionally, in Mr. Martinez's case it is the proper recitation and reach of a federal criminal statute that is in question as opposed to some mysterious new evidence, and thus the government's reliance on *McQuiggin* is misplaced.

In contrast, Mr. Martinez is not arguing that he is "innocent" of the facts as alleged, but that the facts themselves, as alleged by the government, do not constitute a crime under the convicting statutes as they were enacted by Congress. This is completely different from a defendant who is contesting that some mysterious "new evidence" proves that he did not engage in the conduct as accused. Mr. Martinez's contention that he is actually innocent is not based on "new evidence;" it represents the correct application of the facts to the elements of §2422(b) and §2423(a) which should have, but did not, because of his counsel's ineffectiveness, yield a finding of actual innocence.

Having addressed the issues of "new evidence" we now come to the question of how and why the "actual innocence/miscarriage of justice" exception applies to Mr. Martinez. In *Murray*, Supra., at 496, the Supreme Court stated, "we think that in extraordinary cases, where a constitutional violation has probably resulted in the conviction of someone who is actually innocent, a federal habeas court may grant the Writ even in the absence of cause for the procedural default." The Court went on to say that "there is an additional safeguard against miscarriages of justice in criminal cases … That safeguard is the right to effective assistance of counsel, which, as this court has indicated, may in a particular case be violated even by an isolated error of counsel if that error is sufficiently egregious and prejudicial." 477 U.S. at 496, citing *United States v. Cronic*, 466 U.S. at 693-6.

Mr. Martinez's case is indeed one of these "extraordinary cases," and the errors of his counsel were not just "isolated," but manifold and did indeed prejudice Mr. Martinez and thus denied him his constitutional right to effective counsel as well as his right to be heard in his defense at a fair trial. Mr. Martinez's counsel failed to do any meaningful research, or to even devote any serious thought as to how Mr. Martinez's actions did not constitute illegal conduct under the statutes. Mr. Martinez's counsel's ineffectiveness is shown by his failure to recognize that the government's mangled wording of the statutes in its charging papers, changed the scope of conduct from that which was intended to be prohibited by Congress. His counsel's misunderstanding of the elements of §2422(b) and §2423(a) are shown by a comparison between the statutes, as they are handed down by Congress, and the government's interpretation of the statutes' residual clause in its indictment. **TO WIT:**

The residual clause of §2422(b) reads: "or any sexual activity for which any person can be charged with a criminal offense ..."

The residual clause of §2423(a) reads: "or in any sexual activity for which any person can be charged with a criminal offense ..."

Although the two residual clauses of the two statutes differ by one word ("in") they are identical in meaning.

The indictment presented to the Grand Jury and to Mr. Martinez by the government, however, replaces the words "any person can be charged" with "he could have been charged ..."

What Mr. Martinez's counsel failed to understand is that by changing the modifier of the residual clause in the charging papers, the government also changed the meaning of the statute and the scope of conduct it prohibited in its presentation to the court, the jury, and to the defense.

This lack of understanding and failure to research on counsel's part was not confined to these examples but continued throughout his representation of Mr. Martinez. While a single isolated error or even several may not amount to ineffective assistance, when counsel continues to evince abject and consistent ignorance of the very statute he advised his client to proceed to trial against, then there can be no question as to his ineffectiveness. Consequently, it was impossible for Mr. Martinez to "knowingly" and "intelligently" decide to proceed to trial when he was erroneously notified of the charges against him.

This addresses the ineffective assistance of counsel prong of *Murray* which technically is not at issue yet, as this is Mr. Martinez's "gateway" claim. The issue actually at the heart of Mr. Martinez's reply is his claim of actual innocence. This will be discussed in detail infra.

4) "Due diligence" This argument is absolutely incorrect. In *McQuiggin*, Supra., the court stated, "it would be bizarre to hold that a petitioner who asserts a convincing claim of actual innocence may overcome the statutory time bar §2244 (d) (1) (D) erects, yet simultaneously encounter a court-fashioned diligence barrier to pursuit of her petition." *Id.* at 185 L. Ed. 2d 1035. The court then favorably quotes 670 F. 3d at 673 (the 6th Circuit's decision below) which stated, "requiring reasonable diligence effectively makes the concept of the actual innocence gateway claim redundant since petitioners ... seek [an equitable exception only] when they were not reasonably diligent in complying with §2244 (d) (1) (D)."

The government does quote *McQuiggin* in regard to the related timeliness issue in an attempt to undermine Mr. Martinez's "credibility." See "Government's Response ..." page 5, ¶ 1. This is simply wrong. The court in *McQuiggin* stated that timeliness "does bear on the credibility of evidence proffered to show actual innocence." McQuiggin was attempting to introduce stale affidavits in support of his actual innocence claim. Mr. Martinez seeks to proffer no new evidence. As he stated previously the only "new evidence" he asks the court to consider are the federal criminal statutes 2422(b) and 2423(a) as they were handed down by Congress and still in use today.

At any rate, Mr. Martinez would reiterate that in *Mcquigg* it clearly states that a showing of "due diligence" is not required where a movant in a §2255 action successfully shows he is actually innocent.

4) Did Mr. Martinez's conduct fit within the statutory definition of §§ 2422(b) and 2423(a)?

The government, in its response, fails to address this issue and urges the court that "it does not need to address the merit of petitioner's claims ..." either.

This question, however, lies at the heart of Mr. Martinez's actual innocence claim and must be addressed to determine if he has overcome the procedural bar to his ineffective assistance of counsel claims. In *United States v. Campos-Serrano*, 404 U.S. 293 (1971), the Supreme Court stated:

"It has long been settled that 'penal statutes are to be construed strictly,' [citations omitted] and that one 'is not to be subjected to a penalty unless the words of the statute plainly impose it,' [citations omitted] '[w]hen choice has to be made between two readings of what conduct Congress has made a crime, it is appropriate, before we choose the harsher alternative, to require that Congress should have spoken in language that is clear and definite.'" [citations omitted] *Id.* at 404 U.S. 297

Then in *Dunn v.* United States, 442 U.S. 1000 (1979), the Court stated,

"Thus, to ensure that a legislature speaks with special clarity when making the boundaries of criminal conduct, courts must decline to impose punishment for actions that are not 'plainly and unmistakenly' proscribed." *Id.* at 442 U.S. 112, citing *U.S. v. Gradwell*, 243 U.S. 476, 485 (1917)

At Mr. Martinez's trial, testimony was given to the extent that he, "provided information that he had traveled to Wisconsin on Memorial Day weekend 2012. He admitted to having sex with the juvenile on the second day in Wisconsin. (JT Vol. 1, 39-40). Martinez then made another trip in July 2012 to bring the juvenile to Texas to live with him living in his home in Stanton, Texas. The agents testified that Martinez admitted to having sexual intercourse with the juvenile once in Stanton, TX The juvenile's mother and her boyfriend came to Stanton, TX a few days later and picked up the juvenile. *Id.* 40-42

The juvenile testified that she moved in with Martinez at his apartment in Stanton, TX, *Id.* 63. She further testified that she had plans to get married to Martinez. *Id.* A few days after being in Texas, her mother came to Texas to pick her up because the mother was fearful of legal action against the mother. She was fearful because she had allowed her underage daughter (16) to move to Texas with Martinez (28). *Id.* 37, 66-67.

Wanda Tilot, the juvenile's mother, testified that she allowed the juvenile to come down to Texas with Martinez. *Id.* 66. See also brief of Defendant-Appellant in case no.: 13-50876 (5th Cir. 2014).

While Mr. Martinez was forthcoming about having sex with, and planning to marry, the alleged victim, with the consent of her parents, along with moving to Texas together, he at no time enticed a minor to engage in, or caused a minor to travel for the purpose that, the minor engage in prostitution, or [in] any sexual activity for which any person could be charged with a criminal offense. Moreover, the government never made any accusation that Mr. Martinez engaged in any conduct that Congress prohibited under the two statutes he is convicted of violating.

For the purpose of this discussion, Mr. Martinez would contend that only five "facts" regarding his conduct are relevant:

1) He engaged in conversations with a person who was sixteen years of age, in which he,

2) Decided to meet in person after obtaining consent from the parents of the teenager,

3) He did travel to Wisconsin to meet her and her family,

4) He did have sexual intercourse with the teen,

5) He and the teen did travel to Texas, with the consent of the teen's parents, for the purpose of getting married and living together.

In its response, the government does not contend that Mr. Martinez's conduct is, in fact, prohibited conduct under the statutes of conviction, nor does the government compare the facts to the statutes essential elements, it simply asks the court to ignore both the law and the claims Mr. Martinez raised.

Thus, in light of the above, Mr. Martinez would contend that the sole facts the court should consider in regard to determining his guilt or actual innocence under §§ 2422(b) and 2423(a) are the five he set out hereinabove at p. 8, Supra.

So the question squarely before the court at this time is whether or not §§ 2422(b) and 2423(a) as well as the definition of, "or any sexual activity for which any person can be charged with a criminal offense," criminalized the specific conduct engaging in sex with and the marrying of a minor female with the minor female's parents' consent. In order to determine this, we have to carefully examine these statutes.

The first statute, 18 U.S.C. §2422(b), reads as follows:

"(b) Whoever, using the mail or any facility or means of interstate or foreign commerce, or within the special maritime and territorial jurisdiction of the United States knowingly persuades, induces, entices, or coerces any individual who has not attained the age of 18 years, to engage in prostitution or any sexual activity for which any person can be charged with a criminal offense, or attempts to do so, shall be fined under this title and imprisoned not less than 10 years or for life."

The second statute, 18 U.S.C. §2423(a), reads as follows:

"(a) Transportation with intent to engage in criminal sexual activity. A person who knowingly transports an individual who has not attained the age of 18 years in interstate or foreign commerce, or in any commonwealth, territory or possession of the United States, with intent that the individual engage in prostitution, or in any sexual activity for which any person can be charged with a criminal offense, shall be fined under this title and imprisoned not less than 10 years or for life."

Although the two statutes prohibit different conduct, they are identical in their purpose. In a close reading of each it is discovered that one (§2422(b)) prohibits the "enticement" of "any individual who has not attained the age of 18 years, to engage in *prostitution* ..." And that the second (§2423(a)) prohibits the act of "knowingly transporting an individual who has not attained the age of 18 years ... with the intent that the individual engage in *prostitution* ..."

As seen here *Prostitution* is the enumerated predicate offense in both statutes. Prostitution is prohibited by law throughout the entire United States with few exceptions like specific areas in Nevada. In Nevada, the state law authorized prostitution under very limited circumstances. One very specific requirement is that no minor (under the age of 18 years presumably) may engage in prostitution. Thus, it is unlawful for a minor to engage in prostitution anywhere in the United States or its territories and jurisdictions. It is also noteworthy that minors who are caught engaging in prostitution are charged with solicitation in cities across America.

The purpose of 18 U.S.C. §§ 2422(b) and 2423(a) is specifically to punish any person who knowingly causes a minor to engage in prostitution. This is set out in both statutes as the underlying predicate offense. Mr. Martinez, however, was not charged with nor did the government allege that he caused or attempted to cause any minor to engage in prostitution.

The government, in Mr. Martinez's case, relied on the alternative means of both statutes to shoe horn his conduct into a federal case. The alternative means clause, or residual clause, in both statutes allows the prosecution of any person who causes or intends to cause a minor to engage in "*any sexual activity for which any person can be charged with a criminal offense* ..." Thus, to determine if Mr. Martinez is actually innocent, the court must decide if his conduct is in fact a sexual activity for which any person can be charged with a criminal offense. Mr. Martinez contends that it is not because any person, i.e. the alleged victim, is not chargeable for the underlying offense.

The plain reading of both statutes in question shows that Congress intended to prohibit the conduct of causing a minor to engage in Prostitution or any other sexual activity for which "any person," including the minor, could be charged with a criminal offense. Congress went on to clarify its intent by defining the residual clause in 18 U.S.C. §2427 as to include the production of child pornography. Just as with underage prostitution, the production of child pornography is a prohibited act throughout the United States without exception, for which even a minor is chargeable. Congress's intent, to prohibit the conduct of causing a minor to engage in sexual criminal conduct, for which the minor could be charged, is plain in the reading of the residual clause in both statutes.

The residual clauses of §§2422(b) and 2423(a), "or [in] any sexual activity for which any person can be charged with a criminal offense …," were very carefully drafted by Congress exemplifying their specific intent. That intent was to include, as criminal, causing a minor to engage in any other sexually criminal conduct for which the minor may also be charged, i.e. "any person." The plain English reading of the residual clauses expresses Congress's intent to limit the underlying conduct that could trigger both federal statutes. Although at first glance one considers that Congress's intent for "any sexual activity" to trigger the statute, that understanding is not correct. What Congress intended to express is that the sexual activity, that can be used to trigger the statutes, is to be limited to sexual activity for which "any person" can be charged with a criminal offense. Thus, if "any person" (i.e. the minor) is not chargeable for engaging in the specific "sexual activity" accused, then the federal criminal statutes are not triggered.

In Mr. Martinez's case, no minor was chargeable for engaging in any sexual activity. Nor was a minor enticed or transported with the intent that a minor engages in any sexual activity for which the minor could be charged with a criminal offense. Because no minor (any person) was chargeable for the underlying conduct, the conduct was not and is not prohibited by either federal statute. The plain reading of the residual clauses, in §2422(b) and §2423(a), identify that Mr. Martinez's conduct was not criminal conduct under the statutes and because his conduct was never criminal, he is in fact actually innocent.

It is a bedrock tenet of the law that in order for conduct to be criminal, it must be defined by Congress *within the four corners of the statute*. It is clear that Congress could, one day, enact legislation which criminalized Martinez's conduct, but neither the courts nor the government can redraft a statute to provide elements which do not exist. This problem has been addressed in many contexts. The general notion is that the judiciary should not act to fill "gaps" in legislation to correct perceived deficiencies or remedy defectively drafted laws. Perhaps this sentiment was best stated in *Viereck v. U.S.*, 318 U.S. 236 (1942) where the Supreme Court reversed the conviction of a German national who was acting as a propagandist for the Third Reich, disseminating pro-Nazi propaganda while U.S. soldiers were being slaughtered by the Germans in Europe. His actions were obviously not looked upon with favor by the government or the American people in general. The government had accused the defendant of failure to register as a foreign agent. In reversing the conviction, the Court stated:

> "one may be subjected to punishment for a crime in the federal courts only for the commission or omission of an act defined by statute, or by regulation having legislative authority, and then only if punishment is authorized by Congress [citation omitted]. *Id.* at 241.

The government argued for an expansive reading of the statute. In response, the Court stated:

> "The unambiguous words of a statute which imposes criminal penalties are not to be altered by judicial construction so as to punish one not otherwise within its reach, however deserving of punishment his conduct may seem." *Id.* at 243.

The Court emphasized the point that it is not within the judiciary's province to punish an individual's acts which are not prohibited by law even if they would seem to merit such punishment:

> "Even though the specific restriction of Sec. 3(c) were due to defective draftsmanship or inadvertence, which hardly seems to be the case, men are not subjected to criminal punishment because their conduct offends our patriotic emotions or thwarts a general purpose sought to be effected by specific commands which they have not disobeyed. Nor are they to be held guilty of offenses which condemn. For the courts are without authority to repress evil save as the law has proscribed it and then only according to law." *Id.* at 245.

This doctrine has not changed over the years. In October of 2019, the Supreme Court heard oral arguments in the case of *Altitude Express v. Zarda*, 833 F. 3d 100 (2nd Cir. 2018), [below]. In an exchange with the government's attorney during oral argument, Justice Kagan stated the following:

> "For many years the loadstar of this court's statutory interpretation has been the text of the statute, not the legislative history, and certainly not the subsequent legislative history ... This is the usual kind of way in which we interpret statutes now. We look to the laws. We don't look to predictions. We don't look to desires. We don't look to wishes. We look to the laws." As quoted in "The Pivotal Justice," by Margaret Talbot, *The New Yorker*, 11/18/19, p. 41.

CONCLUSION

There is one final thing that Mr. Martinez wishes to make clear – this is not a vagueness case. 18 *U.S.C.* §§2422(b) and 2423(a) are sufficiently precise in their meaning; they just do not criminalize the marriage of a minor to an adult, which is lawful conduct in the state with parental consent. Even when, like in Mr. Martinez's case, the government feels that any sexual activity should trigger the federal statutes, they are still limited by the intent Congress voiced in the words of the law. As Viereck makes clear, even where gaps in a criminal statute are likely due to "defective draftsmanship or inadvertence," citizens are not "to be held guilty of offenses which the statutes have omitted, though by inadvertence, to define and condemn." *Viereck*, Supra., at 245.

Thus, Mr. Martinez is actually innocent because his conduct simply is not prohibited by any federal statute. Because Mr. Martinez has established his actual innocence under federal law, his claims of ineffective assistance of counsel should be allowed to proceed. Moreover, this court should deny the government's motion to dismiss and require its attorney to respond to the constitutional claims raised in Mr. Martinez's original 28 D.S.C. §2255 motion.

Wherefore, above premises considered, Mr. Martinez moves this court to grant this motion in the nature of fairness and equity.

Respectfully submitted on February 10, 2020, by:

Charles Riley Martinez, pro se
Reg.# 10930-380
Federal Correctional Institution
P.O. Box 9000
Seagoville, TX 75159

CERTIFICATE OF SERVICE

I hereby certify that on February 10, 2020, I served a true and correct copy of this motion on the attorney for the government, 400 W. Illinois Ave., Suite 1200, Midland, TX 79701. Delivery of the motion was completed by placing it in the legal mailing system as made available to inmates via U.S. mail, properly addressed, and first-class postage prepaid.

Respectfully submitted on February 10, 2020, by:

Charles Riley Martinez, pro se
Reg.#

CHAPTER FOUR

SECOND IN-TIME §2255

I didn't make this one up myself. However, you should be forewarned, the term "second-in-time §2255" is bound to raise quite a stir in any court where one is filed. That is because this term is rarely used and almost never understood by courts or U.S. Attorneys. As far as my research has shown me, 2018 was the first time it appeared in a court's opinion. Although the principle has preceded the Supreme Court's use of it in *Panetti v. Quarterman*, 551 U.S. 930, 127, S.Ct. 2842, 168 L. Ed. 2d 662 (2007); I believe the phrase was first coined as seen here in *Johnson v. United States*, 724 Fed. Appx. 917 (11th Cir. 2018).

The fifth paragraph of 28 U.S.C. §2255, §2255(e), deprives a sentencing court from having the authority to entertain a second or successive motion for relief if it appears that "such court has denied him relief …" This means that if a prisoner has raised a claim in a §2255 motion, and the court denied that claim, then the court will not have the authority to determine that claim for a second time.

But the Supreme Court has made clear that this provision cannot be held to a literal reading. The Supreme Court has stated that the controlling weight may be given to the denial of a prior motion under §2255 only if:

1) The same claim raised in the second motion was determined against the prisoner in a prior motion;

2) The prior judgment was based on a determination of the merits of the claim the prisoner raised; and

3) The ends of justice would not be served by reaching the merits of the claim raised in the second motion.

Authors Note: This sounds easy at first, but also know that if you raise a different claim in a new motion or the same claim that was not determined on the merits; the successive motion should not be considered if it is an abuse of the §2255 remedy. This means that your motion can be dismissed out of hand if you deliberately withheld or deliberately abandoned one or more of your claims in your first motion.

Another point that must be made about the above three conditions, is elementary but important. Please take special note of the conjunctive between numbers two and three, notice the word "and." This means that all three conditions must apply to determine your second-in-time §2255 is in fact second or successive. The government in its response, however, will suggest that only one or more conditions need apply, just as though the conjunctive between two and three was "or" instead of "and." This is important to understand so pay attention to it.

Denial of a §2255 motion on the basis that the claims it raised could have been made in an earlier §2255 motion has been held by the Supreme Court to have been improper under particular circumstances.

The standard of review of a district court's dismissal of a §2255 motion as "second or successive" is de novo, *Stewart v. United States*, 646 F.3d, 856, 858 (11th Cir. 2011). "Under the Antiterrorism and Effective Death Penalty Act ("AEDPA"), a prisoner who has previously filed a §2255 motion must apply for and obtain authorization from a Court of Appeals before filing a "second or successive" motion, 28 U.S.C. §§2244(b)(3)(A), 2255(h). Absent prior authorization from a Court of Appeals, a district court lacks jurisdiction to consider a second or successive §2255 motion, *United States v. Holt*, 417 F. 3d. 1172, 1175 (11th. Cir. 2005).

The phrase "second or successive" is not self-defining, however, and does not refer to all habeas applications filed second in time, *Stewart*, 646 F. 3d. 859. "[W]hen a petitioner raises a claim that could not have been raised in a prior habeas petition, courts have forgone a literal reading of 'second or successive,'" *Id.* at 860; *Johnson v. United States*, 724 Fed. Appx. 917 (11th Cir. 2018).

The Eleventh Circuit in discussing the AEDPA's gateway provision, second or successive, in *Stewart* said:

> AEDPA dramatically limits successive attempts at habeas relief. If a §2255 motion is deemed "successive," a court may consider it only if it complies with that section's gatekeeping provision, which provides:
>
>> A second or successive motion must be certified as provided in section 2244 by a panel of appropriate court of appeals to contain –

1) newly discovered evidence that, if proven and viewed in light of the evidence as a whole, would be sufficient to establish by clear and convincing evidence that no reasonable factfinder would have found the movant guilty of the offense; or

2) a new rule of constitutional law made retroactive to cases on collateral review by the Supreme Court, that was previously unavailable. 28 U.S.C. §2255(h). AEDPA's restrictions on second or successive motions are meant to forestall abuse of the writ of habeas corpus, see *Felker v. Turpin*, 518 U.S. 651, 664, 116 S.Ct. 2333, 2340, 135 L. Ed. 2d 827 (1996), by, for instance, barring successive motions raising habeas claims that could have been raised in earlier motions where there was no legitimate excuse for failure to do so, see *McCleskey v. Zant*, 499 U.S. 467, 493-95, 111 S.Ct. 1454, 1469-71, 113 L. Ed. 2d 517 (1991). But the Supreme Court has unequivocally explained that the phrase "second or successive" is not self-defining and does not refer to all habeas applications filed second or successively in time, *Panetti v. Quarterman*, 551 U.S. 930, 943-44, 127 S.Ct. 2842, 2853, 168L. Ed. 2d 662 (2007). Rather, it is a term of art that takes its full meaning from the Supreme Court's case law, including decisions predating the enactment of AEDPA. *Id.*, 127 S.Ct. at 2853.

Particularly when a petitioner raises a claim that could not have been raised in a prior habeas petition, courts have forgone a literal reading of "second or successive," see, e.g., *Singleton v. Norris*, 319 F.3d 1018 1023 (8th Cir. 2003) (*en banc*) (finding that Singleton's petition was not successive when it raised a claim that did not arise until he was subject to an involuntary medication order pursuant to *Washington v. Harper* and his execution date had been scheduled); *United States v. Orozco-Ramirez*, 211 F.3d 862, 869, 871 (5th Cir. 2000) ("[Orozco-Ramirez's] claim of ineffective assistance of counsel during [his] out-of-time appeal ... could not have been raised in [his] prior proceeding and, thus, is not 'second or successive')."

But adopting that approach too broadly would threaten Congress's clear intention to limit "second or successive" attempts at post-conviction relief. Therefore, we must confront the difficult task of distinguishing between those previously unavailable claims that Congress contemplated in AEDPA's gatekeeping provisions and those that cannot reasonably be deemed "successive."

The Fifth Circuit addressed this difficulty in *Leal Garcia v. Quarterman*, 573 F. 3d 214, 222 (5th Cir. 2009). It concluded that a subsequent §2254 petition that was based on a defect that did not arise until after the proceedings on the previous petition were completed was not successive, *Id.* at 224. The facts in Leal Garcia are complicated and presented fully in the Fifth Circuit's opinion, but the following facts are most relevant for our purposes.

After Leal Garcia, a Mexican national, filed his first petition for habeas relief, the International Court of Justice ("ICJ") issued its decision in *Case Concerning Avena and Other Mexican Nationals (Mexico v. United States)*, 2004 1. C.J. (Judgment of March 31, 2004) ("Avena") which held that the United States violated the Vienna Convention's guarantee of consular access and ordered that the convictions and sentences of those individuals whose rights were violated be reviewed, *Leal Garcia*, 573 F.3d at 216-18. In response, President George W. Bush signed a declaration ordering states to comply with the mandate in *Avena, Id* at 218. Based on the President's declaration, Leal Garcia filed a state habeas petition requesting review of his conviction and sentence, *Id.* After determining that *Avena* and the President's declaration were not binding on the states, the Texas Court of Criminal Appeals denied Leal Garcia's pending *Avena*-related state petition. *Id.* Leal Garcia then returned to federal court, filing his second federal habeas petition, which challenged the state court's refusal to grant him review in light of *Avena* and the President's declaration. *Id.* at 217, 220 & n.27. The Western District of Texas dismissed that petition for lack of jurisdiction. *Id.* at 217.

On appeal, the Fifth Circuit set out to determine if Leal Garcia's petition was successive under AEDPA, and, therefore, subject to the statute's gatekeeping provisions, *Id.* at 219. Leal Garcia relied on *In re Cain*, 137 F.3d 234 (5th Cir. 1998), to argue that his petition was "non-successive because it [was] based on a claim unavailable to him at the time of his first habeas petition," Leal Garcia, 573 F.3d at 220 (emphasis added). The court rejected the full breadth of Leal Garcia's interpretation because it did not comport with AEDPA's treatment of the term "successive," *Id.* at 221. To adopt Leal Garcia's approach – classifying as "non-successive" any petition based on a claim that was "unavailable" at the time of a first petition – would nullify AEDPA's gatekeeping provisions, *Id.* (explaining that "claims based on new rules of constitutional law (made retroactive by the Supreme Court)," and "claims based on a factual predicate not previously discoverable" are both subject to the gatekeeping provision; therefore, both are previously unavailable and "successive" under AEDPA).

But the court determined that Leal Garcia's claim fell within a small subset of unavailable claims that could not reasonably be categorized as "successive," *Id.* at 222, 224. After noting the AEDPA's gate-keeping provisions are meant to minimize repeated attacks on an underlying judgment, the court stated:

> [I]f the purported defect existed, or the claim was ripe, at the time of the prior petition, the later petition is likely to be held successive even if the legal basis for the attack was not. If, however, the purported defect did not arise, or the claim did not ripen, until after the conclusion of the previous petition, the later petition based on that defect may be non-successive, *Id.* at 222 (emphasis added). The court noted that the President's declaration, meant to make *Avena* enforceable on the states, was not issued until after Leal Garcia's first petition was denied, *Id.* at 223-24. Therefore, "the basis for his claim – Texas's refusal to conduct the review of his conviction – did not occur until well after proceedings on his first petition had concluded," *Id.* at 224. Consequently, Leal Garcia's subsequent petition was not successive under AEDPA. *Id.*

The Fifth Circuit's approach in Leal Garcia is consonant with the Supreme Court's reasoning in *Panetti v. Quarterman*, 551 U.S. at 943-45, 127 S.Ct. at 2853. There, the Court concluded that because the petitioner's *Ford* claim did not ripen until after his first habeas petition was fully adjudicated on the merits his subsequent petition was not "second or successive" under AEDPA. The Court rejected the state's argument that a prisoner contemplating a future *Ford* claim must preserve that claim by filing it in his or her first habeas petition, *Id.* at 943, 946, 127 S.Ct. at 2852, 2854. It explained that, were such an interpretation of "second or successive correct, "the implications or habeas practice would be far reaching and seemingly perverse," *Id.* at 943, 127 S.Ct. at 2852 (quoting *Martinez-Villareal*, 523 U.S. at 644, 118 S.Ct. at 1621). "A prisoner would be faced with two options: forgo the opportunity to raise a *Ford* claim in federal court; or raise the claim in a first federal habeas application (which generally must be filed within one year of the relevant state-court ruling), even though it is premature," *Id.*, 127 S.Ct. at 2852.

Now that the standard for filing a second-in-time §2255 is set firmly in your mind, here are some of the circumstances in which to file one:

- Actual innocence that you can somehow prove is always a dead ringer. Also, an actual innocence claim can always be actionable regardless of the many possible procedural defaults. See *McQuiggin v. Perkins*.

- A change in law that clarifies Congress's intent that is not made retroactive, but does make you actually innocent. This works best when Congress makes clear that they never intended for your conduct to trigger the criminal statute that you are charged with.

- A change in constitutional law (a case) that is made retroactively applicable to cases on collateral review, and that makes a new claim available to you that you have not raised before. Keep in mind that there is a lot of gray area with this third one. Many courts would rather that you file for second or successive authorization in this situation because they *know* that the circuit court will deny it out of hand. Not to worry, sometimes we have to play along and then file the second-in-time motion.

The rest of this chapter is the path that I was forced to travel on behalf of Michael DeAngelo Davis in the Northern District of Texas. I use his case out of the many I have filed because his best exemplifies every possible angle under the second-in-time procedure.

Just a little background, Mr. Davis appealed his case and then filed a §2255 motion. In his quest for review; he *did* raise both claims that I now rely on, which forced me to seek second or successive authorization first. Once he was denied by the Court of Appeals, I was then authorized to file for relief under a second-in-time §2255, because The First Step Act and *United States v. Davis*, 139 S.Ct. 2319 (2019), identified Mr. Michael Davis as actually innocent in both claims.

POST-CONVICTION RELIEF: SECOND LAST CHANCE

MOTION UNDER 28 U.S.C. § 2244 FOR ORDER AUTHORIZING DISTRICT COURT TO CONSIDER
SECOND OR SUCCESSIVE APPLICATION FOR RELIEF UNDER 28 U.S.C. §§ 2254 OR 2255

United States Court of Appeals for the 5th Circuit

Name of Movant Michael D. Davis	Prisoner Number 24604-077	Case Number (leave blank)
Place of Confinement Seagoville F.C.I.		

IN RE: Michael Davis   , MOVANT

---

1. Name and location of court which entered the judgment of conviction from which relief is sought:

   U.S. District Court, Fort Worth, TX

2. Parties' Names: United States _____ vs. Michael Davis

3. Docket Number: 4:93-cr-020-A-1 _____ 4. Date Filed: Unknown

5. Date of judgment of conviction: September 10, 1993 _____ 6. Length of sentence: 457 months

7. Nature of offense(s) involved (all counts):

   Hobbs Act Robbery and possession of a gun 18 U.S.C. §1951 and §924(c)

8. What was your plea? (Check one) [X] Not Guilty   [ ] Guilty   [ ] Nolo Contendere

9. If you pleaded not guilty, what kind of trial did you have? (Check one) [X] Jury   [ ] Judge only

10. Did you testify at your trial? (Check one) [ ] Yes   [X] No

11. Did you appeal from the judgment of conviction? (Check one) [X] Yes   [ ] No

12. If you did appeal, what was the

   Name of court appealed to: Fifth Circuit Court of Appeals

   Parties' names on appeal: United States vs. Davis

   Docket number of appeal: 93-1851 _____ Date of decision: Unknown

   Result of appeal: Affirmed

13. Other than a direct appeal from the judgment of conviction and sentence, have you filed any other petitions, applications for relief, or other motions regarding this judgment in any federal court?   [X] Yes   [ ] No

14. If you answered "Yes" to question 13, answer the following questions:

A. FIRST PETITION, APPLICATION, OR MOTION

(1) In what court did you file the petition, application, or motion? U.S. Supreme Court

(2) What were the parties' names? United States vs. Davis

(3) What was the docket number of the case? Unknown

(4) What relief did you seek? Reverse and Remand

(5) What grounds for relief did you state in your petition, application, or motion? Double Jeopardy

(6) Did the court hold an evidentiary hearing on your petition, application or motion? ☐ Yes ☒ No

(7) What was the result? ☐ Relief granted ☒ Relief denied on the merits

☐ Relief denied for failure to exhaust ☐ Relief denied for procedural default

(8) Date of court's decision: January 9, 1995

B. SECOND PETITION, APPLICATION, OR MOTION

(1) In what court did you file the petition, application, or motion? U.S.D.C. Northern District of TX

(2) What were the parties' names? Davis vs. United States

(3) What was the docket number of the case? Unknown

(4) What relief did you seek? Vacature of sentence

(5) What grounds for relief did you state in your petition, application, or motion? Double Jeopardy

(6) Did the court hold an evidentiary hearing on your petition, application or motion? ☐ Yes ☒ No

(7) What was the result? ☐ Relief granted ☐ Relief denied on the merits

☐ Relief denied for failure to exhaust ☒ Relief denied for procedural default

(8) Date of court's decision: Unknown

C. THIRD AND SUBSEQUENT PETITIONS, APPLICATIONS, OR MOTIONS
For any third or subsequent petition, application, or motion, attach a separate page providing the information required in items (1) through (8) above for first and second petitions, applications, or motions.

D. PRIOR APPELLATE REVIEW(S)

Did you appeal the results of your petitions, applications, or motions to a federal court of appeals having jurisdiction over your case? If so, list the docket numbers and dates of final disposition for all subsequent petitions, applications, or motions filed in a federal court of appeals.

First petition, application, or motion	☐ Yes	Appeal No. __N/A__	☐ No
Second petition, application, or motion	☐ Yes	Appeal No. __N/A__	☐ No
Subsequent petitions, applications or motions	☐ Yes	Appeal No. __N/A__	☐ No
Subsequent petitions, applications or motions	☐ Yes	Appeal No. __N/A__	☐ No
Subsequent petitions, applications or motions	☐ Yes	Appeal No. __N/A__	☐ No
Subsequent petitions, applications or motions	☐ Yes	Appeal No. __N/A__	☐ No

If you did not appeal from the denial of relief on any of your prior petitions, applications, or motions, state which denials you did not appeal and explain why you did not.

15. Did you present any of the claims in this application in any previous petition, application, or motion for relief under 28 U.S.C. § 2254 or § 2255? (Check one)   ☐ Yes   ☒ No

16. If your answer to question 15 is "Yes," give the docket number(s) and court(s) in which such claims were raised and state the basis on which relief was denied.

N/A

17. If your answer to question 15 is "No," why not? This Court will grant you authority to file in the district court only if you show that you could not have presented your present claims in your previous § 2254 or § 2255 application because . . .

A. (For § 2255 motions only) the claims involve "newly discovered evidence that, if proven and viewed in light of the evidence as a whole, would be sufficient to establish by clear and convincing evidence that no reasonable factfinder would have found [you] guilty"; or,

B. (For § 2254 petitions only) "the factual predicate for the claim could not have been discovered previously through the exercise of due diligence" and "the facts underlying the claim, if proven and viewed in light of the evidence as a whole, would be sufficient to establish by clear and convincing evidence that, but for constitutional error, no reasonable factfinder would have found [you] guilty of the offense"; or,

C. (For both § 2254 and § 2255 applicants) the claims involve "a new rule of constitutional law, made retroactive to cases on collateral review by the Supreme Court [of the United States], that was previously unavailable."

The claim in this motion did not become available until the passing of The First Step Act of 2018. In Section 403 of the act, Congress clarified 18 U.S.C. §924(c) of The United States Code. The new act states that, "In general, section 924(c)(1)(C) of title 18, United States code, is amended, in the matter preceding clause (i), by striking 'second or subsequent conviction under this subsection' and inserting 'violation of this subsection that occurs after a prior conviction under this subsection has become final'. As indicated the First Step Act has "clarified" that Mr. Davis, a first time offender under §924(c), was impermissably subjected to an enhanced sentence. This court should grant review because, the Fist Step Act, section 403, is a change in law that provides guidance on the intent of Congress. The decision of Congress in the First Step Act interpreted a previously enacted statute, 18 U.S.C. §924(c). Thus, is considered retroactive because it is substantive. When a change in law alters the range of conduct or the class of persons (i.e. first time offenders like Mr. Davis) that the law punishes. By clarifying the law Congress changed the substantive reach of 18 U.S.C. §924(c), excluding all first time offenders from the reach of it's punishment. See Welch v. United States, 136 S. Ct. 1257; Johnson v. United States, 135 S. Ct. 2251; and Teague v. Lane, 109 S. Ct. 1060.

I did not present the following claims in any previous petition, application, or motion for relief under 28 U.S.C. § 2254: Because the statute of conviction has just recently been "clarified" by Congress on December 21, 2018.

I did not present the claims listed above in any previous petition, application, or motion because

Movant prays that the United States Court of Appeals for the Circuit grant an Order Authorizing the District Court to Consider Movant's Second or Successive Application for Relief Under 28 U.S.C. §§ 2254 or 2255.

_____
Movant's Signature

I declare under Penalty of Perjury that my answers to all questions in this Motion are true and correct. Executed on ____April 8, 2019____
   [date]

_____
Movant's Signature

PROOF OF SERVICE

A copy of this motion and all attachments must be sent to the state attorney general (§ 2254 cases) or the United States Attorney for the United States judicial district in which you were convicted (§ 2255 cases).

I certify that on ___April 8, 2019___ I mailed a copy of this motion and all attachments
   [date]

to _Clerk of the Fifth Circuit of the Court of Appeals_ at the following address:
600 South Maestri Place
New Orleans, LA 70130

_____
Movant's Signature

56

POST-CONVICTION RELIEF: SECOND LAST CHANCE

IN THE UNITED STATES DISTRICT COURT
FOR THE NORTHERN DISTRICT OF TEXAS

MOTION UNDER 28 U.S.C. SECTION 2255,
TO VACATE, SET ASIDE, OR CORRECT SENTENCE BY A
PERSON IN FEDERAL CUSTODY

UNITED STATES OF AMERICA

vs.

Michael Davis
_____
MOVANT (full name of movant)

Seagoville F.C.I.
_____
PLACE OF CONFINEMENT

24604-077
_____
PRISONER ID NUMBER

4:93-cr-020-A-1
_____
CRIMINAL CASE NUMBER

(If a movant has a sentence to be served in the future under a federal judgment which he wishes to attack, he should file a motion in the federal court which entered the judgment.)

INSTRUCTIONS - READ CAREFULLY

1. This motion must be legibly handwritten or typewritten, and signed by the movant under penalty of perjury. Any false statement of a material fact may serve as the basis for prosecution and conviction for perjury. All questions must be answered concisely in the proper space on the form.

2. Additional pages are not permitted except with respect to the facts which you rely upon to support your grounds for relief. No citation of authorities needs to be furnished. If briefs or arguments are submitted, they should be submitted in the form of a separate memorandum.

3. Upon receipt, your motion will be filed if it is in proper order. No fee is required with this motion.

4. If you do not have the necessary funds for transcripts, counsel, appeal, and other costs connected with a motion of this type, you may request permission to proceed *in forma pauperis*, in which event you must execute the declaration provided with this motion, setting forth information establishing your inability to prepay the fees and costs or give security therefor. If you wish to proceed *in forma pauperis*, you must have an authorized officer at the penal institution complete the certificate as to the amount of money and securities on deposit to your credit in any account in the institution.

5. Only judgments entered by one court may be challenged in a single motion. If you seek to challenge judgments entered by different judges or divisions either in the same district or in different districts, you must file separate motions as to each such judgment.

6. Your attention is directed to the fact that you must include all grounds for relief and all facts supporting such grounds for relief in the motion you file seeking relief from any judgment of conviction.

7. When the motion is fully completed, the original and two copies must be mailed to the Clerk of the United States District Court for the Northern District of Texas at the appropriate divisional office whose address is:

Abilene Division	Amarillo Division	Dallas Division	Fort Worth Division
P.O. Box 1218	205 E. 5th St, Rm 133	1100 Commerce, Rm 1452	501 W. 10th St, Rm 310
Abilene, TX 79604	Amarillo, TX 79101	Dallas, TX 75242	Fort Worth, TX 76102

Lubbock Division	San Angelo Division	Wichita Falls Division
1205 Texas Ave., Rm 209	33 East Twohig St, Rm 202	P.O. Box 1234
Lubbock, TX 79401	San Angelo, TX 76903	Wichita Falls, TX 76307

8. Motions which do not conform to these instructions will be returned with a notation as to the deficiency.

MOTION

1. Name and location of court that entered the judgment of conviction you are challenging:

> U.S. District Court
> Fort Worth, Texas

2. Date of the judgment of conviction:

> September 10, 1993

3. Length of sentence: **457 months**

4. Nature of offense involved (all counts):

> Hobbs Act Robbery
>
> Possession of firearm during crime of violence

5. (a) What was your plea? (Check one)

    Not guilty ☒   Guilty ☐   Nolo contendere (no contest) ☐

  (b) If you entered a guilty plea to one count or indictment, and a not guilty plea to another count or
    or indictment, what did you plead guilty to and what did you plead not guilty to?

> N/A

6. If you went to trial, what kind of trial did you have? (Check one)   Jury ☒   Judge Only ☐

7. Did you testify at the trial? (Check one)   Yes ☐   No ☒

8. Did you appeal from the judgment of conviction? (Check one)   Yes ☒   No ☐

9. If you did appeal, answer the following:

Name of Court: **Fifth Circuit**

Result: **Affirmed**

Date of result: **August 22, 1994**

10. Other than a direct appeal from the judgment of conviction and sentence, have you previously filed any petitions, applications, or motions with respect to this judgment in any federal court?

    Yes ☒   No ☐

11. If your answer to 10 was "Yes" give the following information:

    Name of Court: Supreme Court of the United States

    Nature of proceeding:

    > Request for Certiorari

    Grounds raised:

    > Sentence enhancements

    Did you receive an evidentiary hearing on your petition, application or motion?

    Yes ☐   No ☒

    Result: Certiorari denied

    Date of result: January 9, 1995

    As to any *second* petition, application or motion, give the same information:

    Name of Court: U.S. District Court, Northern Division, Fort Worth

    Nature of proceeding:

    > § 2255

    Grounds raised:

    > Mr. Davis has no recollection of the Motion's content

    Did you receive an evidentiary hearing on your petition, application or motion?

    Yes ☐   No ☒

    Result: Dismissed as untimely

    Date of result: July 2, 2001

As to any *third* petition, application or motion, give the same information:

Name of Court: **N/A**

Nature of proceeding:

> **N/A**

Grounds raised:

> **N/A**

Did you receive an evidentiary hearing on your petition, application or motion?

Yes ☐   No ☐   **N/A**

Result: **N/A**

Date of result: **N/A**

Did you appeal to an appellate federal court having jurisdiction, the result of action taken on any petition, application or motion?

First petition, etc.	Yes ☐	No ☒
Second petition, etc.	Yes ☒	No ☐
Third petition, etc.	Yes ☐	No ☐ **N/A**

If you did not <u>appeal</u> from the adverse action on any petition, application or motion, explain briefly why you did not:

> **N/A**

12. State <u>concisely</u> every ground on which you claim that you are being held unlawfully. Summarize <u>briefly</u> the facts supporting each ground. If necessary, you may attach pages stating additional grounds and facts supporting same.

> **CAUTION:** If you fail to set forth all grounds in this motion, you may be barred from presenting additional grounds at a later date.

For your information, the following is a list of the most frequently raised grounds for relief in these proceedings. Each statement preceded by a letter constitutes a separate ground for possible relief. You may raise any grounds which you may have other than those listed. However, you <u>should raise in this petition all available grounds</u> (relating to this conviction) on which you based your allegations that you are being held in custody unlawfully.

<u>DO NOT CHECK ANY OF THESE LISTED GROUNDS.</u> If you select one or more of these grounds for relief, you must allege facts. The motion will be returned to you if you merely check (a) through (j) or any of these grounds.

(a)   Conviction obtained by plea of guilty which was unlawfully induced or not made voluntarily or with understanding of the nature of the charge and the consequences of the plea.

(b)   Conviction obtained by use of coerced confession.

(c)   Conviction obtained by use of evidence gained pursuant to an unconstitutional search and seizure.

(d)   Conviction obtained by use of evidence obtained pursuant to an unlawful arrest.

(e)   Conviction obtained by a violation of the privilege against self-incrimination.

(f)   Conviction obtained by the unconstitutional failure of the prosecution to disclose to the defendant evidence favorable to the defendant.

(g)   Conviction obtained by a violation of the protection against double jeopardy.

(h)   Conviction obtained by action of a grand or petit jury which was unconstitutionally selected and impaneled.

(i)   Denial of effective assistance of counsel.

(j)   Denial of right to appeal.

62

A.   Ground One:

> The First Step Act has clarified 18 U.S.C. § 924(c) in such a way that identifies that Mr. Davis' second 924(c) conviction as unconstitutional.

Supporting FACTS (tell your story briefly without citing cases or law):

> Supporting facts: Mr. Davis is due retroactive application of the First Step Act, section 403, because it is a decision that interprets the reach of 18 U.S.C. § 924(c)(1)(C)(i) and as such is substantive.
>
> See attached Memorandum

B.   Ground Two:

> N/A

Supporting FACTS (tell your story briefly without citing cases or law):

> N/A

C.   Ground Three:

> N/A

Supporting FACTS (tell your story briefly without citing cases or law):

> N/A

D. Ground Four:

> **N/A**

Supporting FACTS (tell your story <u>briefly</u> without citing cases or law):

> **N/A**

13. If any of the grounds listed in 12A, B, C, and D were not previously presented, state briefly what grounds were not so presented, and give your reasons for not presenting them:

> **The ground herein was not made available until the enactment of the First Step Act, on December 21, 2018.**

14. Do you have any petition or appeal now pending in any court as to the judgment under attack?

Yes ☐   No ☒

15. Give the name and address, if known, of each attorney who represented you in the following stages of the judgment attacked herein:

(a) At preliminary hearing:

> **Ira R. Kirkendoll; Paul D. Stickney; Matthew C. Golla**

(b) At arraignment and plea:

Ira R. Kirkendoll; Paul D. Stickney; Matthew C. Golla

(c) At trial:

Ira R. Kirkendoll; Paul D. Stickney; Matthew C. Golla

(d) At sentencing:

Ira R. Kirkendoll; Paul D. Stickney; Matthew C. Golla

(e) On appeal

Ira R. Kirkendoll; Paul D. Stickney; Matthew C. Golla

(f) In any post-conviction proceeding:

Pro Se

(g) On appeal from any adverse ruling in a post-conviction proceeding:

Pro Se

16. Were you sentenced on more than one count of an indictment, or on more than one indictment, in the same court and at approximately the same time?

    Yes ☒   No ☐

17. Do you have any future sentence to serve after you complete the sentence imposed by the judgment under attack?

    Yes ☐   No ☒

    (a) If so, give name and location of court which imposed sentence to be served in the future:

    N/A

    (b) And give date and length of sentence to be served in the future:

    N/A

    (c) Have you filed, or do you contemplate filing, any petition attacking the judgment which imposed the sentence to be served in the future?

        Yes ☐   No ☐   N/A

    Wherefore, movant prays that the Court grant petitioner relief to which he may be entitled in this proceeding.

                                            Signature
                                            _____

                                            N/A
                                            _____
                                            Firm Name (if any)

                                            FCI Seagoville, P.O. Box 9000
                                            _____
                                            Address

                                            Seagoville, TX 75159
                                            _____
                                            City, State & Zip Code

                                            No phone
                                            _____
                                            Telephone (including area code)

I declare (or certify, verify, or state) under penalty of perjury that the foregoing is true and correct.
Executed on   June 14, 2019   (date).

UNITED STATES DISTRICT COURT
FOR THE NORTHERN DISTRICT OF TEXAS
FORT WORTH

	§	
	§	
MICHAEL DAVIS	§	
	§	
v.	§	Case No.
	§	
UNITED STATES OF AMERICA	§	
	§	
	§	

MEMORANDUM OF LAW IN SUPPORT OF 28 U.S.C. §2255 MOTION

I.

INTRODUCTION

In the First Step Act, of December 21, 2018, Congress clarified its intent when it enacted 18 U.S.C. §924(c). In section 403 of the recent act, Congress made clear that it never intended for multiple 924(c)(or stacked) sentences as a result from a single conviction. This most recent clarification makes clear that Mr. Davis was sentenced in violation of Congress's intent. Therefore, his second §924(c) sentence is unconstitutional because it was imposed in violation of the laws of the United States, he is due relief. The clarifying nature of the First Step Act has narrowed the scope of the criminal statute, 18 U.S.C. §924(c). The First Step Act has interpreted the statutes terms in a way that places first time offender out of the reach of §924(c)(1)(C)(i). Thus, Mr. Davis's sentence is clarified as unconstitutional, he is therefore due relief. Accordingly, for these and the other reasons argued herein, the court should grant Mr. Davis's 28 U.S.C. §2255 relief.

II.

BACKGROUND

Davis was indicted on a total of six counts stemming from the alleged robbery of four gas stations in Fort Worth, Texas on December 10, 1992. Four of the counts were for obstruction of commerce by robbery, and two of the counts were for use of a firearm during the commission of a robbery.

Witnesses testified that all of the gas stations sold gas, beer, cigarettes and other goods which were manufactured out-of-state and distributed across states lines. The testimony also revealed that Davis used a handgun in at least two of the robberies. After he fled each of the gas stations he robbed, the stations had to be temporarily closed, thereby interrupting the stream of commerce. When Davis testified at the trial, he admitted robbing the stations, but denied using a handgun in any of them.

The jury convicted Davis on all six counts. The Presentence investigation Report ("PSIR") concluded that Davis's conduct caused the death of Carolyn Overby ("Overby"), an employee working at the Lady Luck Fina station at the time Davis robbed it on December 10, 1992. According to the Assistant Medical Examiner for Tarrant County, Texas, the traumatic event of the robbery caused Overby to suffer a Berry aneurysm at the base of her brain, resulting in her death two days later.

Although Davis filed an objection to the PSIR's finding that his conduct caused Overby's death, at sentencing he failed to present any evidence to contradict that finding. Accordingly, the district court adopted the PSIR's finding that the robbery caused Overby's death as undisputed. The court also found that although Davis did not have the conscious intent to kill, his conduct was such that he should have anticipated that serious injury or death could result. The court concluded that upward departure was authorized under § 5K2.1 of the Sentencing Guidelines, which provides for departure "if death resulted." The court also concluded that an upward departure was warranted because without it Overby's death would not be taken into account by the Sentencing Guidelines.

The district court departed upward on the four obstruction of commerce counts by adding 60 months to the combined offense level under the Sentencing Guidelines, for a total of 157 months for each count running concurrently with one another. In addition, the court imposed a mandatory consecutive sentence of 60 months on one of the firearm counts and a mandatory consecutive sentence of 240 months on the second firearm count.

III

STANDARD OF REVIEW

The clarification announced in the First Step Act is substantive under Teague. By clarifying its intent, in 18 D.S.C. §924(c), Congress changed the substantive reach of the statute by altering the class of persons who are punishable under 18 D.S.C. §924(c)(1)(C)(i). Before the First Step Act, the United States courts believed that the statute allowed multiple (or stacked) sentences in a single conviction under the §924(c) statute. The First Step Act, section 403, however, clarified Congress's intent "by striking 'second or subsequent conviction under this section' and inserting 'violation of this subsection that occurs after a prior conviction under this subsection has become final.'" After the First Step Act, 18 D.S.C. §924(c) (1) (C) (i) no longer applies to the same person engaging in the same conduct. Thus, a first time offender, under §924(c), is no longer subject to the 25 year sentence enhancement, and faces at most 5 years in prison.

No case from the Supreme Court treats statutory interpretation cases as a special class of decisions that are substantive under Teague because they implement the intent of Congress. Instead, decisions that interpret a statute are substantive if and when they meet the normal criteria for a substantive rule: when they alter the range of conduct or the class of persons that the law punishes. Therefore, based on this standard, this court should grant a retroactive effect to the First Step Act, section 403, and grant the relief Mr. Davis is due, see *Welch v. United States*, 136 S.Ct. 1257.

IV.

ARGUMENT

Ground one: The First Step Act has clarified 18 U.S.C. §924(c) in such a way that identifies that

Mr. Davis's second §924(c) conviction as unconstitutional.

The Supreme Court's decision in *Welch v. United States*, 136 S.Ct. 1257, decided that *Johnson v.*

United States was a substantive decision that applied retroactively to a prisoner's case on collateral

review. In Mr. Davis's case the issue before the court is whether the First Step Act's section 403 is a

substantive change in law that should be applied retroactively as well. Mr. Davis contends that it should.

The courts have held that new constitutional rules of criminal procedure generally do not apply

retroactively to cases on collateral review, but new substantive rules do apply retroactively. *Teague v.*

Lane, 489 U.S. 288, 310, 109 S.Ct. 1060, 103 L. Ed. 2d 334; *Schriro v. Summerlin*, 542 U.S. 348, 351,

124 S.Ct. 2519, 159 L. Ed. 2d 442. Substantive rules alter "the range of conduct or the class of persons

that the law punishes." *Id.*, at 353, 124 S.Ct. 2519, 159 L. Ed. 2d 442. Procedural rules, by contrast,

"regulate only the manner of determining the defendant's culpability." Ibid. Under this framework, the

First Step Act, section 403 is substantive. Before the First Step Act, 18 U.S.C. §924(c) could cause an

offender, who was determined to have possessed a weapon twice in one criminal case, to face a prison

sentence of at least 30 years instead of at most 5 years. Since the First Step Act clarified the application

of 18 U.S.C. §924(c)(1)(C)(i), it can no longer mandate or authorize the stacking of two §924(c)

sentences in a single conviction. By the same logic, the First Step Act's, section 403, is not procedural,

since it had nothing to do with the range of permissible methods a court might use to determine whether

a defendant should be sentenced under the act. See *Schriro*, Supra, at 353, 124 S.Ct. 2519, 159 L. Ed. 2d

442.

The question before the court in Mr. Davis's case is not one of guilt or evidence. He seeks to discover whether the First Step Act's section 403 is a substantive act of Congress with retroactive effect in cases (like Mr. Davis's) on collateral review. If so, then Mr. Davis asks this court to grant him relief by resentencing him as mandated by the First Step Act, of 2018.

V.

CONCLUSION

Based on the foregoing, the court should grant Mr. Davis's 28 U.S.C. §2255, resentencing him under the First Step Act.

Submitted on June 14, 2019, by:

_____

Michael Davis, Pro se
Reg. #24604-077
Federal Correctional Institution
P.O. Box 9000
Seagoville, TX 75159

KELLY PATRICK RIGGS

IN THE UNITED STATES COURT OF APPEALS
FOR THE FIFTH CIRCUIT

No. 19-10442

In re: MICHAEL DEANGELO DAVIS,

Movant

A True Copy
Certified order issued Jul 10, 2019

Jyle W. Cayce

Clerk, U.S. Court of Appeals, Fifth Circuit

Motion for an order authorizing
the United States District Court for the
Northern District of Texas to consider
a successive 28 U.S.C. § 2255 motion

Before SMITH, DENNIS, and DUNCAN, Circuit Judges.

PER CURIAM:

In 1993, Michael DeAngelo Davis, federal prisoner # 24604-077, was convicted of four counts of interference with commerce by threats or violence, in violation of 18 U.S.C. § 1951, and two counts of use of a firearm during a crime of violence, in violation of 18 U.S.C. § 924(c). Davis seeks authorization to file a successive 28 U.S.C. § 2255 motion challenging the district court's imposition of a 240-month consecutive sentence for his second § 924(c) offense. He argues that he is entitled to relief based on § 403(a) of the First Step Act of 2018 (First Step Act), which clarified that the consecutive mandatory minimum sentence set forth in § 924(c)(I)(C) should be imposed only if the defendant is being sentenced for a § 924(c) violation that occurred after a prior conviction for violating § 924(c) had become final. See First Ste. Act, Pub. L. No. 115-391, § 403(a), 132 Stat. 5194, 5221·22 (2018).

We will authorize the filing of a second or successive § 2255 motion only if the movant makes a prima facie showing, as required by 28 D.S.C. § 2244(b)(3)(C), that his claims rely on either "newly discovered evidence that, if proven and viewed in light of the evidence as a whole, would be sufficient to

72

establish by clear and convincing evidence that no reasonable factfinder would have found the movant guilty of the offense" or "a new rule of constitutional law, made retroactive to cases on collateral review by the Supreme Court, that was previously unavailable." § 2255(h)(1)-(2); see *In re Arnick*, 826 F.3d 787, 788 (5th Cir. 2016).

Davis's sole argument is based on a newly enacted amendment to a federal statute. He has not shown that his proposed claim is based on newly discovered evidence or on a new rule of constitutional law made retroactive to cases on collateral review by the Supreme Court. Accordingly, IT IS ORDERED that Davis's motion for authorization to file a successive § 2255 motion is DENIED.

MOTION UNDER 28 U.S.C. § 2244 FOR ORDER AUTHORIZING DISTRICT COURT TO CONSIDER
SECOND OR SUCCESSIVE APPLICATION FOR RELIEF UNDER 28 U.S.C. §§ 2254 OR 2255

United States Court of Appeals for the 5th Circuit

Name of Movant	Prisoner Number	Case Number (leave blank)
MICHAEL DAVIS	24604-077	
Place of Confinement		
F.C.I. Seagoville, Tx.		

IN RE: , MOVANT

MICHAEL DAVIS

1. Name and location of court which entered the judgment of conviction from which relief is sought:

U.S. District Court; Northern District of Texas

2. Parties' Names: __United States__ vs. __Michael Davis__

3. Docket Number: __4:93-CR-020-A__   4. Date Filed: _____

5. Date of judgment of conviction: __9-10-1993__   6. Length of sentence: __457 Months__

7. Nature of offense(s) involved (all counts):

Hobbs Act Robbery; and Possession of a Firearm during a crime
of violence, 18 U.S.C. § 924 (C).

8. What was your plea? (Check one)   [X] Not Guilty   [ ] Guilty   [ ] Nolo Contendere

9. If you pleaded not guilty, what kind of trial did you have? (Check one)   [X] Jury   [ ] Judge only

10. Did you testify at your trial? (Check one)   [ ] Yes   [X] No

11. Did you appeal from the judgment of conviction? (Check one)   [X] Yes   [ ] No

12. If you did appeal, what was the

Name of court appealed to: __Fifth Circuit Court of Appeals__

Parties' names on appeal: __United States__ vs. __Michael Davis__

Docket number of appeal: __93-1851__   Date of decision: __8-22-1994__

Result of appeal: __Affirmed conviction and sentence__

13. Other than a direct appeal from the judgment of conviction and sentence, have you filed any other petitions, applications for relief, or other motions regarding this judgment in any federal court?   [X] Yes   [ ] No

14. If you answered "Yes" to question 13, answer the following questions:

A. FIRST PETITION, APPLICATION, OR MOTION

(1) In what court did you file the petition, application, or motion? <u>U.S. District Court</u>

(2) What were the parties' names? <u>Davis</u> vs. <u>United States</u>

(3) What was the docket number of the case? <u>4:01-CV-534-A</u>

(4) What relief did you seek? <u>Vacate sentence</u>

(5) What grounds for relief did you state in your petition, application, or motion? <u>Unavailable</u>

(6) Did the court hold an evidentiary hearing on your petition, application or motion? ☐ Yes ☒ No

(7) What was the result?   ☐ Relief granted   ☐ Relief denied on the merits

☐ Relief denied for failure to exhaust   ☒ Relief denied for procedural default

(8) Date of court's decision: <u>7-02-2001</u>

B. SECOND PETITION, APPLICATION, OR MOTION

(1) In what court did you file the petition, application, or motion? <u>N/A</u>

(2) What were the parties' names? <u>N/A</u> vs.

(3) What was the docket number of the case? <u>N/A</u>

(4) What relief did you seek? <u>N/A</u>

(5) What grounds for relief did you state in your petition, application, or motion?

    N/A

(6) Did the court hold an evidentiary hearing on your petition, application or motion? ☐ Yes ☐ No

(7) What was the result?   ☐ Relief granted   ☐ Relief denied on the merits

☐ Relief denied for failure to exhaust   ☐ Relief denied for procedural default

(8) Date of court's decision: <u>N/A</u>

C. THIRD AND SUBSEQUENT PETITIONS, APPLICATIONS, OR MOTIONS
For any third or subsequent petition, application, or motion, attach a separate page providing the information required in items (1) through (8) above for first and second petitions, applications, or motions.

D. PRIOR APPELLATE REVIEW(S)

Did you appeal the results of your petitions, applications, or motions to a federal court of appeals having jurisdiction over your case? If so, list the docket numbers and dates of final disposition for all subsequent petitions, applications, or motions filed in a federal court of appeals.

First petition, application, or motion	[X] Yes	Appeal No. _01-11064_	[ ] No
Second petition, application, or motion	[ ] Yes	Appeal No. _____	[X] No
Subsequent petitions, applications or motions	[ ] Yes	Appeal No. _____	[X] No
Subsequent petitions, applications or motions	[ ] Yes	Appeal No. _____	[X] No
Subsequent petitions, applications or motions	[ ] Yes	Appeal No. _____	[X] No
Subsequent petitions, applications or motions	[ ] Yes	Appeal No. _____	[X] No

If you did not appeal from the denial of relief on **any** of your prior petitions, applications, or motions, state which denials you did not appeal and explain why you did not.

N/A

15. Did you present any of the claims in this application in any previous petition, application, or motion for relief under 28 U.S.C. § 2254 or § 2255? (Check one)　　　[ ] Yes　　　[X] No

16. If your answer to question 15 is "Yes," give the docket number(s) and court(s) in which such claims were raised and state the basis on which relief was denied.

N/A

17. If your answer to question 15 is "No," why not? This Court will grant you authority to file in the district court only if you show that you could not have presented your present claims in your previous § 2254 or § 2255 application because . . .

A. (For § 2255 motions only) the claims involve "newly discovered evidence that, if proven and viewed in light of the evidence as a whole, would be sufficient to establish by clear and convincing evidence that no reasonable factfinder would have found [you] guilty"; or,

B. (For § 2254 petitions only) "the factual predicate for the claim could not have been discovered previously through the exercise of due diligence" and "the facts underlying the claim, if proven and viewed in light of the evidence as a whole, would be sufficient to establish by clear and convincing evidence that, but for constitutional error, no reasonable factfinder would have found [you] guilty of the offense"; or,

C. (For both § 2254 and § 2255 applicants) the claims involve "a new rule of constitutional law, made retroactive to cases on collateral review by the Supreme Court [of the United States], that was previously unavailable."

I did not present the following claims in any previous petition, application, or motion for relief under 28 U.S.C. § 2254:

> Mr. Davis' convictions and sentences under 18 U.S.C. § 924 (C)(3)(B) are unconstitutional because that portion of the statute has been invalidated.

I did not present the claims listed above in any previous petition, application, or motion because

> Mr. Davis' claim is based on the recent Supreme Court decision in United Stated v. Davis, decided on June 24, 2019

Movant prays that the United States Court of Appeals for the Fifth Circuit grant an Order Authorizing the District Court to Consider Movant's Second or Successive Application for Relief Under 28 U.S.C. §§ 2254 or 2255.

_____
Movant's Signature

I declare under Penalty of Perjury that my answers to all questions in this Motion are true and correct. Executed on _____8 - 21 - 2019_____
                    [date]

_____
Movant's Signature

PROOF OF SERVICE

A copy of this motion and all attachments must be sent to the state attorney general (§ 2254 cases) or the United States Attorney for the United States judicial district in which you were convicted (§ 2255 cases).

I certify that on _____ I mailed a copy of this motion and all attachments
                    [date]

to _____ at the following address:

_____

_____
Movant's Signature

NO STAPLES, TAPE, OR BINDING PLEASE

KELLY PATRICK RIGGS

IN THE UNITED STATES DISTRICT COURT
FOR THE NORTHERN DISTRICT OF TEXAS

MOTION UNDER 28 U.S.C. SECTION 2255,
TO VACATE, SET ASIDE, OR CORRECT SENTENCE BY A
<u>PERSON IN FEDERAL CUSTODY</u>

UNITED STATES OF AMERICA

<u>F.C.I. Seagoville, Texas</u>
PLACE OF CONFINEMENT

vs.

<u>24604-077</u>
PRISONER ID NUMBER

<u>MICHAEL D. DAVIS</u>
MOVANT (full name of movant)

<u>4:93-CR-020-A</u>
CRIMINAL CASE NUMBER

(If a movant has a sentence to be served in the future under a federal judgment which he wishes to attack, he should file a motion in the federal court which entered the judgment.)

INSTRUCTIONS - READ CAREFULLY

1. This motion must be legibly handwritten or typewritten, and signed by the movant under penalty of perjury. Any false statement of a material fact may serve as the basis for prosecution and conviction for perjury. All questions must be answered concisely in the proper space on the form.

2. Additional pages are not permitted except with respect to the facts which you rely upon to support your grounds for relief. No citation of authorities needs to be furnished. If briefs or arguments are submitted, they should be submitted in the form of a separate memorandum.

3. Upon receipt, your motion will be filed if it is in proper order. No fee is required with this motion.

78

If you do not have the necessary funds for transcripts, counsel, appeal, and other costs connected with a motion of this type, you may request permission to proceed *in forma pauperis*, in which event you must execute the declaration provided with this motion, setting forth information establishing your inability to prepay the fees and costs or give security therefor. If you wish to proceed *in forma pauperis*, you must have an authorized officer at the penal institution complete the certificate as to the amount of money and securities on deposit to your credit in any account in the institution.

5. Only judgments entered by one court may be challenged in a single motion. If you seek to challenge judgments entered by different judges or divisions either in the same district or in different districts, you must file separate motions as to each such judgment.

6. Your attention is directed to the fact that you must include all grounds for relief and all facts supporting such grounds for relief in the motion you file seeking relief from any judgment of conviction.

7. When the motion is fully completed, the original and two copies must be mailed to the Clerk of the United States District Court for the Northern District of Texas at the appropriate divisional office whose address is:

Abilene Division
P.O. Box 1218
Abilene, TX 79604

Amarillo Division
205 E. 5th St, Rm 133
Amarillo, TX 79101

Dallas Division
1100 Commerce, Rm 1452
Dallas, TX 75242

Fort Worth Division
501 W. 10th St, Rm 310
Fort Worth, TX 76102

Lubbock Division
1205 Texas Ave., Rm 209
Lubbock, TX 79401

San Angelo Division
33 East Twohig St, Rm 202
San Angelo, TX 76903

Wichita Falls Division
P.O. Box 1234
Wichita Falls, TX 76307

8. Motions which do not conform to these instructions will be returned with a notation as to the deficiency.

MOTION

1. Name and location of court that entered the judgment of conviction you are challenging:

> U.S. DISTRICT COURT: NORTHERN DISTRICT OF TEXAS
>
> FORT WORTH, TEXAS

2. Date of the judgment of conviction:

> SEPTEMBER 10, 1993

3. Length of sentence: 457 MONTHS

4. Nature of offense involved (all counts):

> HOBBS ACT ROBBERY
>
> POSSESSION OF A FIREARM DURING A CRIME OF VIOLENCE

5. (a) What was your plea? (Check one)

Not guilty ☒   Guilty ☐   Nolo contendere (no contest) ☐

(b) If you entered a guilty plea to one count or indictment, and a not guilty plea to another count or or indictment, what did you plead guilty to and what did you plead not guilty to?

> N/A

6. If you went to trial, what kind of trial did you have? (Check one) Jury ☒   Judge Only ☐
7. Did you testify at the trial? (Check one) Yes ☐   No ☒
8. Did you appeal from the judgment of conviction? (Check one) Yes ☒   No ☐
9. If you did appeal, answer the following:

Name of Court: FIFTH CIRCUIT

Result: AFFIRMED

Date of result: 8-22-1994

10. Other than a direct appeal from the judgment of conviction and sentence, have you previously filed any petitions, applications, or motions with respect to this judgment in any federal court?

    Yes [x]   No [ ]

11. If your answer to 10 was "Yes" give the following information:

Name of Court: U.S. DISTRICT COURT, NORTHERN DISTRICT OF TEXAS

Nature of proceeding:

> 28 U.S.C. § 2255

Grounds raised:

> UNAVAILABLE

Did you receive an evidentiary hearing on your petition, application or motion?

    Yes [ ]   No [x]

Result: DISMISSED AS UNTIMELY

Date of result: 7-02-2001

As to any *second* petition, application or motion, give the same information:

Name of Court: N/A

Nature of proceeding:

> N/A

Grounds raised:

> N/A

Did you receive an evidentiary hearing on your petition, application or motion?

    Yes [ ]   No [ ]   N/A

Result: N/A

Date of result: N/A

As to any *third* petition, application or motion, give the same information:

Name of Court: N/A

Nature of proceeding:

N/A

Grounds raised:

N/A

Did you receive an evidentiary hearing on your petition, application or motion?

Yes ☐   No ☐   N/A

Result: N/A

Date of result: N/A

Did you appeal to an appellate federal court having jurisdiction, the result of action taken on any petition, application or motion?

First petition, etc.   Yes ☒   No ☐
Second petition, etc.   Yes ☐   No ☒
Third petition, etc.   Yes ☐   No ☒

If you did not appeal from the adverse action on any petition, application or motion, explain briefly why you did not:

N/A

12. State <u>concisely</u> every ground on which you claim that you are being held unlawfully. Summarize <u>briefly</u> the facts supporting each ground. If necessary, you may attach pages stating additional grounds and facts supporting same.

   CAUTION: If you fail to set forth all grounds in this motion, you may be barred from presenting additional grounds at a later date.

For your information, the following is a list of the most frequently raised grounds for relief in these proceedings. Each statement preceded by a letter constitutes a separate ground for possible relief. You may raise any grounds which you may have other than those listed. However, you <u>should raise in this petition all available grounds</u> (relating to this conviction) on which you based your allegations that you are being held in custody unlawfully.

<u>DO NOT CHECK ANY OF THESE LISTED GROUNDS.</u> If you select one or more of these grounds for relief, you must allege facts. The motion will be returned to you if you merely check (a) through (j) or any of these grounds.

   (a)   Conviction obtained by plea of guilty which was unlawfully induced or not made voluntarily or with understanding of the nature of the charge and the consequences of the plea.

   (b)   Conviction obtained by use of coerced confession.

   (c)   Conviction obtained by use of evidence gained pursuant to an unconstitutional search and seizure.

   (d)   Conviction obtained by use of evidence obtained pursuant to an unlawful arrest.

   (e)   Conviction obtained by a violation of the privilege against self-incrimination.

   (f)   Conviction obtained by the unconstitutional failure of the prosecution to disclose to the defendant evidence favorable to the defendant.

   (g)   Conviction obtained by a violation of the protection against double jeopardy.

   (h)   Conviction obtained by action of a grand or petit jury which was unconstitutionally selected and impaneled.

   (i)   Denial of effective assistance of counsel.

   (j)   Denial of right to appeal.

83

A.   Ground One:

> Mr. Davis' §924 (C)(3)(B) convictions and sentences
> are unconstitutional because that portion of the statute
> has been invalidated.

Supporting FACTS (tell your story briefly without citing cases or law):

> On June 24, 2019, the Supreme Court in DAVIS invalidated
> §924 (C)(3)(B). This recent decision is retroactively
> applicable to cases on collateral review.

B.   Ground Two:

> N/A

Supporting FACTS (tell your story briefly without citing cases or law):

> N/A

C.   Ground Three:

> N/A

Supporting FACTS (tell your story briefly without citing cases or law):

> N/A

D.   Ground Four:

> N/A

Supporting FACTS (tell your story briefly without citing cases or law):

> N/A

13. If any of the grounds listed in 12A, B, C, and D were not previously presented, state briefly what grounds were not so presented, and give your reasons for not presenting them:

> Mr. Davis' claim involves a new rule of constitutional law that has been made retroactive to cases on collateral review by the Supreme Court of the United States that has been unavailable until June 24, 2019.

14. Do you have any petition or appeal now pending in any court as to the judgment under attack?

Yes ☐   No ☒

15. Give the name and address, if known, of each attorney who represented you in the following stages of the judgment attacked herein:

(a) At preliminary hearing:

> Federal Public Defender

(b) At arraignment and plea:

Federal Public Defender

(c) At trial:

Federal Public Defender

(d) At sentencing:

Federal Public Defender

(e) On appeal

Federal Public Defender

(f) In any post-conviction proceeding:

Pro Se

(g) On appeal from any adverse ruling in a post-conviction proceeding:

Pro Se

16. Were you sentenced on more than one count of an indictment, or on more than one indictment, in the same court and at approximately the same time?

Yes ☒   No ☐

17. Do you have any future sentence to serve after you complete the sentence imposed by the judgment under attack?

Yes ☐   No ☒

(a) If so, give name and location of court which imposed sentence to be served in the future:

> N/A

(b) And give date and length of sentence to be served in the future:

> N/A

(c) Have you filed, or do you contemplate filing, any petition attacking the judgment which imposed the sentence to be served in the future?

Yes ☐   No ☐   N/A

Wherefore, movant prays that the Court grant petitioner relief to which he may be entitled in this proceeding.

Signature
_____

Pro Se
Firm Name (if any)

P.O. Box 9000
Address

Seagoville, Tx 75159
City, State & Zip Code

N/A
Telephone (including area code)

I declare (or certify, verify, or state) under penalty of perjury that the foregoing is true and correct.
Executed on ___8-21-2019___ (date).

87

UNITED STATES DISTRICT COURT
NORTHERN DISTRICT OF TEXAS
FORT WORTH DIVISION

MICHAEL DEANGELO DAVIS	§	
Movant,	§	
	§	
VS.	§	NO. 4:19-CV-689-A
	§	(NO. 4:93-CR-020-A)
UNITED STATES OF AMERICA	§	
Respondent.	§	
	§	

ORDER

The court has received and reviewed the motion of Michael DeAngelo Davis under 28 U.S.C. §

2255 to vacate, set aside, or correct sentence and finds that the following order should be entered:

The court ORDERS that:

(1) The Clerk shall provide a true and correct copy of this order to movant;

(2) The Clerk shall provide a true and correct copy of movant's motion and of this order to

respondent, directed to the attention of the Criminal Section Habeas Attorney, United States Attorney's

Office, Fort Worth Division;

(3) By October 3, 2019, the United States Attorney shall file and serve an answer complying with

the provisions of Rule 5(b) of the Rules Governing § 2255 Cases; and

(4) By October 17, 2019, movant shall file and serve any reply he wishes to make to such answer.

SIGNED September 3, 2019.

JOHN McBRYDE
United States District Judge

IN THE UNITED STATES COURT OF APPEALS
FOR THE FIFTH CIRCUIT

No. 19-10945

In re: MICHAEL DEANGELO DAVIS,

Movant

A True Copy
Certified order issued Sep 13, 2019

Tyle W. Cayce

Clerk, U.S. Court of Appeals, Fifth Circuit

Motion for an order authorizing
the United States District Court for the
Northern District of Texas to consider
a successive 28 U.S.C. § 2255 motion

Before ELROD, COSTA, and ENGELHARDT, Circuit Judges.
PER CURIAM:

In 1993, Michael DeAngelo Davis, federal prisoner # 24604-077, was convicted of four counts of interference with commerce by robbery, in violation of 18 U.S.C. § 1951 (Hobbs Act robbery), and two counts of use of a firearm during a crime of violence, in violation of 18 U.S.C. § 924(c). Davis seeks authorization to file a successive 28 U.S.C. § 2255 motion to challenge his § 924(c) convictions. Specifically, he contends that his convictions are invalid in light of the Supreme Court's recent decision in *United States v. Davis*, 139 S.Ct. 2319 (2019).

Before filing a second or successive § 2255 motion in the district court, a movant must obtain an order from this court authorizing the district court to consider the motion. § 2255(h); 28 D.S.C. § 2244(b)(3)(A) & (C). This court may authorize the filing of a second or successive § 2255 motion only if the movant makes a prima facie showing that his claims rely on either "newly discovered evidence that, if proven and viewed in light of the evidence as a whole, would be sufficient to establish by clear and convincing evidence that no reasonable factfinder would have found the movant guilty of the offense" or "a new rule of constitutional law, made retroactive to cases on collateral review by the

Supreme Court, that was previously unavailable." § 2255(h)(1)-(2); *see in re Arnick*, 826 F.3d 787, 788

(5th Cir. 2016).

Although *Davis* held that the residual clause definition of crime of violence, § 924(c)(3)(B), is

unconstitutionally vague, it did not invalidate § 924(c)(3)(A)'s elements clause crime of violence

definition. *Davis*, 139 S.Ct. at 2336. Hobbs Act robbery meets § 924(c)(3)(A)'s elements-based

definition of crime of violence. *See United States v. Bowens*, 907 F.3d 347,353-54 (5th Cir. 2018), cert.

denied, 139 S.Ct. 1299 (2019); *United States v. Buck*, 847 F.3d 267, 274-75 (5th Cir. 2017). Thus, the

Supreme Court's decision in Davis does not provide Davis with a basis for obtaining authorization to

file a successive § 2255 motion. Accordingly, IT IS ORDERED that his motion to file a successive §

2255 motion is DENIED.

POST-CONVICTION RELIEF: SECOND LAST CHANCE

IN THE UNITED STATES DISTRICT COURT
NORTHERN DISTRICT OF TEXAS
FORT WORTH DIVISION

MICHAEL DEANGELO DAVIS
    Movant,

v.

UNITED STATES OF AMERICA
    Respondent.

No. 4:19-CV-689-A
(4:93-CR-020-A)

GOVERNMENT'S MOTION FOR EXTENSION OF TIME

The government respectfully requests a 30-day extension – to November 4, 2019 – to file its response to Davis's motion under 28 U.S.C. § 2255.

The government's response is currently due October 3, 2019. The extension is requested so that the government can provide a thorough brief. Because of the age of the underlying criminal case, electronic records are not available. The original file has been requested from the Federal Records Center.

This extension is not sought for purposes of delay, and it will allow the government to provide the best response possible. The government requests that its deadline to file a response be extended to November 4, 2019.

KELLY PATRICK RIGGS

Respectfully submitted,

ERIN NEALY COX
UNITED STATES ATTORNEY

Brian Portugal
Assistant United States Attorney
Texas Bar No. 24051202
1100 Commerce Street, Third Floor
Dallas, Texas 75242
Telephone: (214) 659-8600
E-mail: brian.portugal@usdoj.gov

CERTIFICATE OF CONFERENCE

I have not spoken to Davis regarding this motion because he is incarcerated.

Brian Portugal
Assistant United States Attorney

CERTIFICATE OF SERVICE

I certify that on September 20, 2019, I filed this motion with the clerk of court for the U.S. District Court, Northern District of Texas. A copy was sent to Michael DeAngelo Davis, Register Number 24604-077, Seagoville FCI, P.O. Box 9000, Seagoville, Texas 75159, by first class mail.

Brian Portugal
Assistant United States Attorney

COPY

IN THE UNITED STATES DISTRICT COURT
NORTHERN DISTRICT OF TEXAS
FORT WORTH DIVISION

CLERK OF DISTRICT COURT
NORTHERN DIST. OF TX
FORT WORTH DIVISION
FILED

DEPUTY CLERK_____

MICHAEL DEANGELO DAVIS
    Movant,

v.

UNITED STATES OF AMERICA
    Respondent.

No. 4:19-CV-689-A
(4:93-CR-020-A)

NOTICE OF SUBSTITUTION OF COUNSEL

The government advises the Court and all parties that this case has been reassigned to Assistant

United States Attorney Brian Portugal, who should be reflected as counsel of record for the United

States of America.

Respectfully submitted,

ERIN NEALY COX
UNITED STATES ATTORNEY

Brian Portugal
Assistant United States Attorney
Texas Bar No. 24051202
1100 Commerce Street, Third Floor
Dallas, Texas 75242
Telephone: (214) 659-8600
E-mail: brian.portugal@usdoj.gov

KELLY PATRICK RIGGS

CERTIFICATE OF SERVICE

I certify that on September 20, 2019, I filed this notice with the clerk of court for the U.S. District

Court, Northern District of Texas. A copy was served on Michael DeAngelo Davis, Register Number

24604-077, Seagoville FCI, P.O. Box 9000, Seagoville, Texas 75159, by first class mail.

Brian Portugal
Assistant United States Attorney

IN THE UNITED STATES DISTRICT COURT
NORTHERN DISTRICT OF TEXAS
FORT WORTH DIVISION

MICHAEL DEANGELO DAVIS §
Movant, §
§
VS. §
§
UNITED STATES OF AMERICA §
Respondent. §
§

NO. 4:19-CV-689-A
(NO. 4:93-CR-020-A)

U.S. DISTRICT COURT
NORTHERN DISTRICT OF TEXAS
FILED

SEP 2 0 2019

CLERK, U.S. DISTRICT COURT
By_____
Deputy

ORDER

Came on for consideration the government's motion for extension of time to file its response to the motion of Michael DeAngelo Davis, movant, under 28 U.S.C. § 2255. The court finds that the motion should be granted.

The court ORDERS that the government's motion be, and is hereby, granted, and the government be, and is hereby, granted an extension of time until November 4, 2019, in which to file its response to movant's motion.

The court further ORDERS that movant be, and is hereby, granted an extension of time until November 18, 2019, in which to file his reply, if any.

SIGNED September 20, 2019.

JOHN McBRYDE
United States District Judge

IN THE UNITED STATES DISTRICT COURT
NORTHERN DISTRICT OF TEXAS
FORT WORTH DIVISION

MICHAEL DEANGELO DAVIS
Movant,

v.

UNITED STATES OF AMERICA
Respondent.

No. 4:19-CV-689-A
(4:93-CR-020-A)

MOTION TO DISMISS OR TRANSFER SECTION 2255 MOTION
AS SECOND OR SUCCESSIVE

The Court should dismiss or transfer Davis's Section 2255 motion as a second or successive motion that

he has not received authorization to file.

STATEMENT OF THE CASE

Davis was found guilty by a jury of four counts of obstruction of commerce by robbery (Hobbs Act

robbery), in violation of 18 U.S.C. § 1951, and two counts of using or carrying a firearm during and in

relation to a crime of violence, in violation of 18 U.S.C. § 924(c). (CR No. 5-1 at 56-68, 77-81)[1] On

September 15, 1993, the Court entered judgment, sentencing Davis to 457 months' imprisonment. (CR

No. 5-1 at 96-97.) Davis appealed, but the Court of Appeals affirmed this Court's judgment on August

22, 1994. *United States v. Davis*, 30 F.3d 613 (5th Cir.). In 2001, he filed a motion under 28 U.S.C. §

2255, which the Court denied. (CV-1 Nos. 1 &2.) On August 30, 2019, the Clerk of Court docketed

this, his second, motion under Section 2255. (CV-2 No.1.) Davis filed a motion for authorization to file

a successive motion with the Court of Appeals, but that court has not yet ruled. See *In re Davis*, No. 19-

10945 (5th Cir.).

---

[1] "CR No. __" refers to the docket of the underlying criminal proceeding, *United States v. Davis*, No. 4:93-CR-020-A. "CV-1 No. __" refers to the docket of Davis's first Section 2255 action, No. 4:01-CV-534-A. "CV-2 No.__ "refers to the docket of this Section 2255 action.

GROUND FOR DISMISSAL OR TRANSFER

Before proceeding in the district court, a prisoner who wants to file a second or successive motion to vacate, set aside, or correct sentence under 28 D.S.C. § 2255 must obtain authorization from a panel of the appropriate circuit court of appeals. See 28 D.S.C. §§ 2255(h), 2244(b)(3)(A); *see also Reyes-Requena v. United States*, 243 F.3d 893, 898 (5th Cir. 2001). Until circuit court authorization is granted, a district court lacks jurisdiction over a successive Section 2255 motion. *See United States v. Key*, 205 F.3d 773, 774-75 (5th Cir. 2000).

In this circuit, if a movant files a second or successive Section 2255 motion before obtaining authorization from the court of appeals, the district court has two options. First, it may dismiss the motion for lack of jurisdiction. *In re Hartzog*, 444 F. App'x 63, 65 (5th Cir. 2011) (citing *Key*, 205 F.3d at 774). Alternatively, it may transfer the motion to the circuit court. *Id.; see also In re Epps*, 127 F.3d 364, 365 (5th Cir. 1997) (approving the practice of transferring a successive motion to the circuit court and establishing procedures in the circuit court to handle the transfers).

This Court should dismiss or transfer Davis's Section 2255 motion because it lacks jurisdiction over the matter. There is no dispute that Davis has yet to receive authorization from the Fifth Circuit to proceed with a successive motion. Thus, Section 2255, Section 2244, and well-established case law make clear that this Court has no jurisdiction over Davis's successive motion. 28 U.S.C. §§ 2244(b)(3)(A), 2255(h); *Key*, 205 F.3d at 774-75. Dismissal or transfer are appropriate because they align with longstanding Fifth Circuit precedent, permit the Fifth Circuit to resolve the authorization issue before initiating any district court litigation, and are faithful to the limitations placed on successive Section 2255 motions by Congress.

CONCLUSION

Davis's Section 2255 motion should be dismissed or transferred as an unauthorized second or successive motion over which the Court lacks jurisdiction.

KELLY PATRICK RIGGS

Respectfully submitted,

ERIN NEALY COX
UNITED STATES ATTORNEY

Brian Portugal
Assistant United States Attorney
Texas Bar No. 24051202
1100 Commerce Street, Third Floor
Dallas, Texas 75242
Telephone: (214) 659-8600
E-mail: brian.portugal@usdoj.gov

CERTIFICATE OF CONFERENCE

I have not spoken to Davis regarding this motion because he is incarcerated.

Brian Portugal
Assistant United States Attorney

CERTIFICATE OF SERVICE

I certify that on September 29, 2019, I filed this motion with the clerk of court for the U.S. District Court, Northern District of Texas. A copy was sent to Michael DeAngelo Davis, Register Number 24604-077, Seagoville FCI, P.O. Box 9000, Seagoville, Texas 75159, by first class mail.

Brian Portugal
Assistant United States Attorney

3

POST-CONVICTION RELIEF: SECOND LAST CHANCE

IN THE UNITED STATES DISTRICT COURT
NORTHERN DISTRICT OF TEXAS
FORT WORTH DIVISION

MICHAEL DEANGELO DAVIS
      Movant,

v.

UNITED STATES OF AMERICA
      Respondent.

No. 4:19-CV-689-A
(4:93-CR-020-A)

<u>NOTICE OF SUBSTITUTION OF COUNSEL</u>

The government advises the Court and all parties that this case has been reassigned to Assistant

United States Attorney Brian Portugal, who should be reflected as counsel of record for the United

States of America.

Respectfully submitted,

ERIN NEALY COX
UNITED STATES ATTORNEY

Brian Portugal
Assistant United States Attorney
Texas Bar No. 24051202
1100 Commerce Street, Third Floor
Dallas, Texas 75242
Telephone: (214) 659-8600
E-mail: brian.portugal@usdoj.gov

KELLY PATRICK RIGGS

CERTIFICATE OF SERVICE

I certify that on September 29, 2019, I filed this motion with the clerk of court for the U.S. District

Court, Northern District of Texas. A copy was sent to Michael DeAngelo Davis, Register Number

24604-077, Seagoville FCI, P.O. Box 9000, Seagoville, Texas 75159, by first class mail.

Brian Portugal
Assistant United States Attorney

UNITED STATES DISTRICT COURT
NORTHERN DISTRICT OF TEXAS
FORT WORTH DIVISION

MICHAEL DAVIS

V.

UNITED STATES OF AMERICA

Civ. Case No. 4:19-CV-689-A

Crim. Case No. (4:93-CR-020-A)

DAVIS'S RESPONSE IN OPPOSITION TO GOVERNMENT'S MOTION TO DISMISS

Mr. Davis moves this court to deny the governments' motion to dismiss or transfer his Section 2255 motion as second or successive. This court has the authority to decide his claim in this §2255 proceeding because his motion IS NOT a second or successive §2255 motion.

Under the A.E.D.P.A., a prisoner who has previously filed a §2255 motion must apply for and obtain authorization from a Court of Appeals before filing a "second or successive" §2255 motion. 28 U.S.C. §2244(b)(3)(A), 2255(h). Absent prior authorization from a Court of Appeals, a District Court lacks jurisdiction to consider a second or successive §2255 motion. *United States v. Holt*, 417 F. 3d. 1172, 1175 (11th Cir. 2005).

The Court of Appeals, however, In *Johnson v. United States*, 724 Fed. Appx. 917 (11th Cir. 2018) held that:

"The phrase 'second or successive' is not self-defining, however, and does not refer to all habeas applications filed second in time. *Stewart*, 646 F. 3d. at 859. 'When a petitioner raises a claim that could not have been raised in a prior habeas petition, courts have foregone a literal reading of "second or successive,"' *Id.* at 680"

Mr. Davis's claim could not have been raised in a prior §2255 motion because his claim is based on a new rule of constitutional law that was established on June 24, 2019. See *United States v. Davis* et al, 139 S.Ct. 2319; 204 L. Ed. 2d 757 (June 24, 2019). Thus, Mr. Davis's §2255 motion cannot be labeled as second or successive under current circuit precedent.

Wherefore, based on the foregoing, Mr. Davis moves this court to deny the government's motion to dismiss and order the government to answer his claims on their merits.

Submitted on November 18, 2019, by:

_____
Michael DeAngelo Davis, pro se
Reg.# 24604-077
Federal Correctional Institution P.O. Box 9000
Seagoville, TX 75159

CERTIFICATE OF SERVICE

I certify that on November 18, 2019, I served a copy of the foregoing pleading on the U.S. Attorney via U.S. Mail, properly addressed with first class postage prepaid.

Submitted on November 18, 2019, by:

_____
Michael DeAngelo Davis, pro se
Reg.# 24604-077

UNITED STATES DISTRICT COURT
NORTHERN DISTRICT OF TEXAS
FORT WORTH DIVISION

COPY

MICHAEL DEANGELO DAVIS
Movant,

V.

UNITED STATES OF AMERICA
Respondent.

No. 4:19-CV-689-A
(4:93-CR-020-A)

REPLY TO DAVIS'S RESPONSE TO MOTION' TO DISMISS OR TRANSFER
SECTION 2255 MOTION
AS SECOND OR SUCCESSIVE

In his response to the government's motion to dismiss or transfer, Davis contends that his Section 2255motibn cannot be deemed second or successive because, he argues, his claim was not available until the Supreme Court issued its decision in *United States v. Davis*, 139 S.Ct. 2319 (2019). (CV No. 12 at 1-2.) In support he cites an unpublished opinion from another circuit. (*Id.*)

Davis misunderstands the standard for successive motions by conflating the question of whether a motion is successive with the question of whether a successive motion meets the standard for authorization. The line of authority in his cited case dealt with situations where a motion was not successive because the claim could not arise until some later event after the, first motion. See *Johnson v. United States*, 724 F. App'x 917 (11th Cir, 2018), (quoting *Stewart v. United States*, 646 F.3d856, 860(11th Cir. 2011)). *Stewart* illustrates this with its citations to decisions of the Eighth and Fifth Circuits: one case dealt with a claim that did not arise until the movant was subject to involuntary medication in advance of execution of a death sentence, and the other case dealt with ineffective assistance of counsel during an out-of-time appeal that was the remedy of prior ineffective assistance. *See Stewart*, 646 F.3d at 860 (citing *Singleton v. Norris*, 319 F.3d 1018, 1023 (8th Cir. 2003) (*en bane*) & *United States v. Orozco-Ramirez*, 211 F.3d 862, 869, 871 (5th Cir. 2000)).

103

In contrast, Davis's claim – that 18 D.S.C. § 924(c)(3)(B) is unconstitutionally vague and therefore cannot be applied to him – was available before the Supreme Court's new decision, even if there was no binding authority supporting that claim. As such, Davis's motion is still successive. Because it is successive, the question becomes whether it should be authorized for presentation because it rests on (i) "newly discovered evidence that, if proven and viewed in light of the evidence as a whole, would be sufficient to establish by clear and convincing evidence that no reasonable factfinder would have found the movant guilty of the offense" or (ii) "a new rule of constitutional law, made retroactive to cases on collateral review by the Supreme Court, that was previously unavailable." 18 D.S.C. § 2255(h)(1)-(2). That question, however, is a jurisdictional threshold that Congress reserved for the Circuit Court of Appeals. *See* 18 D.S.C. § 2255(h); 28 U.S.C. § 2244(b)(3)(A) & (C).

Accordingly, because it is clear that Davis is trying to present a successive motion, dismissal or transfer to the Circuit Court of Appeals remains the correct jurisdictional disposition. And, in any event, the Fifth Circuit has now denied Davis authorization to file a successive motion, so this Court can dismiss this action with full confidence that transferring it would be futile, *See In re Davis*, 19-10945 (5th Cir. 2019).

Respectfully submitted,

ERIN NEALY COX
UNITED STATES ATTORNEY

Brian Portugal
Assistant United States Attorney
Texas Bar No. 24051202
1100 Commerce Street, Third Floor
Dallas, Texas 75242
Telephone: (214) 659-8600
E-mail: brian.portugal@usdoj.gov

<u>CERTIFICATE OF SERVICE</u>

I certify that on December 10, 2019, I filed this motion with the clerk of court for the U.S. District Court, Northern District of Texas. A copy was sent to Michael DeAngelo Davis, Register Number 24604-077, Seagoville FCI, P.O. Box 9000, Seagoville, Texas 75159, by first class mail.

Brian Portugal
Assistant United States Attorney

IN THE UNITED STATES DISTRICT COURT
NORTHERN DISTRICT OF TEXAS
FORT WORTH DIVISION

MICHAEL DEANGELO DAVIS	§	
Movant,	§	
	§	
VS.	§	NO. 4:19-CV-689-A
	§	(NO. 4:93-CR-020-A)
UNITED STATES OF AMERICA	§	
Respondent.	§	
	§	

ORDER

Came on for consideration the motion of Michael DeAngelo Davis under 28 U.S.C. § 2255 to vacate, set aside, or correct sentence by a person in federal custody. This is a second or successive motion under 28 U.S.C. § 2255. See Civil Action No. 4:01-CV-534-A. Movant not having obtained leave to file the motion, the court lacks jurisdiction to consider it. 28 D.S.C. § 2255 (h).

The court ORDERS that the above-referenced motion be and is hereby dismissed for lack of jurisdiction.

Pursuant to Rule 22(b) of the Federal Rules of Appellate Procedure, Rule 11(a) of the Rules Governing Section 2255 Proceedings for the united states District Court's, and 28 U.S.C. § 2253 (c) (2), for the reasons discussed herein, the court further ORDERS that a certificate of appealability be, and is hereby, denied, as movant has not made a substantial showing of the denial of a constitutional right.

SIGNED December 11, 2019.

JOHN McBRIDE
United States District Judge

IN THE UNITED STATES DISTRICT COURT
NORTHERN DISTRICT OF TEXAS
FORT WORTH DIVISION

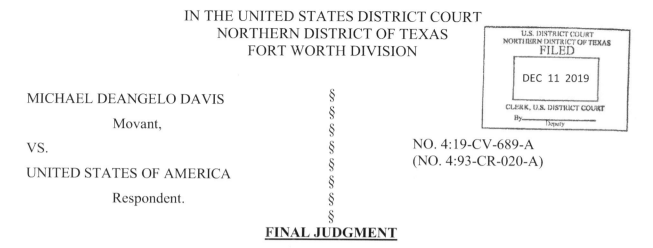

MICHAEL DEANGELO DAVIS	§	
Movant,	§	
	§	
VS.	§	NO. 4:19-CV-689-A
	§	(NO. 4:93-CR-020-A)
UNITED STATES OF AMERICA	§	
Respondent.	§	
	§	

FINAL JUDGMENT

Consistent with the order signed this date,

The court ORDERS, ADJUDGES, and DECREES that the motion of Michael DeAngelo Davis to

vacate, set aside, or correct sentence pursuant to 28 U.S.C. § 2255 be, and is hereby, dismissed for lack

of jurisdiction.

SIGNED December 11, 2019.

JOHN McBRYDE
United States District Judge

KELLY PATRICK RIGGS

UNITED STATES DISTRICT COURT
NORTHERN DISTRICT OF TEXAS
FORT WORTH DIVISION

Michael DeAngelo Davis

V.

United States of America

Case No.:

4:19-CV-689-A

NOTICE OF APPEAL

Mr. Davis appeals from the district court's December II 2019, judgment because it creates a circuit

split as to the definition of second or successive. Additionally, Mr. Davis is actually innocent of his 18

U.S.C. §924(c) conviction and is likely being denied review because he is an uncounseled black man. In

recent decision it is easy to see that prisoners who are white and/or can afford counsel receive

preferential treatment. See *Buck v. Davis*, 137 S.Ct. 759.

Submitted on December 27, 2019, by:

Michael DeAngelo Davis, Pro se
Reg. # 24604-077
Federal Correctional Institution
P.O. Box 9000
Seagoville, TX 75159

CERTIFICATE OF SERVICE

I certify that on December 27, 2019, I served all parties to this action.

Michael DeAngelo Davis, Pro se
Reg.# 24604-077

United States Court of Appeals
FIFTH CIRCUIT
OFFICE OF THE CLERK

LYLE W. CAYCE
CLERK

TEL. 504·310·7700 600
S. MAESTRI
PLACE, Suite 115
NEW ORLEANS, LA 70130

January 14, 2020

#24604-077
Mr. Michael DeAngelo Davis
FCI Seagoville
P.O. Box 9000
Seagoville, TX 75159-9000

No. 20-10028   USA *v.* Michael Davis
                 USDC No. 4:19-CV-689

Dear Mr. Davis,

We have docketed your appeal. You should use the number listed above on all future correspondence.

You should carefully read the following sections

Filings in this court are governed strictly by the Federal Rules of Appellate Procedure, **NOT** the Federal Rules of Civil Procedure. We cannot accept motions submitted under the Federal Rules of Civil Procedure. We can address only those documents the court directs you to file, or motions filed under the FED. R. APP. P. in support of the appeal. See FED. R. APP. P. and 5ᵀᴴ CIR. R. 27 for guidance. Documents not authorized by these rules will not be acknowledged or acted upon.

<u>Court Fees</u>

You must pay a filing fee for your notice of appeal unless the district court has entered an order exempting you from paying the fee under FED. R. APP. P. 24. The $505.00 Court of Appeals docketing fee is due within 15 days from this date, and you must notify this office once this is done. If you do not pay the filing fee or file a motion with the district court clerk for leave to proceed in *forma pauperis* on appeal, we will dismiss your appeal without further notice, see 5ᵗʰ CIR. R. 42.3.

ATTENTION ATTORNEYS: Attorneys are required to be a member of the Fifth Circuit Bar and to register for Electronic Case Filing. The "Application and Oath for Admission" form can be printed or downloaded from the Fifth Circuit's website, www.ca5.uscourts.gov. Information on Electronic Case Filing is available at www.ca5.uscourts.gov/cmecf/.

The clerk's office offers brief templates and the ability to check the brief for potential deficiencies prior to docketing to assist in the preparation of the brief. To access these options, log in to CM/ECF and from the Utilities menu, select 'Brief Template' (Counsel Only) or 'PDF Check Document.'

We recommend that you visit the Fifth Circuit's website, www.ca5.uscourts.gov and review material that will assist you during the appeal process. We especially call to your attention the Practitioner's Guide and the 5th Circuit Appeal Flow Chart, located in the Forms, Fees, and Guides tab.

Sealing Documents on Appeal: Our court has a strong presumption of public access to our court's records, and the court scrutinizes any request by a party to seal pleadings, record excerpts, or other documents on our court docket. Counsel moving to seal matters must explain in particularity the necessity for sealing in our court. Counsel do not satisfy this burden by simply stating that the originating court sealed the matter, as the circumstances that justified sealing in the originating court may have changed or may not apply in an appellate proceeding. It is the obligation of counsel to justify a request to file under seal, just as it is their obligation to notify the court whenever sealing is no longer necessary. An unopposed motion to seal does not obviate a counsel's obligation to justify the motion to seal.

Sincerely,

LYLE W. CAYCE, Clerk

By: Connie Brown

Connie Brown, Deputy Clerk
504-310-7671

cc:

Ms. Karen S. Mitchell
Ms. Leigha Amy Simonton

UNITED STATES DISTRICT COURT
NORTHERN DISTRICT OF TEXAS
FORT WORTH DIVISION

Michael DeAngelo Davis

Case No.: 4:19-CV-689

V.

United States of America

Motion for leave to proceed
In Forma Pauperis on Appeal

Mr. Davis moves this court to grant him leave to proceed in appeal In Forma Pauperis. The record reflects that this court denied Mr. Davis §2255 relief notwithstanding issues that include actual innocence. This court has and continues to deny Mr. Davis the appointment of counsel. Good cause exists because, as the recent First Step Act reveals, he is serving an unlawful stacked 18 U.S.C. §924(c) sentence and is deprived of his due relief solely because of his ignorance of law. Mr. Davis swears that he is unable to pay the cost of appeal and provides a six-month commissary account report as proof.

Wherefore, Mr. Davis moves this court to grant this motion and grant him leave to proceed In Forma Pauperis.

Respectfully submitted on January 28, 2020 by:

_____
Michael D. Davis, Pro se
Reg.# 24604-077

KELLY PATRICK RIGGS

CERTIFICATE OF SERVICE

I certify that. on January 28, 2020, I served a copy of this motion on the Clerk of the Court of

Appeals for the Fifth Circuit and the attorney for the government via U.S. mail, properly addressed, first

class postage prepaid by placing them in the legal mailing system as made available to inmates at

Seagoville FCI

Submitted,

Michael D. Davis, Pro se
Reg.# 24604-077
Federal Correctional Institution
P.O. Box 9000
Seagoville, Tx 75159

IN THE UNITED STATES DISTRICT COURT
FOR THE ___Northern___ DISTRICT OF TEXAS
Fort_Worth_____ DIVISION

_____Michael D. Davis_____
Plaintiff's name and ID Number

_____Seagoville, F.C.I._____
Place of Confinement

CASE NO. 4:19-CV-689_____
(Clerk will assign the number)

v.

**APPLICATION TO PROCEED
IN FORMA PAUPERIS**

_____United States_____
Defendant's name and address

I, ___Michael Davis___, declare, depose, and say that I am the Plaintiff in the above entitled case. In support of my motion to proceed without being required to prepay fees, costs or give security therefor, I state that because of my poverty, I am unable to pay in advance the filing fee for said proceedings or to give security for the filing fee. I believe I am entitled to relief.

I further declare that the responses which I have made to questions and instructions below are true.

1.   Have you received, within the past 12 months, any money from any of the following sources?

a. Business, profession or form of self-employment?	Yes	[No]
b. Rent payments, interest or dividends?	Yes	[No]
c. Pensions, annuities or life insurance payments?	Yes	[No]
d. Gifts or inheritances?	[Yes]	No
e. Family of friends?	[Yes]	No
f. Any other sources?	Yes	[No]

If you answered YES to any of the questions above describe each source of money and state the amount received from each during the past 12 months.

_____See Attached_____

_____

2.   Do you own cash, or do you have money in a checking or savings account, including any funds in prison accounts?

[Yes]   No

If you answered YES, state the total value of the items owned.

_____See Attached_____

_____

Exhibit IV-2

- 1 -

KELLY PATRICK RIGGS

IN THE UNITED STATES DISTRICT COURT
FOR THE NORTHERN DISTRICT OF TEXAS
FORT WORTH DIVISION

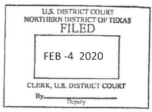

MICHAEL DEANGELO DAVIS, §
                         §
VS.   §
                         §
UNITED STATES OF AMERICA §
                         §

Case No.: 4:19-CV-689-A

(Criminal No.4:93-CR-020-A(1))

ORDER GRANTING MOTION TO PROCEED ON APPEAL IN FORMA PAUPERIS

Defendant Michael DeAngelo Davis has filed a motion for leave to proceed on appeal in forma pauperis accompanied by a completed certificate of inmate trust account. After review and consideration of the motion and inmate account certificate, the court concludes the motion should be granted. Therefore,

The court ORDERS that the motion for leave to proceed on appeal in forma pauperis (doc. 19), be and is hereby, GRANTED.

SIGNED February 4, 2020.

JOHN H. McBRYDE
United States District Judge

114

United States Court of Appeals
FIFTH CIRCUIT
OFFICE OF THE CLERK

LYLE W. CAYCE
CLERK

TEL. 504·310·7700 600
S. MAESTRI
PLACE, Suite 115
NEW ORLEANS, LA 70130

February 05, 2020

#24604-077
Mr. Michael DeAngelo Davis
FCI Seagoville
P.O. Box 9000
Seagoville, TX 75159-9000

No. 20-10028   USA v. Michael Davis
USDC No. 4:19-CV-689

Dear Mr. Davis,

We have docketed the appeal as shown above and ask you to use the case number above in future inquiries.

Before this appeal can proceed you must apply for a certificate of appealability (COA) to comply with 28 O.S.C. § 2253. If you wish to proceed, address your motion for COA to this court. Also send a separate brief supporting the motion. In the brief set forth the issues, clearly give supporting arguments. Your "motion for COA" and "brief in support" together may not exceed a total of 30 pages. You must file 2 legible copies within 40 days from the date of this letter. If you do not do so we will dismiss the appeal, see 5ᵀᴴ CIR. R. 42. Note that 5ᵀᴴ CIR. R. 31.4 and the Internal Operating Procedures following rules 27 and 31 provides the general sense of the court on the disposition of a variety of matters, which includes that except in the most extraordinary circumstances, the <u>maximum</u> extension for filing briefs is 30 days in criminal cases and 40 days in civil cases.

<u>Reminder as to Sealing Documents on Appeal:</u> Our court has a strong presumption of public access to our court's records, and the court scrutinizes any request by a party to seal pleadings, record excerpts, or other documents on our court docket. Counsel moving to seal matters must explain in particularity the necessity for sealing in our court. Counsel do not satisfy this burden by simply stating that the originating court sealed the matter, as the circumstances that justified sealing in the originating court may have changed or may not apply in an appellate proceeding. It is the obligation of counsel to justify a request to file under seal, just as it is their obligation to notify the court whenever sealing is no longer necessary. An unopposed motion to seal does not obviate a counsel's obligation to justify the motion to seal.

KELLY PATRICK RIGGS

Sincerely,

LYLE W. CAYCE, Clerk

By: _____
Melissa B. Courseault, Deputy Clerk
504-310-7701

cc:

Ms. Leigha Amy Simonton

Appeal No.: 20-10028

IN THE

UNITED STATES COURT OF APPEALS

Michael DeAngelo Davis

V.

UNITED STATES OF AMERICA

On Appeal from the U.S. District Court

For the Northern District of Texas

[Case No.: 4:19-CV-689]

MOTION FOR ISSUANCE OF A CERTIFICATE

OF APPEALABILITY

Mr. Davis is proceeding in pro se and respectfully moves this Court of Appeals to issue a Certificate of Appealability. He is currently deprived of his constitutional right to liberty without due process of law. As Mr. Davis has demonstrated in the attached application for a Certificate of Appealability, he is actually innocent of any conduct that warrants a second or subsequent 18 U.S.C. §924(c) sentence. In Mr. Davis's case, he is a first-time offender, under the law, but yet he was sentenced as though he was a second time offender, in violation of the mandates of Congress.

Once Mr. Davis discovered that the First Step Act of 2018, and the recent Supreme Court decision in *United States v. Davis et. al.* identified him as actually innocent of the 20-year sentence under §924(c), he asked the district court to appoint counsel. His motion was never answered. Mr. Davis then began his own misguided litigation to pursue relief.

The proceeding eventually resulted in Mr. Davis's second-in-time §2255 motion being filed in pro se because he was once again denied the appointment of counsel. Mr. Davis has, to the best of his ability, shown that he is actually innocent and due relief.

117

KELLY PATRICK RIGGS

Mr. Davis's application for a Certificate of Appealability demonstrates that the district court's

judgment, to dismiss his §2255 motion, is questionable, and thus, due further consideration.

Mr. Davis desires to appeal the district court's judgment, as is authorized by 28 U.S.C. §2253(a)

and shows that his case is due consideration pursuant to §2253(c)(1), §2253(c)(2), and Appellate Rule

22(b)(1). See also *Miller-El v. Cockrell*, 537 U.S. 322, 336; 123 S.Ct. 1029; 154 L. Ed. 2d 931 (2003).

Wherefore, above premises considered, Mr. Davis moves this court to grant him his requested

relief.

Respectfully submitted on March 9, 2020, by:

Michael DeAngelo Davis, Pro se
Reg. #24604-077
Federal Correctional Institution
P.O. Box 9000
Seagoville, TX 75159

CERTIFICATE OF SERVICE

I hereby certify that on March 9, 2020, I served a copy of the foregoing motion and application for

Certificate of Appealability, on all parties via U.S. mail as provided to prisoners for legal mail, first

class postage prepaid and affixed thereto, and properly addressed to: The Clerk of U.S. Court of

Appeals for the Fifth Circuit, and

Brian Portugal

Assistant United States Attorney 1100 Commerce Street

Third Floor

Dallas, TX 75242

Respectfully submitted on March 9, 2020, by:

Michael DeAngelo Davis, Pro se
Reg. #24604-077
Federal Correctional Institution P.O. Box 9000
Seagoville, TX 75159

118

POST-CONVICTION RELIEF: SECOND LAST CHANCE

Appeal No.: 20-10028

IN THE

UNITED STATES COURT OF APPEALS

Michael DeAngelo Davis

V.

UNITED STATES OF AMERICA

On Appeal from the U.S. District Court

For the Northern District of Texas

APPLICATION FOR ISSUANCE OF A CERTIFICATE OF APPEALABILITY

_____
Michael DeAngelo Davis
Reg. #24604-077

KELLY PATRICK RIGGS

UNITED STATES COURT OF APPEALS
FOR THE FIFTH CIRCUIT

Michael DeAngelo Davis

Appeal No. 20-10028

V.

[Civ. No. 4:19-CV-689]

United States of America

APPLICATION FOR ISSUANCE OF A CERTIFICATE OF APPEALABILITY

Mr. Davis, proceeding in pro se and invoking the Supreme Court's controlling doctrine of *Haines v. Kerner*, 404 U.S. 519, 520-521, moves this court to issue a Certificate of Appealability (herein after COA). He seeks the issuance of a COA, pursuant to 28 U.S.C. §2253(c)(2), authorizing him (Mr. Davis) to appeal from the district court's December 11, 2019, order to dismiss his 28 U.S.C. §2255 motion for a lack of jurisdiction.

NATURE OF THE PROCEEDING

On August 21, 2019, Mr. Davis filed an instant motion under 28 U.S.C. §2255. In his motion, he argued that he is actually innocent of the second 20-year sentence under 18 U.S.C. §924(c)(3)(B). Moreover, in the First Step Act, congress clarified its intent by explaining that neither the government nor the Court was authorized to seek or impose a second (stacked) §924 (c) sentence upon a defendant sentenced under 18 U.S.C. §924(c) for the first time. Thus, his confinement for the second §924(c) sentence is an unconstitutional violation of the Thirteenth Amendment because:

1) In the recent case of *United States v. Davis, et. al.*, The Supreme Court held that the residual clause of 18 U.S.C. §924 (c)(3)(B) was unconstitutionally void for vagueness. Additionally, the Supreme Court gave instructions for courts to forego the use of The Modified Categorical Approach and return to the

Categorical Approach, thus removing the crime of Hobbs Act Robbery from §924's force clause as well. *See 18 U.S.C. §924 (c)(3)(A).*

2) Mr. Davis is actually innocent of the second or stacked §924(c) sentence because Congress never intended, nor did it authorize courts to impose a second §924(c) sentence upon a defendant who had never been sentenced under §924(c) previously. Mr. Davis's actual innocence is established in the words of the First Step Act, Section 403. In the Act, Congress clarified its intent that the 20-year sentence should only be imposed upon a defendant previously sentenced under §924(c) in an earlier case that had already been decided against him. Mr. Davis had never before been sentenced under 18 U.S.C. §924(c). Thus, the court was without authorization to impose the second §924(c) sentence. Mr. Davis is actually innocent. *See Mcquiggin v. Perkins* (2013).

PROCEDURAL STATUS OF THE CASE

An application to the judges of the Court of Appeals for a Certificate of Appealability is appropriate at this time because:

1) The district court entered a final, appealable judgment in this case on December 11, 2019, that dismissed Mr. Davis's motion that he filed under 28 U.S.C. §2255.

2) Mr. Davis desires to appeal the judgment, as is authorized by 28 U.S.C. §2253(a). However, §2253(c)(1) and appellate rule 22(b)(1) require that a Certificate of Appealability be issued as a pre-condition of proceeding with the appeal.

3) A timely notice of appeal was filed in this case on December 27, 2019.

4) After the district court dismissed Mr. Davis's §2255 motion, the court failed to grant or deny a Certificate of Appealability.

5) On January 28, 2020, Mr. Davis followed the instruction of the Court of Appeals by filing a motion for leave to proceed in Forma Pauperis in the district court.

6) On February 4, 2020, the district court granted Mr. Davis's re- quested relief to proceed in Forma Pauperis on appeal.

STANDARD OF REVIEW

A federal prisoner, whose §2255 motion is denied by a federal district court, does not have an absolute right to appeal. Federal law requires that the prisoner first obtain a Certificate of Appealability (herein after "COA") from a Circuit Judge of the appropriate Court of Appeals. 28 U.S.C. §2253 (c) (1). A COA may be issued "only if the applicant has made a substantial showing of the denial of a constitutional right." §2253(c) (2). Until the prisoner secures a COA, the Court of Appeals may not rule on the merits of his case. *Miller-El v. Cockrell*, 537 U.S. 322, 336; 123 S.Ct. 1029; 154 L. Ed. 2d 931 (2003).

The Supreme Court, in *Buck v. Davis*, 137 S.Ct. 759; 197 L. Ed. 2d 1 (2017), said that: "A Court of Appeals should limit its examination [at the COA stage] to a threshold inquiry into the underlying merit of [the] claims, and ask only if the District Court's decision was debatable. *Miller-El*, 537 U.S., at 327, 348, 123 S.Ct. 1029, 154 L. Ed. 2d 931." [internal quotations omitted].

The Supreme Court has emphasized that the COA inquiry is not co-extensive with a merit's analysis. At the COA stage, the only question is whether the prisoner has shown that "jurists of reason could disagree with the district court's resolution of his constitutional claims or that jurists could conclude the issues presented are adequate to deserve encouragement to proceed further." *Miller-El*, 537 U.S., at 327; 123 S.Ct. 1029; 154 L. Ed. 2d 931. This threshold question should be decided without "full consideration of the factual or legal bases adduced in support of the claims." Id., at 336; 123 S.Ct. 1029; 154 L. Ed. 2d 931. "When a Court of Appeals sidesteps [the COA] process by first deciding the merits of an appeal, and then justifying its denial of a COA based on its adjudication of the actual merits, it is in essence deciding an appeal without jurisdiction." Id., at 336-337; 123 S.Ct. 1029; 154 L. Ed. 2d 931.

Therefore, in the case of Michael D. Davis, the sole question before the Fifth Circuit of the United States Court of Appeals, is whether jurists of reason could have debated whether the District Court had jurisdiction to reach the merits of his §2255 motion.

ISSUE OF THE CASE

Mr. Davis questions if the district court abused its discretion, by failing to make an informed choice among the many alternatives to the established procedural defaults.

According to the precedential rulings of the Supreme Court of the United States, the district court has abused its discretion by determining its jurisdiction without an understanding of, and correctly applying, the governing law and the many procedural default rulings.

ABUSE OF DISCRETION

A review of a district court's judgment for abuse of discretion has three essential components:

1) Was the Court's judgment under the Court's discretion, as authorized by law?

2) Did the district court understand its own discretion and, if so, did the district court provide its Honest Service by exercising its sound discretion?

- The failure to exercise choice in a situation calling for choice is an abuse of discretion.

- Adhering to uniform policy in a situation calling for a case-specific balancing is an abuse of discretion.

3) Did the district court exercise its discretion erroneously?

- An informed choice among alternatives requires that the district court's determination be based upon a firm factual foundation; Therefore, does the record reveal sufficient facts upon which the district court's determination was based?

- Did the district court judge understand and correctly apply the governing law or did the judge rely on an improper factor?

In Mr. Davis's case the district court abused its discretion by deciding that it did not have jurisdiction to reach the merits of his second-in-time §2255. The court's error is based on a failure to understand and/or apply actual innocence as cause for Mr. Davis's procedural default.

REASONS TO GRANT A CERTIFICATE OF APPEALABILITY

Denial of Constitutional Right – Mr. Davis is currently incarcerated for a crime that he is actually innocent of. Mr. Davis was indicted on a total of six counts stemming from the alleged robbery of four gas stations in Fort Worth, Texas on December 10, 1992. Four of the counts were for obstruction of commerce by robbery, and two of the counts were for use of a firearm during the commission of a robbery. 18 *U.S.C.* §1951 and §924(c). At sentencing, the court imposed a mandatory consecutive sentence of 60 months on one of the firearm counts and a mandatory consecutive sentence of 240 months on the second firearm count. See 18 U.S.C. §924(c)

Mr. Davis's actual innocence was established with the passing of the First Step Act of 2018. In Section 403(a), 132 Stat. at 5221-22, Congress clarified 18 U.S.C. §924(c). The new act states that, "In general, Section 924(c)(1)(C) of title 18, United States Code, is amended, in the matter preceding clause (i), by striking 'second or subsequent conviction under this subsection' and inserting 'violation of this subsection that occurs after a prior conviction under this subsection has become final.'" As indicated, the First Step Act has "clarified" that Mr. Davis, a first-time offender under §924(c), was impermissibly subjected to a second mandatory sentence of 240 months, and because his 240 month sentence was not authorized by an act of Congress, he is actually innocent under the law.

The Supreme Court, in *Murray v. Carrier*, 477 U.S. 478, 495-6 (1986), stated, "We think that in extraordinary cases, where a constitutional violation has probably resulted in the conviction of someone who is actually innocent, a federal habeas court may grant the writ even in the absence of cause for the procedural default." See also *McQuiggin v. Perkins*, 569 U.S. 383: 133 S.Ct. 1924 (2013), holding that actual innocence, if proved, may serve as a gateway to overcome procedural default.

Mr. Davis's case is one of those extraordinary cases where his actual innocence should serve to invoke the review of a United States district court. A COA should be issued and his case remanded.

Jurists of Reason Could Debate the District Court's Judgment – Mr. Davis's actual innocence would cause jurists of reason to find the district court's decision debatable. The first and most important judicial officer in Mr. Davis's case is the district judge who dismissed the action which Mr. Davis seeks to appeal.

The district judge, on February 4, 2020, issued an order granting Mr. Davis's motion seeking leave to proceed on appeal In Forma Pauperis. The controlling law, concerning proceeding in forma pauperis, is 28 U.S.C. §1915. Subsection 1915(e)(2)(B)(1) states that, "… the court shall dismiss the case at any time if the court determines that – the action or appeal – is frivolous or malicious."

In today's judicial atmosphere, resources are scarce because of newly enacted law like the First Step Act and Supreme Court decisions like *United States v. Davis et. al.* Thus, it is unreasonable to conclude that a wise district judge would waste judicial resources by granting in forma pauperis status to a prisoner advancing a frivolous claim. It is likewise unreasonable to conclude that a district judge would fail to consider the reasonableness of the appeal prior to granting or denying a motion as important as a motion for leave to proceed In Forma Pauperis. Mr. Davis believes that the district judge reconsidered his own judgment after reading Mr. Davis's notice of appeal. Thus, District Judge John H.

McBryde appears to be a jurist of reason who found his own judgment debatable in light of all available information.

Mr. Davis's case also represents a Circuit Court split as to the definition of 'second or successive.' See *United States v. Holt*, 417 F.3d. 1172 (11th Cir. 2005); *Johnson v. United States*, 724 Fed. Appx. 917 (11th Cir. 2018) citing Stewart, 646 F. 3d. at 859. Mr. Davis also contends that every judge in America who follows that actual innocence serves as a gateway to procedural default are jurists of reason who would find the district court's decision debatable.

PROCEDURAL PREREQUISITES FOR ACTION

As shown in this filing, Mr. Davis has satisfied all of the procedural prerequisites to action by this court on this application for a Certificate of Appealability:

1) Mr. Davis has filed a timely notice of appeal;

2) Mr. Davis promptly followed the instructions of this court to move for leave to proceed In Forma Pauperis;

3) Mr. Davis has made more than a good faith effort to conform this application to all of the requirements set out in the Federal Rules of Appellate Procedure, Rule 22 and Fifth Circuit Rules pertaining to motions seeking the issuance of a Certificate of Appealability.

4) Mr. Davis has served all interested parties to this action with a copy of this application and the supporting papers, as is reflected in the attached Certificate of Service.

CONCLUSION

For the reasons set out above, Mr. Davis respectfully requests that this court issue the requested Certificate of Appealability on all the issues set forth in this application.

Respectfully submitted on March 9th, 2020, by:

Michael DeAngelo Davis, Pro se
Reg. #24604-077
Federal Correctional Institution
P.O. Box 9000
Seagoville, TX 75159

CHAPTER FIVE

SECOND-OR-SUCCESSIVE AUTHORIZATION

Looking back on my years as a Jailhouse Lawyer leaves me truly amazed at what a judge will do to maintain the conviction of Americans who are actually innocent. Yes, they will, and they have ignored the facts of innocence. As you have now seen in the case of Mr. Davis in chapter four, it is the law as it relates to the facts that determines guilt or innocence. That means that a change in either fact or law should make a difference in whether a defendant was actually innocent, or actually guilty. And when such a change is discovered, then the defendant is due review of his or her claim under the law.

Since the passing of the Antiterrorism and Effective Death Penalty Act, in 1996, motions for Post-Conviction Relief under §2255 have been doled out at pretty much one-to-a-customer. But the law also holds that a prisoner can file a second §2255 after the Supreme Court has issued a ruling that changed Constitutional law and has declared the ruling to be made retroactive to cases on collateral review. See 28 U.S.C. §2255(h)(2). The law also holds that a second §2255 motion can be filed where a prisoner has discovered new and compelling evidence that they (the prisoner) were actually innocent of the offense of conviction. See 28 U.S.C. §2255(h)(1).

The two circumstances that are described above strike at the very heart of both habeas corpus and post-conviction relief – you are innocent of something.

> *Important Note: You will find that for the purpose of post-conviction proceedings, the court and the government will use the terms "actual innocence," "fundamental miscarriage of justice," and "factual innocence" interchangeably. But all these combined* do not *limit a claim to an assertion that you did not engage in certain conduct. As with Mr. Davis in the previous chapter, he did rob four gas stations, but he is not guilty of violating 18 D.S.C. §924(c)(1)(C). Just as I have proven in many cases that a conviction under 21 D.S.C. §841 does not automatically constitute a sentence under the Career Criminal Act.*

This is pretty simple if you have found a new constitutional law or a new fact that shows that you are actually innocent of a crime or a particular sentence, then you have the right to raise a claim.

It is also pretty simple if there has been a change in constitutional law that was made retroactive, or you have found new evidence that proves you are actually innocent, then you have a lawful right to review. This includes changes that will affect only the length of your sentence.

> *Authors Note: Before going on, I do recommend that you read 28 U.S.C. §2244 and 28 U.S.C. §2255(h) for yourself. Having a good understanding of these two laws, which control the authorization of second or successive §2255 filings, will bring clarity to what is coming in the rest of this chapter.*

Now that you have read §2244, I want you to pay particular attention to §2244(b)(3)(D), "the court of appeals shall grant or deny the authorization to file a second or successive application not later than 30 days after the filing of the motion." This time limit is not in your favor. What this means is that the court of appeals must employ its "if in doubt deny" policy when time gets short.

In almost all situations where the Supreme Court has made a change to constitutional law that is to be applied retroactively, the number of applications for second or successive authorizations received by the Court increases by nearly 100-fold. To make up for the additional workload the court of appeals separates the applications, counseled applications in one class and pro se applications in another. The counseled applications are then passed to the court's staff attorneys and given reasonable consideration. The pro se filings, however, are passed to clerks and interns to practice on. Their only responsibility is to, at a minimum, deny the application before the end of thirty days. In my practice as a jailhouse lawyer, I have filed many motions seeking second or successive authorization. After the Supreme Court decision in *Johnson v. United States*, 576 U.S. __ , 135 S.Ct. __ ; 192 L. Ed. 2d 569 (2015), I had filed a little over twenty §2244 motions to the Court of Appeals for the Fifth Circuit. To my surprise, all but three were denied – eight of the responses from the Court were identical all the way down to having the wrong names and histories in the Court's opinions.

The important thing here is that three were granted. Those three identified that the applicant had been "actually innocent" of being an armed career criminal. So, as you consider your own situation, ask yourself, 'what am I actually innocent of doing or being? When you have that answer, present it to the court clearly.

While a showing of cause is usually necessary under the Cause and Prejudice requirement for federal Post-Conviction Relief from a conviction or sentence, the Supreme Court has recognized an exception to the rule. That exception is often called the "actual innocence exception," or the courts have also used other terms such as "fundamental miscarriage of justice" or "ends of justice."

Let me also stress to you that a pro se litigant must effectively show rather than just say, "actual innocence." An example of a motion for second or successive authorization can be found in the appendix. But before you go to the form, read and understand what the Supreme Court said in the cases that follow:

In *Murray v. Carrier*, 477 U.S. 478; L. Ed. 2d 397; 106 S.Ct. 2639 (1986), the Supreme Court expressed that it remained confident that most victims of a fundamental miscarriage of justice would in fact meet the cause and prejudice standard. The Supreme Court also added that (1) it did not pretend that this would always be the case; and (2) accordingly, in an extraordinary case where a constitutional violation has probably resulted in the conviction of one who is actually innocent, a federal habeas corpus court may grant the writ even in the absence of a showing of cause for the procedural default.

With respect to a case, which involved a denial to the defense of discovery of some statements by an alleged victim, the Supreme Court has, in the past, ruled that the accused's federal habeas corpus petition would have to be dismissed for failure to establish cause for a procedural default; unless, it was determined on remand that the statements in question contained material that would establish the accused's *actual innocence*.

In *Smith v. Murray*, 477 U.S. 527; 91 L. Ed. 2d 434; 106 S.Ct. 2661 (1986), the Supreme Court recognized that, while a cause and prejudice test generally applies for the purpose of excusing a procedural default, a federal habeas corpus court may grant the writ, even in the absence of a showing of cause for the procedural default, where a constitutional violation has probably resulted in the conviction of one who is actually innocent. Be mindful that, according to the Supreme Court, the concept of "actual" is distinct from "legal" innocence. Therefore, it does not translate easily into the context of an alleged error at the sentencing phase of a criminal proceeding.

As indicated by this case, the Supreme Court is quick to rule that it is clear on the record that an application of the cause and prejudice test would not result in a finding that a fundamental miscarriage of justice occurred. In addition, the Supreme Court concedes that "Profound Societal Costs" that attend the exercise of federal habeas corpus jurisdiction and rejects the suggestion that there is anything fundamentally unfair about enforcing procedural-default rules in cases devoid of any substantial claim that the alleged error undermined the accuracy of the guilt or sentencing determination.

Although a cause and prejudice test generally applies for the purposes of excusing a procedural default, a federal habeas corpus court may grant the writ, even in the absence of a showing of cause for the procedural default. As discussed earlier, a showing of cause is not necessary where a constitutional violation has probably resulted in the conviction of one who is actually innocent.

In *Dugger v. Adams*, 489 U.S. 401; 103 L. Ed. 2d 435; 109 S.Ct. 1211 (1989), the Supreme Court seemed to recognize that, in an *extraordinary* case involving a state death sentence, a federal court may grant the writ even in the absence of a showing of cause. But the Supreme Court also cautioned, that for such purposes, a fundamental miscarriage of justice does not result whenever there is a substantial claim that a constitutional violation undermined the accuracy of a sentencing decision. The Supreme Court here demonstrated that if an error is, by its nature, the kind of error that might have affected the accuracy of a death sentence, it is far from demonstrating that an individual defendant probably is "actually innocent" of the sentence that the defendant received.

In *McCleskey v. Zant*, 499 U.S. 467; 113 L. Ed. 2d 517; 111 S.Ct. 1454 (1991), the Supreme Court ruled that, under 28 U.S.C. §2244(b) and under Rule 9(b) of rules governing [28 U.S.C.] §2254 cases, a cause and prejudice standard generally applies in determining whether a federal court will decline to entertain a claim in a second or subsequent federal habeas corpus petition. The Court opined that even when considering denial for abuse of the writ, for inexcusable neglect in failing to raise the claim in a prior such petition, the petitioner may still proceed if the petitioner cannot show cause.

Stating that the failure to raise the claim in an earlier petition may nonetheless be excused if the petitioner can show that a fundamental miscarriage of justice would result from a failure to entertain the claim. The Supreme Court recognized that, in a limited class of habeas corpus cases involving procedural defaults, federal courts retain the authority to issue the writ in extraordinary circumstances when a constitutional violation probably has caused the conviction of one who is innocent of the crime.

In cases involving an allegation of "abuse of the writ," the Supreme Court added, allowing an exception for a fundamental miscarriage of justice would (1) give meaningful content to an otherwise unexplained "ends of justice" inquiry mandated in such cases; and (2) serve as an additional safeguard against compelling an innocent person to suffer an unconstitutional loss of liberty, thus providing a guarantee that the ends of justice would be served in full.

In *Sanders v. United States*, 373 U.S. 1; 10 L. Ed. 2d 148; 83 S.Ct. 1068 (1963), a case that involved a federal prisoner's petition for Post-Conviction Relief under 28 U.S.C. §2255 – the Supreme Court noted that the phrase "ends of justice" had originally been drawn from the text of the 1948 version of 28 U.S.C. §2244. The statute at that time contained a paragraph that applied to both state and federal prisoners. As easily recognized today, §2244 is quite different in text and in meaning from its original 1948 version. Nonetheless, the Supreme Court has said that even after the numerous amendments that changed the meaning of the once controlling law, the "ends of justice" inquiry remained appropriate with respect to a successive petition by a prisoner.

In *Kuhlmann v. Wilson*, 477 U.S. 436; 91 L. Ed. 2d 364; 106 S.Ct. 2616 (1986), the Supreme Court in its majority opinion, expressed the view that under 28 U.S.C. §2244(b) the ends of justice required federal courts to entertain a second or successive habeas corpus petition by a prisoner convicted in a state criminal trial, based on a federal constitutional claim already rejected on the merits in a previous federal petition, only where the prisoner supplemented the constitutional claim with a colorable showing of "factual innocence." Members of the Court also express the view that while such a showing of innocence was sufficient for purposes of the ends of justice inquiry, other showings in which prisoners advance potentially meritorious claims and provide good justification for returning to court a second time with the same claim might, in the discretion of a Federal District Court, justify making relief available. Finally, the third view was expressed that, when a district court is confronted with the question whether the ends of justice would be served by entertaining a prisoner's petition raising a claim that had been rejected in a prior federal petition, one of the facts that might properly by considered is whether the prisoner can advance a colorable claim of innocence, although this fact is not an essential element of every just determination.

More recently still, the Supreme Court has established the "actual innocence" exception to the cause and prejudice standard. The high court has continuously held that a federal court may hear the merits of a successive, abusive, or procedurally defaulted claim if failure to hear the claim would constitute a miscarriage of justice.

In *Sawyer v. Whitley*, 120 L. Ed. 2d 269; 112 S.Ct. 2514 (1992), the Supreme Court observed that: (1) the actual innocence exception is very narrow; and (2) in order to make the exception workable, it has to be subject to determination by relatively objective standards. The Supreme Court provided, as an example of "actual innocence" in the non-capital context, a case where the state has convicted the wrong person of the crime, such as an instance where (1) another person has credibly confessed to the crime; and (2) it is evident that the law has made a mistake.

Although most of you are not subject to the death penalty, let me also say that the Supreme Court has found it near impossible to develop a similar framework that can apply with uniformity in the capital sentencing context. But, the Supreme Court has decided that for federal habeas corpus petitioners, to effectively show their "actual innocence" of a state death sentence, they must show by clear and convincing evidence that but for a federal constitutional error, no reasonable juror would have found the petitioner eligible for the death penalty under applicable state law.

According to the Supreme Court, this standard allows a petitioner to show that: (1) there were no aggravating circumstances; or (2) some other condition of eligibility was not met. This standard does not, however, extend to allowing a petitioner to show the existence of additional mitigating evidence which affected only the ultimate discretionary decision between the death penalty and life in prison. For a very good example of how the exception is effectively applied in a capital case, see *Buck v. Davis*, 137 S.Ct. 759; 197 L. Ed. 2d 1 (2017).

Again, I cannot stress enough to pro se litigants the need to *show*, rather than just say, "actual innocence."

CHAPTER SIX

RULE 60(B)

For those of you who don't know already, let me say that Rule 60(b) relief is likely the most elusive creature you can see in a post-conviction proceeding. It is my opinion that this is true because of two things: (1) 28 D.S.C. §2255 is not truly adequate in its intended purpose of providing expeditious relief from an erroneous sentence, if it were Rule 60(b) would never be invoked in a post-conviction proceedings; and (2) 90 percent, and maybe even more, of all judges and lawyers fail to continue their education, most having no clue how §2255 or Rule 60(b) is supposed to work. The bottom line is that the courts view all Americans as guilty of something, and all bar members as omnipotent beings who make no mistakes.

This chapter is my feeble attempt to illustrate how Rule 60(b) relief can be obtained in a post-conviction proceeding. My intention here is to explain this phenomenon in a way that everyone – even lawyers – can understand. Keep in mind, first and foremost, that Rule 60(b) is one of the many Federal Rules of Civil Procedure. As such, Rule 60(b) would not ordinarily have any purpose in a criminal case. But because a §2255 action is not completely criminal nor is it completely civil in nature, the parties may rely on both the Federal Rules of Criminal Procedure and The Federal Rules of Civil Procedure in a §2255 proceeding; see Rules Governing Section 2255 proceedings, Rule 12, in the appendix.

The most important thing you can do before you start to write anything with "Rule 60(b)" on it, is to read all of Rule 60, which is available in the appendix of this book. I say this because there is more to the rule than what you read about in its subsection (b).

The Text of Rule 60(b) reads as follows:

> (b) **Grounds for Relief from a Final Judgment, Order, or Proceeding.** On motion and just terms, the court may relieve a party or its legal representative from a final judgment, order, or proceeding for the following reasons:
>
> (1) mistake, inadvertence, surprise, or excusable neglect;
>
> (2) newly discovered evidence that, with reasonable diligence, could not have been discovered in time to move for a new trial under Rule 59(b);
>
> (3) fraud (whether previously called intrinsic or extrinsic), misrepresentation, or misconduct by an opposing party; (4) file judgment is void;
>
> (5) the judgment has been satisfied, released, or discharged; it is based on an earlier judgment that has been reversed or vacated; or applying it prospectively is no longer equitable; or
>
> (6) any other reason that justified relief.

If you're thinking that this rule has some hardcore teeth after reading it, I would agree with you – except you'll find that the courts have reworded and redefined this rule many times over the years. As an example, if a federal criminal defendant, proceeding pro se, could truly rely on Rule 60(b)(3), then almost every §2255 proceeding would be reopened automatically. This is true only because the courts have sidestepped a federal defendant's right to counsel at appeal. After the Supreme Court's decision in *Massaro v. United States*, 538 U.S. 500, the courts have committed the greatest fraud America has ever seen. The courts have circumvented Congress's intent in 18 U.S.C. §3006A (c), in all federal criminal cases, for the sole purpose of sustaining the 80 billion dollar a year federal budget required to operate the Wayward Criminal Justice System. Today the Bureau of Prisons alone is paid $102.60 per day per inmate … even the innocent ones.

Also, consider that the judge who will evaluate your Rule 60(b) motion is the same judge who denied your §2255, and almost no judge is willing to admit what they are doing.

Keep in mind that when Rule 60 was drafted as a rule of civil procedure, that was where it was expected to be used. Never had anyone considered that it would have any bearing in a post-conviction proceeding affecting a criminal sentence. Because of this, the courts are quick to deny review of any motion listing any of the first five reasons. If a court were to grant a 60(b) motion in a post-conviction proceeding, based on any of the grounds list in reasons 1-5, it would undermine the public's confidence in the court's integrity and the public's expectation of the fair administration of the justice in federal criminal cases.

A good example of my previously stated opinion is the fact that I have found only one Supreme Court case to discuss the issue of the applicability of Rule 60(b)(3). As the rule indicates, it authorized the granting of relief to a party in the event of fraud, and if the high court were to recognize the widespread fraud that pervades our federal courts, it would quickly reduce The American Criminal Justice System down to the illegal slave trade it actually is. In *Klapprott v. United States*, 335 U.S. 601; 93 L. Ed. 266; 69 S.Ct.384 (1949), the Supreme Court considered a wide range of applications for Rule 60(b)(3) and 60(b)(4); that included reasons such as fraud on the court, misrepresentation, or other misconduct of an adverse party; and even the granting of relief from a void judgment. Consider for a moment what would happen if fraud and misrepresentation by the government were actionable in §2255 cases that followed the guilty plea of a defendant who was forced to rely on the representation of a panel lawyer or a federal defender. That is right, over half of all federal "Ghost dope" and child pornography sentences would be vacated.

After considering all the reasonable exclusions of this rule's applicability, you will find that only one provision of Rule 60(b) remains: Rule 60(b)(6).

Rule 60(b)(6) authorized a court to relieve a party from a final judgment for "any other reason that justifies relief," Fed. R. Civ. P., Rule 60(b)(6). Although this sounds simple enough, it is not. The courts have been whittling away at the rule's application ever since 1949. In *Buck v. Davis*, 137 S.Ct. 759; 197 L. Ed. 2d 1 (2017), the Supreme Court decided that relief is available under Rule 60(b)(6) only in extraordinary circumstances, which they claim will rarely occur in the habeas corpus and post-conviction proceedings. The Court went on to indicate that, in determining whether extraordinary circumstances are present, the Court may consider a wide and undefined range of factors. These factors may include the risk of injustice to the parties and the risk of undermining the public's confidence in the judicial process.

Now we have come full circle, "extraordinary circumstances" in the Court's narrow dogmatic view means "actual innocence" or "miscarriage of justice." What's more is that a "claim of actual innocence is not cognizable in a §2255 motion," even when the evidence of innocence is clear in the record, see *Jordan v. Sec'y Dept. of Corr.*, 485 F. 3d 1351, 1356 (11th Cir. 2007) as quoted by Judge Karon Owen Bowdre in the case of *Kelly Patrick Riggs v. United States*, Northern District of Alabama, Case No.: 2:15-cv-8043-KOB.

Further study of federal cases will show that the use of complex procedures, the denial of counsel at first tier collateral review, and the inapplicability of an actual innocence claim in a §2255 proceeding all conspire to help the courts maintain the conviction of tens of thousands of innocent Americans. And, a Rule 60(b)(6) motion is the first place that federal defendants are authorized to show that they are actually innocent. Bear in mind that actual innocence is the only "extraordinary circumstance" that allows review. Your claims in your 60(b)(6) motion must show that your §2255 proceeding was unreliable because it was somehow defective.

The last basic principle to consider before moving on to actual practice instruction is that Rule 60(b)(6) relief is different from the relief that is available under Rule 60(b)(1)-60(b)(5), so don't try to mix them together. In *Liljeberg v. Health Services Acquisition Corp.*, 486 U.S. 847; 100 L. Ed. 2d 855; 208 S.Ct. 2194 (1988), the Supreme Court gave the opinion that Rule 60(b)(1)-60(b)(5), which give specific reasons on which to grant relief, and Rule 60(b)(6), which authorizes relief for "any other reason justifying relief ..." are very different in the scope of reasons for which they can grant relief. Because of the potential to raise a claim under the "miscarriage of justice" or "actual innocence" exceptions, motions under Rule 60(b)(6) don't suffer from the "reasonable time" – 1 year – limitation period contained in Rule 60(b). The Court indicated that Rule 60(b)(6) provides federal courts a broad authority to grant relief, but that extraordinary circumstances are required to make a motion under the "other reasons" language of Rule 60(b)(6).

> *Authors Note: Do not try to overcome the timeliness of a Rule 60 (b)(1)-60(b)(5) claim by raising it in a motion titled Rule 60(b)(6). The Supreme Court has made clear that a motion under Rule 60(b)(6) may not be based on any of the grounds that are listed in Rules 60(b)(1)-60(b)(5), and that Rule 60(b)(6) may not be relied upon to get around the 1-year limitations period of Rule 60(b) as particularly applied to Rules 60(b)(1)-60(b)(3), see Pioneer Inv. Servo Co. v. Brunswick Assocs. Ltd. Partnership, 123 L. Ed. 2d 74; 113 S.Ct. 1489 (1993).*

RULE 60(B) VS. §2255 MOTIONS

A book that has the intended purpose of showing people how to succeed at something will not usually dwell too much on those who have failed in the past, but just this once I'm going to share with you a loser. Not to show you what not to do, but because the judge in this case gave a very good summary of the legitimate uses of a 60(b) motion in a post-conviction context. I also recommend that you read this case for yourself in the law library, because here I have omitted internal quotations and some citations to save space.

ADAMS v. UNITED STATES
911 F. 3d 397 (7th Cir. 2018)
In Part

A. Legitimate uses for Rule 60(b) and §2255 motions.

Not even an omniscient judge could anticipate the many complexities that can come to pass in law and life. Rule 60, therefore, "gives district courts the power and discretion to modify their judgments when truly new facts come to light or when the judge recognizes an error and believes it should be corrected." *Kennedy v. Schneider Elec.*, 893 F. 3d 414, 419 (7th Cir. 2018). But as we have noted time and again, Rule 60(b) provides relief only in the most "extraordinary situations where a judgment is the inadvertent product of special circumstances and not merely erroneous application of law." And a party invoking Rule 60(b) must claim grounds for relief that could not have been used to obtain a reversal by means of a direct appeal. *Banks v. Chicago Bd. of Educ.*, 750 F. 3d, 663, 667 (7th Cir. 2014). Not only is Rule 60(b) relief available only in extraordinary circumstances, but once a district court has denied that relief, those "proceedings are subject to only limited and deferential appellate review." *Gonzalez v. Crosby*, 545 U.S. 524, (2005). We review a court's decision to deny Rule 60(b) for an abuse of discretion only. *Pearson v. Target Corp.*, 893 F. 3d, 980, 984 (7th Cir. 2018).

Rule 60(b) relief is thus different than post-conviction relief under 28 U.S.C. §2255 which is meant to challenge a sentence "upon the ground that the sentence was imposed in violation of the Constitution, or laws of the United States, or that the court was without jurisdiction to impose such sentence, or that the sentence was in excess of the maximum authorized by law, or is otherwise subject to collateral attack ..." 28 U.S.C. §2255(a). Ordinarily a defendant has but one chance at post-conviction relief under 28 U.S.C. §2255 to set aside or correct his sentence, except in the case of newly discovered evidence or a new rule of retroactively applied constitutional law. See 28 U.S.C. §2255(h). The Antiterrorism and Effective Death Penalty Act requires a prisoner to receive the prior approval of the Court of Appeals before filing a second or successive motion under §2255. See 28 U.S.C. §2255(h); *Nunez v. United States*, 96 F. 3d 990, 991 (7th Cir. 1996). "No matter how powerful a petitioner's showing, only this [appellate] court may authorize the commencement of a second or successive petition .... From the district court's perspective, it is an allocation of subject-matter jurisdiction to the court of appeals. A district court must dismiss a second or successive petition, without awaiting any response from the government, unless the court of appeals has given approval for its filing." Nunez, 96 F. 3d at 991.

Therefore, if a Rule 60(b) motion is, in its essence, merely asking for relief that one would ask for in a motion under §2255, such a motion would be subject to the same restrictions or requirements for successive habeas petitions. *Gonzalez*, 545 U.S. at 529-30. According to the Supreme Court, therefore, a prisoner may not use a Rule 60(b) motion to "attack the federal court's previous resolution of a [habeas or §2255] claim on the merits." Such an attack, the court reasoned, is essentially just another claim for post-conviction relief. As the Supreme Court explained in Gonzalez:

> First, any claim that has already been adjudicated in a previous petition must be dismissed. §2244(b)(1). Second, any claim that has not already been adjudicated must be dismissed unless it relies on either a new and retroactive rule of constitutional law or new facts showing a high probability of actual innocence. §2244(b)(2). Third, before the district court may accept a successive petition for filing, the court of appeals must determine that it presents a claim not previously raised that is sufficient to meet §2244(b)(2)'s new-rule or actual-innocence provisions. *Gonzalez*, 545 U.S. at 529-30.

> A prisoner could, however, file a viable 60(b) motion after a failed §2255 attempt, if his claim is that a procedural error precluded him from receiving a determination on the merits – for example, a claim that the federal court misapplied a statute of limitations, errantly determined that a party had failed to exhaust, or a claim of fraud on the court. *Id.* at 532 & n.4, 5. See also, *Bradley v. Lockett*, 549 F. Appx. 545, 550-52 (7th Cir. 2013). In short, no matter what label a litigant gives to the motion, any post-judgment motion in a criminal proceeding that falls within the scope of §2255 is considered a motion under §2255. See *Melton v. United States*, 359 F. 3d 855, 857 (7th Cir. 2004). In other words, if it looks like a successive §2255 motion, it is a successive §2255 motion even if it is dressed in Rule 60(b) clothing. Thus, when a petitioner has already been heard in post-conviction proceedings and then attempts to reopen those proceedings by moving under Rule 60(b), the district court's first task is to determine whether the petitioner "has in reality filed an unauthorized second or successive petition." *Ramirez v. United States*, 799 F. 3d 845, 850 (7th Cir. 2015). Otherwise Rule 60 could be used to circumvent the statutory limitation on successive motions under §2255. See *Gonzalez*, 545 U.S. at 531-32.

RULE 60(B)(6) IN ACTUAL PRACTICE

I wish there were a place in the law library where prisoners could find a clear and definite path to relief. Unfortunately, one does not exist. That is why advocates like me write books – to pass on what we have learned that works. Just as you won't find a definite path to follow, nor will you find a formatted Rule 60(b) motion form to fill out.

Remember also that district courts do not grant §2255 motions that are filed by prisoners filing in pro se. Likewise, you will find that courts do not grant Rule 60(b)(6) motions filed by prisoners either. Yes, you must go to the court of appeals for relief. When you petition the court of appeals, you will find that you will have to get a COA, just like in a §2255 proceeding. But what is different is that the appellate court will review the denial of a Rule 60(b) motion for abuse of discretion. As you may remember from a previous chapter, I outlined the criteria of an abuse of discretion. So, as you prepare to write your motion for relief under Federal Rules of Civil Procedure, Rule 60(b), try to keep your next step in mind and prepare for it.

PRACTICE POINTERS

First, let us consider what a Rule 60(b) motion is really asking for. If I had to say it in a single word, that word would be "rehearing." You are specifically asking the court to reopen your §2255, because something out of the court's control caused the court to get it wrong. Keep in mind that this is not a very popular position to take with any court. So, try this, "The court was deprived of the ability to rule correctly" … *i.e.* not the court's fault.

Second, do not under any circumstance raise any issue that could have been determined in your first §2255 motion, see 28 U.S.C. §2255(a). If you do raise such an issue, you have just filed an unauthorized "second or successive" motion that will be dismissed instantly.

Third, the key to a successful Rule 60(b) motion, one that is not considered second or successive, is the "extraordinary circumstances" of the case.

Last, but definitely not least, are the facts that support your 60(b) claim. A 60(b) motion, just like a §2255 motion, should be long on the facts and light on the law. And of course, your appeal of a denial of 60(b) relief should be for an abuse of discretion.

The remainder of this chapter is dedicated to providing you with some important examples to follow. The first is the opinion of the 7th Circuit Court of Appeals in *Ramirez v. United States*, 799 F. 3d 845 (7th Cir. 2015). This Court's opinion is important because it is the first identifiable and successful application of the *Martinez* exception in a federal criminal case. I suggest you read and understand this opinion before you even start your outline.

Next, you will find two examples of 60(b)(6) motions. You will notice that they are different. In both cases the movants (federal defendants in criminal cases) are actually innocent. What is different is that in Mr. Mercer's case, his actual innocence is the extraordinary circumstance; and in Mr. Riggs's case (although he too is actually innocent) it is the court's attempt to conceal the fact that he is actually innocent. To make this simple, notice that Mr. Mercer had to present the recorded facts that established his actual innocence; and Mr. Riggs had to prove only that the court refused to hear the ground that would have proved his actual innocence.

As far as I know, these are the two most up-to-date examples of 60(b)(6) filings in federal criminal cases. Those motions are very personalized to their application, so use them with caution. These motions are included as examples of effective format only. I suggest that you use them once you have effectively personalized them for your own use. Please refer to Chapter Two of this book before you start writing.

Ramirez v. United States
799 F. 3d 845 (7th Cir. 2015)

CASE SUMMARY: District court improperly denied defendant's motion under Fed. R. Civ. P. 60(b)(6) without discussing how post-conviction counsel's performance affected the integrity of proceedings, which was an abuse of discretion. A remand was required so that the district court could consider the merits of his contentions.

OVERVIEW: HOLDINGS: [1] – No one informed defendant about an alternative path to relief after his post-conviction lawyer abandoned him and left without a jurisdictionally-out-of-time appeal, and defendant did not conceal pertinent information from the court; [2] – The district court's decision on defendant's Fed. R. Civ. P. 60(b)(6) motion was based on a clear error of law, as it dismissed his effort to raise a claim about the assistance of post-conviction counsel; [3] – Defendant was effectively unable to raise his ineffective assistance claim until collateral review because he was in the typical situation of needing to develop the record more fully before he could proceed; [4] – Trial counsel's performance was deficient as the lack of desire to uncover the truth was deficient and defendant showed that his sentence would have been different had counsel objected.

OUTCOME: Judgment reversed and remanded.

Opinion

In 2008 Israel Ramirez pleaded guilty to possessing marijuana with intent to distribute. His presentence investigation report classified him as a career offender based on two earlier state convictions for assault. Despite the fact that his convictions were for "intentional, knowing, or reckless" assault, counsel did not object to the PSR's characterization, and the district court sentenced Ramirez as a career offender. In so doing, the court treated the Texas convictions as crimes of violence under U.S.S.G. §4Br.2(a)(2)'s residual clause, which defines as a "crime of violence" for purposes of career-offender status at sentencing any federal or state offense punishable by imprisonment of more than one year "that otherwise involves conduct that presents a serious potential risk of physical injury to another."

Ramirez retained new counsel and moved to vacate his sentence under 28 U.S.C. §2255, arguing that sentencing counsel was ineffective for failing to object to the career-offender designation. The district judge denied the motion and, because post-conviction counsel failed to keep Ramirez informed about the post-conviction proceedings, R3mirezdidnot submit a timely request for a certificate of appealability. He tried filing a late request, but when it was dismissed for lack of jurisdiction, he moved under Federal Rule of Civil Procedure 9 b2(6) for relief from the judgment. He argued that post-conviction counsel was ineffective for causing him to miss the appeal deadline (among other reasons). The district judge denied the motion on the belief that there is a rigid rule under which there is no right to counsel on collateral review. See *Coleman v. Thompson*, 501 U.S. 722, 752, 111 S.Ct. 2546, 115 L. Ed. 2d 640 (1991). This would have been correct before the Supreme Court's decisions in *Trevino v. Thaler*, 133 S.Ct. 1911, 185 L. Ed. 2d 1044 (2013), and *Martinez v. Ryan*, 132 S.Ct. 1309, 182 L. Ed. 2d 272 (2012). In those two decisions, however, the Court significantly changed its approach to claims of ineffective assistance of counsel at initial-review collateral proceedings. We conclude that the argument Ramirez raises is cognizable under Rule 60(b), see *Gonzalez v. Crosby*, 545 U.S. 524, 125 S.Ct. 2641, 162 L. Ed. 2d 480 (2005), and thus that a remand is required so that the district court may consider the merits of his contentions.

I

This appeal arises out of a series of events that began with Ramirez's two convictions in Texas. According to an offense report tendered by the prosecution at Ramirez's first Texas plea hearing, Ramirez had run in front of his wife's moving car, opened the passenger door, and gotten into the car. When his wife stopped to wave down a police officer, he grabbed her by her hair and punched her in the mouth. According to the offense report prepared for a second Texas prosecution, Ramirez went to his wife's house and banged on her door. When she refused to let him in, he broke the house windows and her car windshield, and then kicked in the front door, pulled her hair, and knocked her to the floor. He grabbed her arm and started to drag her away. These incidents led to two separate indictments for "intentionally, knowingly, or recklessly" causing "bodily injury" to his wife by "striking her with his hand"; Ramirez pleaded guilty in both cases. See TEX. PENAL CODE §22.01(a)(1) (1999).

In 2008 Ramirez pleaded guilty to the conviction that gives rise to this proceeding – possessing marijuana with intent to distribute. See 21 U.S.C. §841(a)(1). Ramirez's presentence investigation report listed, among other convictions, the two incidents in which he had assaulted his wife; it specified that he had been charged with assault to a family member for striking his wife with his hand. The probation officer concluded that these two "crimes of violence" rendered Ramirez a career offender. See U.S.S.G. §§ 4B1.1(a); 4B1.2(a). Ramirez's lawyer did not contest the probation officer's conclusion.

In the course of determining Ramirez's advisory sentencing range, the district court agreed with that assessment. The career-offender designation resulted in a guidelines imprisonment range of 262 to 327 months. (Without career-offender status, the range would have been 151 to 188 months. See U.S.S.G. Sent. Table (2008).) The court sentenced Ramirez to a within-guide-lines term of 300 months' imprisonment.

On appeal, Ramirez's trial counsel moved to withdraw under *Anders v. California*, 386 U.S. 738, 744, 87 S.Ct. 1396, 18 L. Ed. 2d 494 (1967). We rejected that motion on the ground that a colorable challenge to Ramirez's career-offender classification existed. *United States v. Ramirez*, No. 09-1815, 2009 U.S. App. LEXIS 29885 (7th Cir. Nov. 4, 2009). The government conceded error, admitting that the documents before the district court did not establish that Ramirez had been convicted of crimes of violence. Brief for Appellee at 12, *United States v. Ramirez*, 606 F. 3d 396 (7th Cir. 2010) (No. 09-1815). Rejecting that concession, we affirmed the conviction. We first held that the Texas assault statute was divisible (meaning that there were three ways in which it might be violated-through intentional, knowing, or reckless behavior). On appeal, however, the plain-error standard applied. That left Ramirez with the burden of showing that he had been convicted under the "reckless" branch of the statute. He failed to do so for lack of evidence, and so his sentence for the drug offense stood. *United States v. Ramirez*, 606 F. 3d 396,398 (7th Cir. 2010).

At that point, Ramirez obtained new counsel, who filed a motion under 28 U.S.C. §2255 asserting, as relevant here, that trial counsel was ineffective at sentencing for failing to object to Ramirez's classification as a career offender. The district judge denied the motion and declined to issue a certificate of appealability because, he wrote, Ramirez (still) had not produced any documents to show that he had been convicted of reckless assault and thus had not shown that he was prejudiced by counsel's omission. The proceeding went awry, however, when post-conviction counsel let Ramirez down in three ways: he did not inform Ramirez of the court's decision; he failed to file any post judgment motions; and he failed to file a notice of appeal.

Once he learned that counsel had deserted him, Ramirez filed an untimely pro se notice of appeal from the section 2255 motion denial; we dismissed for lack of appellate jurisdiction. *Ramirez v. United States*, No. 13-3511 (7th Cir. Jan. 21, 2014); see 28 U.S.C. §2107(a); *Bowles v. Russell*, 551 U.S. 205,

210-211, 127 S.Ct. 2360, 168 L. Ed. 2d 96 (2007). Ramirez then moved to vacate the district court's judgment under Federal Rule of Civil Procedure 60(b)(6), arguing that the ineffectiveness of his post-conviction counsel – who had failed to request any of the Texas court documents and worse, had deserted him – constituted an extraordinary circumstance warranting the reopening of the judgment. The district judge denied the Rule 60(b)(6) motion because, he wrote, the right to counsel does not extend to proceedings under section 2255, and because Ramirez still had not shown that he was prejudiced by any of trial counsel's omissions because he never produced any documents showing he had been convicted of nonviolent assault. Ramirez appealed the denial of his Rule 60(b)(6) motion, and this court certified for appeal the question whether trial counsel was ineffective at sentencing. We also instructed the parties to address whether the district court abused its discretion in denying Ramirez's Rule 60(b) (6) motion in light of Trevino and Martinez.

II

Ramirez argues that the district court did commit an abuse of discretion when it denied his Rule 60(b)(6) motion. One way in which a court may take a decision that lies outside the boundaries of its discretion is by basing that decision on a material error of law. Ramirez asserts that the district court incorrectly relied on Coleman's absolute rule that counsel's performance on a post-conviction motion can never justify relief from a judgment, rather than on Trevino and Martinez. Relying on such cases as *Nash v. Hepp*, 740 F. 3d 1075 (7th Cir. 2014), the government replies that these new cases at most amount to a mundane change in the law that does not amount to an extraordinary circumstance for purposes of Rule 60(b)(6). It also argues that Trevino, Martinez, and *Maples v. Thomas*, 132 S.Ct. 912, 181 L. Ed. 2d 807 (2012) (a third case in the new line), apply only to petitions for relief filed by state prisoners under 28 U.S.C. §2254, not to motions filed by federal prisoners under 28 U.S.C. §2255.

A

The first question we must address is whether Ramirez was entitled to use a Rule 60(b) motion, or if he has in reality filed an unauthorized second or successive petition without the necessary permission of this court. See 28 U.S.C. §§2244, 2255(h). If this was a proper use of Rule 60(b), the next question is whether Ramirez has shown enough to earn a consideration of his arguments on the merits.

We are satisfied that Ramirez's motion was not a disguised second or successive motion under section 2255, and thus may be evaluated on its own merit. Ramirez is not trying to present a new reason why he should be relieved of either his conviction or his sentence, as provided in 28 U.S.C. §2255(a). He is instead trying to reopen his existing section 2255 proceeding and overcome a procedural barrier to its adjudication. Recall that on direct appeal this court found enough merit in Ramirez's claims that we rejected counsel's Anders submission and required the case to go forward. Appellate counsel never obtained the relevant records from the Texas courts, however, and so the appeal failed for lack of proof. When Ramirez sought to remedy these failures in a motion under section 2255, post-conviction counsel failed to remedy that critical omission, despite the central role that it played in our disposition of the direct appeal. We do not know if that omission was intentional or not, although if the records had been unfavorable to Ramirez, it is hard to see why the prosecutor did not obtain them. Most importantly, post-conviction counsel abandoned Ramirez on appeal, thus depriving him of the opportunity to pursue his Sixth Amendment claims.

Gonzalez held that in rare circumstances, a motion under Rule 60(b) may be used by a prisoner. There the Court confirmed that "Rule 60(b) has an unquestionably valid role to play in habeas cases." 545 U.S. at 534. But that role is restricted. The "movant seeking relief under Rule 60(b)(6) [must] show extraordinary circumstances justifying the reopening of a final judgment." *Id.* at 535 (internal quotation marks omitted). A change in law alone will not suffice for this purpose. *Id.* at 536 (change in Supreme

Court's interpretation of the AEDPA statute of limitations did not qualify); Nash, 740 F. 3d at 1078; *Hill v. Rios*, 722 f. 3d 937, 938 (7th Cir. 2013); see also *Cox v. Horn*, 757 F. 3d 113, 115 (3rd Cir. 2014) ("for relief to be granted under Rule 60(b)(6), 'more' than the concededly important change of law wrought by Martinez is required – indeed, much 'more' is required"); but see *Adams v. Thaler*, 679 F. 3d 312 (5th Cir. 2012) (stating that change in decisional law effected by Martinez did not justify use of Rule 60(b); not discussing any other equitable considerations).

We agree with the Third Circuit's approach in Cox, in which it rejected the absolute position that the Fifth Circuit's Adams decision may have reflected, to the effect that intervening changes in the law never can support relief under Rule 60(b)(6). The Third Circuit held instead that "intervening changes in the law rarely justify relief from final judgments under 60(b)(6)." 757 F. 3d at 121. It explained that it had "long employed a flexible, multi-factor approach to Rule 60(b)(6) motions, including those built upon a post-judgment change in the law, that takes into account all the particulars of a movant's case." *Id.* at 122. In fact, it pointed out, this position may not be inconsistent with that of the Fifth Circuit, which reviewed other equitable factors in a later case similar to Adams before rejecting the petitioner's claim. See *Dias v. Stephens*, 731 F. 3d 370 (5th Cir. 2013).

Rule 60(b)(6) is fundamentally equitable in nature. See *Liljeberg v. Health Servs. Acquisition Corp.*, 486 U.S. 847, 863-64, 108 S.Ct. 2194, 100 L. Ed. 2d 855 (1988); *DiVito v. Fidelity & Deposit Co. of Md.*, 361 F. 2d 936, 939 (7th Cir. 1966); see also Charles Alan Wright, Arthur R. Miller & Mary Kay Kane, Federal Practice and Procedure §2857 at 321 (3d ed. 2012). It thus requires the court to examine all of the circumstances, bearing in the need for the party invoking the rule to demonstrate why extraordinary circumstances justify relief. Pertinent considerations include, though are not limited to, a change in the Supreme Court's approach to the fundamental rules for deciding habeas corpus cases; the diligence of the petitioner; whether alternative remedies were available but bypassed; and whether the underlying claim is one of which relief could be granted.

In Nash, for example, we noted a number of factors that showed collectively that extraordinary circumstances for purposes of Rule 60(b)(6) did not exist, despite the change in law brought about by Martinez, Maples, and Trevino. Nash could have appealed notwithstanding the actions of his counsel, because the court itself instructed him about the proper measures to take. (Wisconsin law treats post-conviction relief in an unusual way, insofar as it allows defendants to raise a claim of ineffectiveness of counsel simultaneously with a direct appeal.) Where Nash "easily could have remedied counsel's omission and started the plenary post-conviction process anew," 740 F. 3d at 1079, there was no abuse of discretion in denying Nash's motion under Rule 60(b)(6). Similarly, in Hill the petitioner chose not to file a petition for rehearing with this court or a petition for certiorari with the Supreme Court, after he failed to persuade a panel that his remedy under section 2255 was inadequate. As we put it there, "[a] litigant who bypasses arguments on appeal cannot depict his own omission as an 'extraordinary' event that justifies post-judgment relief." 722 F. 3d at 938-39. Furthermore, Hill had never alerted this court during his earlier appeal that he had filed an earlier motion under section 2255 and that was why he was seeking to take advantage of the safety-valve clause of section 2255(e). See generally *Webster v. Daniels*, 784 F. 3d 1123, 1135-39 (7th Cir., 2015) (*en banc*). It ill behooved him to seek a new opportunity to raise points that he could have advanced earlier. We thus found no abuse of discretion in denying Hill's motion under Rule 60(b)(6).

Nash and Hill follow Gonzalez's admonition that extraordinary circumstances will exist only rarely. At the same time, however, as the Third Circuit said in Cox, "rarely" does not mean "never." Like the petitioner in Nash, Ramirez points to his abandonment by counsel as the extraordinary circumstance that justifies reopening his section 2255 proceeding. Unlike Nash, however, the remainder of the equities in Ramirez's case do not undermine his application for relief. No one – not a court, not his lawyer – informed him about an alternative path to relief after his post-conviction lawyer abandoned him and left him with only a jurisdictionally-out-of-time appeal. Ramirez did not conceal pertinent information from the court. The district court's decision on his Rule 60(b)(6) motion, dated November 19, 2013, was based on a clear error of law: the court dismissed his effort to raise a claim about the assistance of post-conviction counsel with these words:

> Next, Ramirez argues he is entitled to relief because his habeas counsel was ineffective. The right to effective assistance of counsel, however, does not extend to §2255 proceedings. *Cannon v. United States*, 326 F. App'x 393, 395, (7th Cir. 2009) (citing 28 U.S.C. §2254(i)).1 As such, Ramirez is not entitled to relief based on his counsel's performance. At the time the court wrote those words, all three of the Supreme Court decisions on which Ramirez relies were on the books: Maples was handed down on Jan. 18, 2012; Martinez on Mar. 20, 2012; and Trevino on May 28, 2013. The court's error of law is therefore plain.

B

The change in law between Coleman, on the one hand, and Martinez, Maples, and Trevino on the other, plays only a part in our evaluation of Ramirez's Rule 60(b)(6) motion. The ineffectiveness of his post-conviction attorney is the other critical point. Martinez held that the procedural default that occurred when Martinez's post-conviction counsel did not raise a claim of ineffective assistance of counsel in his state collateral proceeding would not bar his petition under 28 U.S.C. §2254, where "the state collateral proceeding was the first place to challenge his conviction on grounds of ineffective assistance." 132 S.Ct. at 1313. The Court explained that "if, in the [State's] initial-review collateral proceeding, there was no counselor counsel in that proceeding was ineffective," procedural default would not "bar a federal habeas court from hearing a substantial claim of ineffective assistance at trial." rd. at 1320 (emphasis added). In Martinez, state law required the petitioner to wait until the initial-review collateral proceeding before raising such a claim. A year later, in Trevino, the Court extended Martinez's holding to cases in which the state did not require defendants to wait until the post-conviction stage, but "[t]he structure and design of the [state] system in actual operation ... [made] it virtually impossible for an ineffective assistance claim to be presented on direct review." 133 S.Ct. at 1915. The question is whether these holdings apply to some or all federal prisoners who bring motions for post-conviction relief under section 2255. We already have answered this in the affirmative, in *Choice Hotels Intern., Inc. v. Grover*, 792 F. 3d 753 (7th Cir. 2015), where we wrote that "[a]lthough *Maples* and *Holland* [*v. Florida*, 560 U.S. 631, 130 S.Ct. 2549, 177 L. Ed. 2d 130 (2010)] were capital cases, we do not doubt that their holdings apply to all collateral litigation under 28 U.S.C. §2254 or §2255." *Id.* at 755. A closer look at the issue convinces us that this position was correct.

In *Massaro v. United States*, 538 U.S. 500, 123 S.Ct. 1690, 155 L. Ed. 2d 714 (2003), the Supreme Court considered the case of a man who did not raise any claim relating to ineffectiveness of trial counsel on his direct appeal, and so was trying to raise such an argument in a motion under section 2255. The United States argued that the ineffectiveness claim was procedurally defaulted, because Massaro could have raised it on direct appeal. The Supreme Court rejected that position and held instead that there is no procedural default for failure to raise an ineffective-assistance claim on direct appeal, even if new counsel handles the direct appeal and even if the basis for the claim is apparent from the trial record. *Id.* at 503-4. Indeed, the Court criticized the practice of bringing these claims on direct appeal, because "the issue would be raised for the first time in a forum not best suited to assess those facts." *Id.* at 504. This court has been equally if not more critical of the practice of trying to raise ineffective assistance claims on direct appeal:

Raising ineffective assistance on direct appeal is imprudent because defendant paints himself into a corner. We've explained why the contention is doomed unless the contention is made first in the district court and a full record is developed – which happens occasionally but did not happen here. Yet although the argument has trifling prospect of success, the defense has much to lose …. [W]hen an ineffective-assistance claim is rejected on direct appeal, it cannot be raised again on collateral review …

Ever since Massaro the judges of this court have regularly asked counsel at oral argument whether the defendant is personally aware of the risks of presenting an ineffective-assistance argument on direct appeal and, if so, whether defendant really wants to take that risk. We encourage counsel to discuss that subject with the defendant after argument and to consider withdrawing the contention. We asked that question at oral argument of this appeal, and counsel assured us that Flores is aware of the risks and wants the contention resolved now. That is his prerogative, foolish though the choice seems to the judiciary. *United States v. Flores*, 739 F. 3d 337, 341-42 (7th Cir. 2014). See also, e.g., *United States v. Moody*, 770 F. 3d 577, 582 (7th Cir. 2014) (ineffective assistance claim "should be pursued in a collateral proceeding under 28 U.S.C. §2255"); *United States v. Bryant*, 754 F. 3d 443, 444 (7th Cir. 2014) ("[a] claim of ineffective assistance need not, and usually as a matter of prudence should not, be raised in a direct appeal, where evidence bearing on the claim cannot be presented and the claim is therefore likely to fail even if meritorious"); *United States v. Harris*, 394 F. 3d 543, 558 (7th Cir. 2005) ("only the rarest and most patently egregious of ineffective assistance claims are appropriately brought on direct appeal"); *United States v. Trevino*, 60 F. 3d 333, 338 (7th Cir. 1995) ("we have often cautioned that a defendant who presents an ineffective assistance claim for the first time on direct appeal has little to gain and everything to lose").

Because the federal courts have no established procedure (such as the one Wisconsin uses, for instance) to develop ineffective assistance claims for direct appeal, the situation of a federal petitioner is the same as the one the Court described in Trevino: as a practical matter, the first opportunity to present a claim of ineffective assistance of trial or direct appellate counsel is almost always on collateral review, in a motion under section 2255. There may be rare exceptions, as Massaro acknowledged, for a case in which trial counsel's ineffectiveness "is so apparent from the record" that it can be raised on direct appeal or even noticed by the appellate court on its own. 538 U.S. at 508-09. But Ramirez's is not one of them.

Even if this is so, the government argues, we should not apply the principles set forth in Martinez and Trevino because they involved petitions brought under 28 U.S.C. §2254, not motions under section 2255. The government's position finds some support in dicta from *United States v. Lee*, 792 F. 3d 1021 (8th Cir. 2015). But Lee turned on an antecedent problem: the petitioner's motion under Rule 60(b) there was properly denied because it required precertification under section 2244(b)(3) and the court of appeals refused to take that step. The court also noted that Lee had not been diligent: instead of presenting his supporting evidence in his motion under section 2255, he just included a footnote saying that such evidence could be provided later. 792 F. 3d at *4, 2015 U.S. App. LEXIS 12009. The court also indicated that Martinez and Trevino might be limited to section 2254 cases, but that comment was not necessary to the result.

Neither Martinez nor Trevino suggested that, for these purposes, the difference between sections 2254 and 2255 was material. What does matter is the way in which ineffective assistance of counsel claims must be presented in the particular procedural system. This varies among the states, and between the states and the federal system, but we already have explained why in the great majority of federal cases, ineffectiveness claims must await the first round of collateral review. Moreover, if review were to be more restricted on either the state or the federal side, federalism concerns suggest that it would be the state side. Most of the rules that govern petitions under section 2254 are mirrored in section 2255, including importantly the procedure for handling second or successive petitions. We can think of no reason why Martinez and Trevino should be read in the way the government advocates. The same principles apply in both the section 2254 and the section 2255 contexts, as this case illustrates. Ramirez was effectively unable to raise his ineffective assistance claim until collateral review because he was in the typical situation of needing to develop the record more fully before he could proceed.

As we already have noted, post-conviction counsel failed to notify Ramirez that the district court had denied his section 2255 motion, and this omission allowed the deadline for filing a notice of appeal to lapse. See *Ramirez v. United States*, No. 13-3511 (7th Cir. Jan. 21, 2014). Counsel's abandonment deprived Ramirez of the ability to press his ineffective-assistance argument on appeal. See *Maples*, 132 S.Ct. at 923-24 (holding that attorney abandonment is extraordinary circumstance allowing federal court to disregard state procedural bar to hearing habeas petition); Holland, 560 U.S. at 652-53. We see no reason to distinguish between actions at the state level that result in procedural default and the consequent loss of a chance for federal review, and actions at the federal level that similarly lead to a procedural default that forfeits appellate review. See *Washington v. Ryan*, 789 F. 3d 1041, 1047-48 (9th Cir. 2015) (explaining that counsel's abandonment can be extraordinary circumstance when abandonment resulted in lost ability to appeal); *Mackey v. Hoffman*, 682 F. 3d 1247, 1253 (9th Cir. 2012) (relief available under Rule 60(b) (6) when federal habeas corpus petitioner has been grossly neglected by counsel "in a manner amounting to attorney abandonment").

C

All that remains is to determine whether the argument left hanging after counsel abandoned Ramirez has "some merit." Martinez, 132 S.Ct. at 1318. We think it does. Ramirez argues that trial counsel performed deficiently at sentencing by failing to object to his classification as a career offender, and that this prejudiced him because, based on the record in the district court, the underlying convictions were not, categorically, crimes of violence. See *Begay v. Unites States*, 553 U.S. 137, 128 S.Ct. 1581, 170 L. Ed. 2d 490 (2008).

We agree with Ramirez that trial counsel's performance was deficient. An attorney's failure to object to an error in the court's guidelines calculation that results in a longer sentence for the defendant can demonstrate constitutionally ineffective performance. See *United States v. Jones*, 635F. 3d 909,916 (7th Cir. 2011). Ramirez points out that sentencing counsel believed at the time that Ramirez had the requisite convictions to make him a career offender. But by that time, Begay had been decided and counsel should have known that the two Texas convictions were suspect. See *Begay*, 553 U.S. at 141. Counsel also said that he unsuccessfully had tried to get the Texas records. He complained that he would have had to subpoena them from the Texas county in which Ramirez was convicted, and that this "would have been extremely difficult to do and time consuming." This lack of desire to uncover the truth was deficient. See *Strickland v. Washington*, 466 U.S. 668, 690, 1045, Ct. 2052, 80 L. Ed. 2d 674 (1984); *Wilson v. Mazzuca*, 570 F. 3d 490, 502 (2d Cir. 2009) (deficient performance includes errors arising from "oversight, carelessness, ineptitude, or laziness"). (Ramirez's new counsel obtained the records with little difficulty, and they are now available to this court.)

The next question is whether counsel's deficiency prejudiced Ramirez. See Strickland, 466 U.S. at 688-94; *Pidgeon v. Smith*, 785 F. 3d 1165, 1171 (7th Cir. 2015). The Texas statute under which Ramirez was twice convicted criminalizes "intentional, knowing, or reckless" assault. The district court concluded that counsel's performance did not prejudice Ramirez because Ramirez never met his burden to show that he was convicted of nonviolent assault. The parties also debate whether Ramirez could make that showing now. But at the time of sentencing, it was the government's burden, not Ramirez's, to show (using acceptable materials) that Ramirez's earlier convictions were for knowing or intentional conduct, not reckless actions. See *Johnson v. United States*, 559 U.S. 133, 137, 130 S.Ct. 1265, 176 L. Ed. 2d 1 (2010) (without evidence to suggest otherwise, sentencing judge must presume conviction rested on the least serious act in divisible statute). In his ineffective assistance claim, Ramirez needed to show only that his sentence would have been different had counsel objected to his characterization as a career offender. See Jones, 635 F. 3d at 916. As the government conceded on direct appeal, it could not meet its burden; neither the charging papers nor the plea colloquy shed any light on which version of assault was the basis for Ramirez's two Texas convictions. Brief for Appellee at 12, *United States v. Ramirez*, 606 F. 3d 396 (7th Cir. 2010) (No. 09-1815); see *Descamps v. United States*, 133 S.Ct. 2276, 2281-82, 186 1. Ed. 2d 438 (2013); *Shepard v. United States*, 544 U.S. 13, 24-25, 125 S.Ct. 1254, 161 1. Ed. 2d 205 (2005). Any objection by counsel would have been sustained.

Resisting this conclusion, the government directs us to two statements made by Ramirez's ex-wife in which she describes how he attacked her. Because these statements, to which Ramirez stipulated at the plea hearing, depict a violent crime, the government asserts that he was not prejudiced by counsel's failure to object to the PSR. See Shepard, 544 U.S. at 24-25; *Taylor v. United States*, 495 U.S. 575, 599-600, 110 S.Ct. 2143, 109 L. Ed 2d 607 (1990); *United States v. Woods*, 576 F. 3d 400, 405 (7th Cir. 2009). But those statements shed light only on "what the defendant did," not "what crime the conviction represents." Ramirez, 606 F. 3d at 398. They do not clarify whether Ramirez was charged with and convicted of intentional, knowing, or reckless assault. Just because he might have been convicted of the more serious conduct does not mean necessarily that he was; it is commonplace for defendants to be convicted on a lesser offense than the facts would have supported. We are left with a record in which none of the permissible documents reveals which of the three possible states of mind was used for Ramirez's convictions. See Shepard, 544 U.S. at 24-25; Taylor, 495 U.S. at 599-600; Woods, 576 F. 3d at 405.

We note in closing that Ramirez was classified as a career offender under §4B1.2(a)(2)'s residual clause. See Ramirez, 606 F. 3d at 398 (writing that Texas's assault offense "does not have, as an element, the use or threatened use of physical force, and it is not specifically enumerated in the Guideline, so it can be a crime of violence only under the residual clause of §4B1.2(a)(2)"). In *Johnson v. United States*, 135 S.Ct. 2551, 192 L. Ed. 2d 569 (2015), the Supreme Court held that the identically worded residual clause of the Armed Career Criminal Act is unconstitutionally vague. Compare U.S.S.G. §4B1.2(a)(2) with 18 U.S.C. §924(e)(2)(B)(ii). We have interpreted both residual clauses identically, see *United States v. Billups*, 536 F. 3d 574, 579 n.1 (7th Cir. 2008); *United States v. Upton*, 512 F. 3d 394, 404 (7th Cir. 2008) (abrogated on other grounds by *United States v. Miller*, 721 F. 3d 435, 443 (7th Cir. 2013); *United States v. Rosas*, 410 F. 3d 332, 335-36 (7th Cir. 2005), and so we proceed on the assumption that the Supreme Court's reasoning applies to section 4B1.2 as well. This is a point, however, that neither side has briefed, and it may warrant attention on remand. We note that the U.S. Sentencing Commission is now seeking comments on a proposal to change the guideline language to make it conform to Johnson. See U.S. Sentencing Commission News Release, "U.S. Sentencing Commission Seeks Comment on Revisions to Definition of Crime of Violence." We leave any issue about the effect of Johnson on the Guidelines for another day.

III

We conclude that Ramirez's situation fits the framework articulated in Maples, Trevino, and Martinez. The district court was apparently unaware of those decisions and thus categorically denied Ramirez's motion under Rule 60(b)(6) without discussing how post-conviction counsel's performance affected the integrity of the proceedings. We agree with Ramirez that this amounted to an abuse of discretion. We therefore Vacate the denial of the Rule 60(b) motion and Remand with instructions to grant the Rule 60(b) motion and reopen the proceedings under section 2255. The record is insufficient to determine if Ramirez has other qualifying convictions that might support affirmance of the sentence on other grounds. That and other pertinent issues may be raised on remand.

UNITED STATES DISTRICT COURT
WESTERN DISTRICT OF OKLAHOMA

Donovan G. Mercer	
V.	No.: 5:14-CR-280-PRW
UNITED STATES	

MOTION FOR RELIEF PURSUANT TO FED R. CIV P., RULE 60(b)(6)

Mr. Mercer moves this court to issue an order, setting aside the judgment to deny his previously filed §2255 motion, pursuant to Rule 60(b)(6) of the Federal Rules of Civil Procedure.

It's because of the extraordinary circumstances in Mr. Mercer's case that requires this court to set its previous judgment aside. Federal Rules of Civil Procedure, Rule 60(b)(6) is the proper vehicle to set the court's judgment aside because no other grounds under Rule 60(b) nor any other procedure is available to grant the relief that justice requires. In particular, and more fully exhibited in the testimony of FBI Agent Ken Rogers, in Mr. Mercer's trial, and FBI Agent Robert Harden, in Mr. Mercer's §2255 hearing, Mr. Mercer is actually innocent and stands convicted based solely on evidence that the FBI falsified. Moreover, because of the FBI's conduct in Mr. Mercer's case, the government was sent on a fool's errand. TO WIT:

I.

This case involves the accuracy of evidence and testimony, offered for the first time in Mr. Mercer's §2255 hearing, that has a substantial propensity to establish his actual innocence and proving the existence of his alibi defense. This dispute is identified by the conflicting statements given by two different FBI agents in two separate proceedings.

147

II.

Mr. Mercer's §2255 proceeding was presided over by the Honorable Patrick R. Wyrick, of the United States District Court for the Western District of Oklahoma, who entered a judgment in favor of the United States. This judgment was appropriately appealed to the United States Court of Appeals for the Tenth Circuit, which affirmed the judgment of the district court.

III.

Subsequently, by virtue of discovery and investigation conducted by court-appointed appellate counsel, it was discovered that the court was deprived of a meaningful opportunity to evaluate Mr. Mercer's grounds for §2255 relief because the FBI injected additional false testimony at the §2255 hearing.

The record reflects that Mr. Mercer's §2255 was initially denied without a hearing. Mr. Mercer appealed. The Court of Appeals granted a Certificate of Appealability on two issues;

1) The Ares Report reports times as "CDT" and "CST," presumably standing for Central Daylight Time and Central Standard Time. But if the Ares Report already used Central Time, why did the prosecutor advise the defense counsel to add 5 hours to the report time to get the correct local time in Oklahoma?

2) Assuming the Ares Report lists times that "previously downloaded files were shared," as the government asserted, R. Vol. II at 238 (first emphasis added), then why do the times set forth in the Ares Report appear to precede the times listed in GE 401?

Accordingly, the government was burdened with providing proof at the §2255 hearing, to establish the accuracy of its Exhibit 401. See *United States v. Glover*, 97 F. 3d 1345, 1347 (10th Cir. 1996).

On remand, the government called a single witness, Mr. Harden, to answer the Circuit Court's first question – why do we need to add 5 hours to the Ares Report? In answer, Mr. Harden stated his "belief" that an unnamed law enforcement "tool" that was used to produce the Ares Report made an error when reporting the download times:

> "My belief is that the tool converts the time to Central Time, standard or daylight, when it did not need to perform the conversion."

See proceeding Transcript Volume 2, at page 22.

Based on Mr. Harden's testimony, the Ares Report tool determined that a download occurred at a specific time, which it was programed to determine was Coordinated Universal Time, and converted the time to Central Time by subtracting five hours (for daylight savings time) – when in fact the pre-converted time already was Central Time. Therefore, according to Mr. Harden, to make up for the program's error, five hours must be added to the download times that are reported by the faulty program. To use the example from the court's last decision, based on Mr. Harden's testimony, if the tool said a download time was 12:09 p.m. on July 9, 2012, five hours would have to be added, to fix the program's error, so that it would reflect the correct time of 5:09 p.m.

Mr. Harden went on in an attempt to answer the Circuit Court's second question – Why do the times set forth in the Ares Report appear to precede the times listed in the government's evidence 401? His answer came in three parts:

First, he claimed that version 6.3 of the Internet Evidence Finder – a different tool from the one used to populate the Ares Report (see Volume 2, pages 19-20) – produced download times in Exhibit 401 claiming to be Coordinated Universal Time. (see Volume 2, page 16; see also Volume 1, page 447). The government introduced as Hearing Exhibit 4 the first page of a multi-page report using version 6.3. That page is a spreadsheet with a column labeled "Downloaded Date/Time – (UTC) (MM/DD/YYYY)." See Volume 1, page 447.

Second, Mr. Harden testified that the tool – like the tool used to prepare the Ares Report – was programmed with an error that caused it to misstate the time zone. The tool was programmed to state that the download times were in Coordinated Universal Time when in fact the download times were in local time, in Mr. Mercer's case, that was Central Time. See Volume 2, page 16-17.

Third, Mr. Harden testified that to correct the program's output error, we must substitute "COT" (or "CST") for the program's display of "UTC."

Mr. Harden also testified that he conducted his own independent test by downloading a Bible Study file (inappropriately trying to bolster his credibility by bringing potentially false religious devotions into evidence) to confirm his opinion that Exhibit 401 correctly listed download times in Central Time. (Volume 2, page 22). The test, he claimed, also confirmed his opinion that the Ares Report correctly listed download times in Coordinated Universal Time requiring the addition of five hours to convert the time to Central Time.

The court's ability to provide a reliable judgment suffered from multiple problems. The first problem is in noting that Mr. Harden's explanation is not even close to credible. He testified about two different decryption tools – Internet Evidence Finder and a second and unspecified software application used to decrypt ShareH.net and ShareL.net to produce the Ares Report. These two programs were presumably created by two different software companies and were made available to law enforcement nationwide to reliably decrypt Ares and other peer-to-peer networking software, and were both purchased by the FBI at different times for use in internet crime investigations and prosecutions. Mr. Harden, who claims to have worked for the FBI continuously since graduating from Central Oklahoma University, was not involved in creating either program (See Volume 1, page 403), and apparently had no experience using either tool. (See generally Volume 2, pages 4-33).

Notwithstanding his lack of experience with the investigative tools, Mr. Harden testified that "both applications suffered from the same time 'bug.'" Evidence Finder 6.3 reported download times that it said was in Universal Coordinated Time, but that was, according to Mr. Harden, a "bug." In fact, he specifically said that, Internet Evidence Finder 6.3 was reporting download times in Central Time. And to correctly read its report, he said, the §2255 court should substitute Central Time for Universal Coordinated Time. Mr. Harden testified that the unnamed different tool that was used to create the Ares Report, reported download and share times in Central Time. But this was incorrect, according to his testimony. What this tool actually did, Mr. Harden said, was make three errors:

1) it determined the download/share times in Universal Coordinated Time; 2) it converted the download/share times to Central Time by subtracting five hours from it; and 3) it labeled that time is "CST" or " CDT," (i.e. Central Time). See Volume 2, page 21-22.

Mr. Harden further testified that, to fix these three errors the §2255 court should simply add five hours to the time this tool reported. This would ultimately allow the court to "FIX" the evidence in the government's favor. Mr. Harden's resolve and his explanation of the two software application's errors is extraordinary and virtually inconceivable. It is not likely to be in the realm of possibility that both applications in fact have these exceptional, rare, and coincidental time quirks and errors.

Mr. Harden testified that the Government's Exhibit 401 was populated using "the Ares downloads document," and not the "Ares ShareH.dat report." In a thorough review of the court's record, it is clear that Mr. Harden's testimony is less than clear. But the reference to "Ares ShareH.dat report" is apparently a reference to what the Court of Appeals identified as the Ares Report, which lists both download times and the times when files were shared or made available for sharing. But his testimony on this critical factual issue was based solely on naked hearsay, and not even hearsay from Mr. Rogers, who testified at Mr. Mercer's trial. Mr. Harden said that his information on how the government's Exhibit 401 was populated was "based on my understanding and conversations with the case agent, SA Farabow," who was not a forensics expert. See Vol. 2, page 14. When asked whether the Ares Report was used to populate Exhibit 401, Mr. Harden continued offering hearsay, saying that it was his "understanding" that the Ares Report was not used.

On a critical issue, not even an expert witness is permitted to "act as mere conduits for hearsay," *Williams v. Illinois*, 567 U.S. 50, 80 (2012); See *United States v. Mejia*, 545 F. 3d, 197, 197 (2nd Cir. 2008) ("The expert may not, however, simply transmit that hearsay to the jury"). The Supreme Court held in *Williams* that an experts' "out-of-court statements cannot be accepted for their truth" since "[her] opinion is only as good as the independent evidence that establishes its underlying premise." '567 U.S., at 80. Unfortunately, because the government provided the court with only Mr. Harden as a witness, the court was forced to not only decipher his testimony, but also base its decision on Mr. Harden's hearsay testimony. See Volume 1, page 391-93. Mr. Mercer reminds that his claim is not based on grounds that can be determined in a §2255 proceeding. But that his claim is that the court was unable to reach a reliable decision based on Mr. Harden's false and hearsay testimony given during the §2255 hearing.

Additionally, when the district court had "clarifying question[s]," it repeatedly relied on the government's attorney himself to answer them. See Volume 2, page 15-17.

After answering that "the Ares download document" was used to populate the government's Exhibit 401; Mr. Harden, when cross-examined gave a patently different hearsay answer – that his "understanding" was that Exhibit 401 was populated by both "the output of Internet Evidence Finder and Ares download Excel document." See 'Volume 2, page 24.

When asked to explain why Internet Evidence Finder 6.3 reported download times in Coordinated Universal Time, Mr. Harden simply answered yes to the government's leading questions, including whether it was the result of a programming "bug" in version 6.3. See Volume 2, page 17-18.

Mr. Harden also said that he "cross-check[ed]" the download times in the old and new Internet Evidence Finder versions against the times in Exhibit 401 and "found that the download dates and times in Internet Evidence Finder match and fell within the time ranges listed in the government's Exhibit 401." Vol. 2, page 13. But that simply begged the question that the Court of Appeals asked the District

Court to resolve – whether version 6.3 reported download times in Coordinated Universal Times, as it said it did.

Mr. Harden testified that he conducted his own "testing" of Internet Evidence Finder, both versions, to determine how it was reporting download times. He did this by downloading a Bible Study Guide. He claimed that when the file was downloaded he used a clock or a watch; he testified that both versions correctly reported the download time "regardless of the column header" showing "UTC" in version 6.3. He also claims that he ran the test on the Ares Report tool; it reported a download time that was five hours before the download was completed; so he had to add five hours to make the report he offered in evidence reflect the correct download time.

His "test" was underwhelming. It consisted of downloading – on one occasion – the Bible Study Guide and recording the download time on his watch/clock and comparing that download time to the download times reported by ShareH.dat and ShareL.dat. It would be reasonable to infer from that test that on one occasion the two tools reported different download times and the Ares Report tool was incorrect. But Mr. Harden's testimony, and his test, failed to answer the basic questions:

1) Did two different software applications have download time errors, and if so, why? Specifically, why did Internet Evidence Finder 6.3 report download times in Universal Coordinated Time if it purportedly was reporting download times in Central Time? and 2) Why did the Ares Report tool report download times in Central Time if it actually was reporting download times in Universal Coordinated Time? Without the answers to these two questions, it is impossible to know whether the software was malfunctioning when Government's Exhibit 401 was created or, for that matter, when Mr. Harden was conducting the test. Nor is it possible to know whether both Mr. Rogers and Mr. Harden were engaging in some type of operator error when they were using Internet Evidence Finder.

IV.

On remand, the Court of Appeals ordered the district court to resolve two questions. The main factual issue before the district court was the accuracy of Government's Exhibit 401. In preparation for the hearing, the district court appointed Mr. Patrick Quillian, a lawyer from the Criminal Justice Act Panel, to represent Mr. Mercer. Unfortunately for Mr. Mercer, his new lawyer provided grossly ineffective assistance of counsel prior to, and at the evidentiary hearing. Mr. Mercer's new lawyer failed to refine Mr. Mercer's claim in a brief to the court. Mr. Mercer's counsel put on no evidence on Mr. Mercer's behalf. Mr. Mercer's counsel did not object to Mr. Harden's ignorance, his offering of hearsay evidence, nor did counsel object to the obvious evidentiary problems in the government's presentation at the hearing. Although Mr. Harden's hearsay testimony weakened substantially Mr. Harden's own credibility, Mr. Mercer's inability to object through competent counsel deprived the district court of the ability to reach an informed decision.

In the face of Mr. Harden's lack of knowledge and his reliance on the alleged information of others, who did not testify, it was Mr. Mercer's own counsel who concealed the fact that the government could not carry its post-remand burden of establishing the accuracy and credibility of the Government's Exhibit 401.

Although Mr. Mercer is aware that a habeas petitioner is barred from making a claim that habeas counsel provided ineffective assistance of counsel, he is also aware that a §2255 proceeding is not a habeas proceeding, but is a first-tier collateral review also known as a post-conviction relief proceeding.

Mr. Mercer's claims, under Fed. R. Civ. P., Rule 60(b)(6), are extraordinary for two reasons: One, Mr. Mercer is actually innocent; and two, the district court used the §2255 process to circumvent Congress's intent in 18 U.S.C. §3006A. The law that requires a criminal court to appoint counsel to a defendant states that, "A person for who counsel is appointed shall be represented at every stage of the proceedings from his initial appearance ... through appeal ..." 18 U.S.C. §3006A(c). In Mr. Mercer's case, however, and that of all other federal defendants, he was deprived of an opportunity to raise a meaningful ineffective assistance of trial counsel claim on direct appeal, with the assistance of counsel. It is because the U.S. District Courts misapply the Supreme Court's holdings in *Massaro v. United States*, 538 U.S. 500 (2003), that no federal defendant that suffers from the ineffectiveness of defense counsel may raise such a claim or direct appeal where such a claim can be raised with the assistance of counsel. In *Massaro*, the Supreme Court held that "… ineffective assistance claims ordinarily will be litigated in the first instance in the district court …" The lower courts since *Massaro* have thus concluded that an ineffectiveness claim should be reserved for collateral review. This effect ultimately led all circuit courts to dismiss all I.A.C. claims raised in direct appeals, notwithstanding the Supreme Court's *Massaro* holding that: "This Court does not hold that ineffective assistance claims must be reserved for collateral review, as there may be cases [such as Mr. Mercer's] in which trial counsel's ineffectiveness is so apparent from the record that appellate counsel will raise the issue on direct appeal or the obvious deficiencies in representation will be addressed by the appellate court Sua Sponte."

In Mr. Mercer's case the district court appointed counsel not once or twice but three times, none of which would provide anything more than substandard assistance. The effects of the district court's choices were disastrous. Because of counsel's failures, Mr. Mercer was deprived of an opportunity to raise a claim that trial counsel was ineffective in a direct appeal. It is because of the lower court's belief, that the *Massaro* holding forbids the raising of an ineffective assistance claim in a direct appeal, that Mr. Mercer's right to appellate counsel, Congress's intent in 18 U.S.C. §3006A, is circumvented.

In Mr. Mercer's first-tier collateral proceeding, under 28 U.S.C. §2255, he was required to raise all his meaningful ineffective assistance of trial counsel claims without the benefit of counsel. Thus, because of the federal procedural framework, Mr. Mercer was once again deprived of a meaningful opportunity to raise an ineffective assistance of trial counsel claim with the benefit of his constitutional and statutory right to the effective assistance of counsel.

In spite of these procedural faults in the federal system, Mr. Mercer still stumbled his way through to the Tenth Circuit Court of Appeals and was granted a remand for further proceedings. The district court once again appointed substandard counsel who failed to even object to the obvious presentation of hearsay evidence.

Although Mr. Mercer's §2255 counsel was woefully deficient, he cannot turn back the clock to raise a claim against his §2255 counsel's ineffectiveness in his original §2255 as the federal procedure requires. These conditions create a procedural default that cannot be overcome by a trained federal lawyer, much less a pro se litigant who cannot afford the cost of competent counsel.

A finding that the defendant's federal law (§2255) "procedural default" that rests on an independent and adequate federal ground, ordinarily prevents a federal court from considering any additional federal constitutional claims, see *Coleman v. Thompson_*, 501 U. S. 722, 729-730. However, the Supreme Court has subsequently held that, "A prisoner may obtain federal review of a defaulted claim by showing cause for the default and prejudice from a violation of federal law. *Martinez*, Supra, at 10, 132 S.Ct. 1309." *Trevino v. Thaler*, 133 S.Ct. 1309; 182 L. Ed. 2d 272 (2012). In *Martinez*, the Supreme Court recognized a "narrow exception" to *Coleman*'s statement, "That an attorney's ignorance or inadvertence in a post-conviction proceeding does not qualify as a cause to excuse a procedural default." 566 U.S. 1, 9. The exception allows a federal habeas court to find "cause" to excuse such default where (1) the ineffective assistance of trial counsel claim was a "substantial" claim; (2) the "cause" consisted of there being "no counsel" or only "ineffective" counsel during the initial collateral review proceeding; (3) the collateral review proceeding was the "initial" review proceeding with respect to the "ineffective-assistance-of-trial counsel claim"; and (4) the law requires that the claim "be raised in an initial-review collateral proceeding."

V.

The record reflects that Mr. Mercer's post-conviction counsel, Mr. Quillian, failed to provide both competent counsel and his due diligence in Mr. Mercer's §2255 post-conviction proceedings. Thus, due to counsel's failures, the court was unable to identify that Mr. Mercer is actually innocent and that Mr. Mercer was deprived of his constitutional and statutory right to raise a claim, that he received ineffective assistance of trial counsel, in a direct appeal with the assistance of reasonably competent counsel.

VI.

It is irrelevant whether Mr. Quillian's conduct was intentional or the result of completely innocent oversight. This failure of Mr. Quillian to provide his honest service to Mr. Mercer, in the very least resulted in a taint to this court's judgment. Because Mr. Quillian allowed, or simply failed to understand, the impact of introduction of not only false but also hearsay evidence without objection; he inadvertently deprived the district court of its ability to evaluate the case and to rule fairly. This set of circumstances deprived Mr. Mercer of his reasonable expectation to an unquestionably impartial and informed court in his §2255 post-conviction proceeding.

VII.

There was and still is no other remedy available to Mr. Mercer to remedy this miscarriage of justice because: 1) actual innocence is not cognizable in a §2255 proceeding; 2) the lower court's understanding of *Massaro* deprives Mr. Mercer of an opportunity to raise a meaningful claim of ineffectiveness of trial counsel in direct appeal with the assistance of competent counsel; and (3) Mr. Mercer was deprived of an opportunity to raise the claim that Mr. Quillian deprived Mr. Mercer of his hones t service, in Mr. Mercer's original §2255 motion, because it hadn't yet happened.

Mr. Mercer's claim is cognizable only in a motion under Fed. R. Civ. P., Rule 60(b)(6), because

his claim that the courts have fashioned a rule that circumvents the intention of Congress in 18 U.S.C.

§3006A, is extraordinary.

VIII.

The extraordinary circumstances raised by this motion are not grounds for relief under any other

provision of Rule 60(b), nor are they actionable in a §2255 post-conviction proceeding. This motion

may not be recharacterized as a second or successive §2255 motion. A Rule 60(b) motion should be

treated as a successive habeas petition if it "seeks to add a new ground for relief" or "attacks the federal

court's previous resolution of a claim on the merits." *Gonzalez v. Crosby*, 545 U.S. 525, 532; 125 S.Ct.

2641, 2648; 162 L. Ed. 2d 480 (2005). But when the Rule 60(b) motion attacks "some defect in the

integrity of the federal habeas proceeding," and not the merit issue, it is not an impermissible successive

motion.

Wherefore, based on the foregoing, Mr. Mercer moves this court to relieve him from the judgment

to deny his §2255 motion.

Respectfully submitted on March 30, 2020, by:

_____

Donovan G. Mercer, Pro se
Reg. #29076-064
Federal Correctional Institution
P.O. Box 9000
Seagoville, TX 75159

CERTIFICATE OF SERVICE

I, hereby, certify that on March 30, 2020, I served a copy of this motion on the U.S. attorney via

U.S. mail, properly addressed, and first class postage affixed thereto, by placing it in the prison legal

mail system as it is available to prisoners.

Respectfully submitted on March 30, 2020, by:

_____

Donovan G. Mercer, Pro se
Reg. #

UNITED STATES DISTRICT COURT
NORTHERN DISTRICT OF ALABAMA
SOUTHERN DIVISION

Kelly Patrick Riggs	Case No.:
V.	2:15-cv-8043-KOB
United States of America	[2:12-cr-287-KOB-JEO]

MOTION FOR RELIEF FROM FINAL JUDGMENT IN §2255 PROCEEDING PURSUANT TO FED. R. CIV. P., RULE 60(b)(6)

Mr. Riggs moves this court to relieve him from the final judgment denying his §2255, because the court, failed to address all his grounds for relief as required by *Clisby v. Jones*, 960 F. 2d. 925 (11th Cir. 1992) (en banc).

JURISDICTION

The district court has exclusive authority, under Fed. R. Civ. P., Rule 60(b)(6), to relieve Mr. Riggs from its final judgment because it failed to reach the merit of the claims raised in ground three of his amended §2255 motion. Pursuant to Rule 60(b), a district court may relieve a party from final judgment, order, or proceeding on certain grounds, including any reason that justifies relief. Fed. R. Civ. P., Rule 60(b). A Rule 60(b) motion should be treated as a successive habeas petition if it "seeks to add a new ground for relief" or "attacks the federal court's previous resolution of a claim on the merits." *Gonzalez v. Crosby*, 545 U.S. 525, 532, 125 S.Ct. 2641, 2648, 162 L. Ed. 2d 480 (2005). But when the Rule 60(b) motion attacks "some defect in the integrity of the federal habeas proceeding," and not the merit issue, it is not an impermissible successive motion.

STATEMENT OF THE CASE

On or about November 11th, 2015, Mr. Riggs submitted an instant motion seeking Post-Conviction Relief pursuant to 28 U.S.C. §2255. His primary claims – although poorly particularized because of his

159

ignorance of law – were based on four basic events: 1) he and his defense counsel, Glennon F. Threatt, Jr., suffered from two distinct and separate conflicts of interest; 2) that he had been outright denied counsel at a critical, pre-guilt, stage of the criminal proceeding; 3) he suffered from a constructive denial of counsel at a critical stage; and 4) he had been abandoned by counsel on direct appeal. After years of delay in the United States district court, Mr. Riggs was granted leave to amend and/or clarify his §2255.

In the amended §2255, Mr. Riggs concisely presented four grounds for relief: 1) his guilty plea was not intelligent, knowing, and voluntary; 2) counsel was ineffective because he had a conflict of interest; 3) that he had been deprived of counsel in his criminal case; and 4) he is actually innocent.

On May 2, 2018, the district court denied Mr. Riggs's §2255 motion based on three of his four grounds, "(1) his guilty plea was not intelligent, knowing, and voluntary; (2) counsel was ineffective because he had a conflict of interest; and (3) he is actually innocent."

ARGUMENT

Mr. Riggs was deprived of his right to due process in his §2255 proceeding because the court failed to reach the merits of the third ground in his amended motion. The Eleventh Circuit of the United States court of appeals has routinely held that "when a district court fails to address the claims presented in a §2255 habeas petition, we vacate without prejudice and remand the case for consideration of all remaining claims." *Clisby v. Jones*, 960 F. 2d 925, 936 (11th Cir. 1992) (en banc). In *Clisby*, the district court dismissed thirteen of the petitioner's claims, granted habeas relief of one claim, and reserved judgment on the remaining five claims. *Id.* at 935. "In response, we expressed concern over the 'growing number of cases in which [we were] forced to remand for consideration of issues, the district court chose not to resolve.'" *Id.* at 935-36. "We acknowledged the disruptive effect that such 'piecemeal litigation' had on a state's criminal justice system. *Id.* at 935. Accordingly, in an effort to streamline habeas procedure, we exercise our supervisory authority and instructed district courts to resolve all claims for relief raised in a petition for writ of habeas corpus pursuant to §2254, 'regardless of whether habeas relief is granted or denied' *Id.* at 936. We have defined a 'claim for relief' as 'any allegation of a Constitutional violation.' *Id.*"

In Mr. Riggs's 2255 proceeding the district court failed to address an entire ground for relief. Ground three in Mr. Riggs amended §2255 raised three separate claims of outright denial of counsel. The district court did however state in a footnote, on page 8 of its memorandum that "the record confirms that Mr. Riggs was represented by counsel at every stage of his criminal proceeding." Although mentioned in a footnote, the district court failed to mention, let alone address, a single issue of merit in Mr. Riggs ground three.

In a second footnote, on page 8 of the court's memorandum, the court expressed that Mr. Riggs, "attempts to assert a claim of ineffective assistance about Ms. Barnett's actions ..." In this, the district court outright lies. Mr. Riggs, in his ground three, did not claim that Ms. Barnett (an assistant Federal Public defender) had provided ineffective assistance of counsel. Mr. Riggs accused Ms. Barnett and Glennon F. Threatt, Jr. of ATTEMPTED MURDER and conspiracy to murder a federal defendant – Mr. Riggs. Moreover, Mr. Riggs's ground three particularizes several claims against defense counsel Brett M. Bloomston as providing ineffective assistance of trial counsel. But yet the district court failed to even acknowledge Mr. Bloomston as trial counsel at all.

Finally, the district court discusses Mr. Riggs's arguments concerning how the federal defenders' office helped to conceal evidence and testimony in DeAndre Washington's murder. What the district court leaves out however, is that Mr. Riggs specifically named United States District Judge Karon Owen Bowdre, as the official who received not only the report about DeAndre Washington's murder but also a threat to murder Gary (Sambo) Hazelrigg, who was subsequently murdered in 2015.

It is likely because Mr. Riggs accused District Judge Karon Owen Bowdre of being an accessory after the fact in DeAndre Washington's murder and a facilitator in Gary Hazelrigg's murder, that she refused to address the merit in Mr. Riggs's case. Moreover, Judge Bowdre must continue to deny Mr. Riggs any review on the merits of his claims to maintain her own credibility. In the event Judge Bowdre were to rule in the interest of justice, in Mr. Riggs's case, it would lend credence to Mr. Riggs's claim that she is indeed culpable in three murder investigations. Thus, an equitable ruling on Mr. Riggs's ground three would shatter Judge Bowdre's public reputation and the people's confidence in the Northern District of Alabama.

CONCLUSION

Wherefore, Mr. Riggs moves this court to grant him relief from the final judgment in his §2255 proceeding, so it may determine the merit of ground three in his amended §2255. In the alternative, Mr. Riggs asks that Judge Bowdre recuse herself due to her personal interest in the outcome of this case. This motion will be, as all others in this proceeding have been, made available for public opinion in Mr. Riggs's books, and Post-Conviction Relief Series available on Amazon.com. (Amazon.com/author/KellyPatrickRiggs)

Submitted on April 1, 2019, by:

Kelly Patrick Riggs, Pro se
Reg.#
Federal Correctional Institution
P.O. Box 9000
Seagoville, TX 75159-9000

CERTIFICATE OF SERVICE

This motion has been served on all parties as required by rule and law.

Submitted on April 1, 2019, by:

Kelly Patrick Riggs, Pro se
Reg.#
Federal Correctional Institution
P.O. Box 9000
Seagoville, TX 75159-9000

IN THE UNITED STATES DISTRICT COURT
FOR THE NORTHERN DISTRICT OF ALABAMA
SOUTHERN DIVISION

KELLY PATRICK RIGGS,   ]
                                         ]
    Petitioner,   ]
                                         ]
v.   ]   2:15-cv-8043-KOB
                                         ]
UNITED STATES OF AMERICA,   ]
                                         ]
    Respondent.   ]

ORDER

This matter comes before the court on Mr. Riggs's "Motion for Relief From Final Judgment in §
2255 Proceeding Pursuant to Fed. R. Civ. P., Rule 60(b)(6)." (Doc. 88). The court previously denied
Mr. Riggs's § 2255 motion and motion for a certificate of appealability on May 2,2018. (Docs. 76 &
77). Now, Mr. Riggs attempts to use Fed. R. Civ. P. 60(b)(6) to get another bite of the proverbial apple.
For the following reasons, the court DENIES the motion. (Doc. 88).

In his Rule 60(b)(6) motion, Mr. Riggs claims that the court failed to address his claim that "he had
been deprived of counsel in his criminal case." Mr. Riggs is mistaken. The court *did* address that issue
and denied it. (Doc. 76 at 8 fn 2).

The court also doubts that Fed. R. Civ. P. 60(b)(6) provides an avenue for Mr. Riggs to raise this
issue at this juncture because he has failed to show exceptional circumstances to warrant its application.
Crapp v. City of Miami Beach, 242 F.3d 1017, 1020 (11th Cir. 2001) (Relief under Rule 60(b)(6) is "an
extraordinary remedy which may be invoked only upon a showing of exceptional circumstances.")

In his objections to the court's order denying his § 2255 motion filed less than two weeks after the
court denied his habeas motion, Mr. Riggs previously raised this same argument that the court failed to
address his denial of counsel issue. (Doc. 78). Mr. Riggs then appealed the court's denial of his § 2255
motion to the Eleventh Circuit on May 17, 2018 (doc. 81), but the Circuit Court denied Mr. Riggs's
motion for a certificate of appealability on July 20, 2018 (doc. 87). So, when the Eleventh Circuit

denied Mr. Riggs's motion for a certificate of appealability, it had before it this same issue and denied Mr. Riggs any relief.

The court notes that Mr. Riggs waited over eight months after the Eleventh Circuit's ruling to file this current motion. The Eleventh Circuit has spoken, and this court has done all it can do in this case. The court DENIES the motion for relief from final judgment. (Doc. 88).

DONE and ORDERED this 11th day of April, 2019.

KARON OWEN BOWDRE
CHIEF UNITED STATES DISTRICT JUDGE

UNITED STATES DISTRICT COURT
NORTHERN DISTRICT OF ALABAMA
SOUTHERN DIVISION

Kelly Patrick Riggs

v.   Case No.: 2:15-cv-8043-KOB

United States of America

NOTICE OF APPEAL

Mr. Riggs gives notice of appeal from the courts judgment to deny his 60(b) motion, pursuant to Federal Rules of Appellant Procedure, Rules 3(a)(1); and Rule 4(a)(1)(A). Mr. Riggs specifically seeks to determine if the eleventh Circuit for the U.S. Court of Appeals has delegated its authority to [Judge] Karon Owen Bowdre, and if she subsequently overruled and/or invalidated the Eleventh Circuit's holding in *Clisby v. Jones*, 960 F. 2d 925 (11th Cir. 1992) (en banc) holding that a district courts are to resolve all constitutional claims in petitions before granting or denying relief.

Submitted on April 30, 2019, by:

x_____
Kelly Patrick Riggs, Pro Se
Reg. #
Federal Correctional Institution
P.O. Box 9000
Seagoville, TX 75159

CERTIFICATE OF SERVICE

I certify that I have served a copy of this notice on the clerk of this court, the clerk of the court of appeals, the government, and the Washington Post, properly addressed to each, first-class postage pre-paid. Submitted on April 30, 2019, by:

x_____
Kelly Patrick Riggs, Pro Se
Reg. #
Federal Correctional Institution

KELLY PATRICK RIGGS

P.O. Box 9000
Seagoville, TX 75159

POST-CONVICTION RELIEF: SECOND LAST CHANCE

Appeal No. 19-11778-G

IN THE UNITED STATES COURT OF APPEALS FOR THE ELEVENTH CIRCUIT

Kelly Patrick Riggs

v.

UNITED STATES OF AMERICA

On Appeal From The U.S. District Court

for the Northern District of Alabama

Civil No.: 2:1S-cv-8043-KOB

APPLICATION FOR ISSUANCE OF A CERTIFICATE OF APPEALABILIY

Kelly Patrick Riggs, Pro se
Reg. #
Federal Correctional Institution
P.O. Box 9000
Seagoville, TX 75159

UNITED STATES COURT OF APPEALS
FOR THE ELEVENTH CIRCUIT

Kelly Patrick Riggs	Appeal No.: 19-11778-G
v.	[Civil Case No.: 2:15-cv-8043-KOB]
United States of America	

APPLICATION FOR ISSUANCE OF A CERTIFICATE OF APPEALABILITY

Mr. Riggs is proceeding in pro se and is invoking the Supreme Court controlling doctrine of *Haines v. Kerner*, 404 U.S. 519, 520-21. He moves this court to issue a certificate of appealability (hereinafter COA). He seeks the issuance of a COA, pursuant to 28 U.S.C. §2253(c)(2), authorizing him (Mr. Riggs) to appeal from the district court's April 11, 2019, order to deny his April 1, 2019, motion for relief pursuant to Federal Rules of Civil Procedure, Rule 60(b). Mr. Riggs contends that the district court's denial of relief without addressing his constitutional claims for relief is an abuse of discretion. See *Peterson v. Sec'y, Dep't of Corr.*, 676 Fed. Appx. 827 (11th Cir. 2017).

Jurisdictional Statement

Mr. Riggs filed a motion seeking to be relieved of the district court's judgment. The district court was vested with jurisdiction pursuant to Federal Rules of Civil Procedure, Rule 60(b). Attached.

The district court denied the motion on April 11, 2019. Mr. Riggs filed his timely notice of appeal on April 30, 2019. This court has the jurisdiction to issue a C.O.A. pursuant to 28 D.S.C. §§ 1291 and 2253(c), because the district court abused its discretion by denying Mr. Riggs 60 (b) motion. The record is plain that he has presented at minimum two constitutional claims that have gone unresolved. See *Clisby v. Jones*, 960 F. 2d 925 (11th Cir. 1992) (en bane).

Mr. Riggs files this application for a C.O.A. because the district court issued its judgment, disposing of his motion, without reaching the merits of his constitutional claims.

Statement of the Issues

1) Mr. Riggs asks: If the district court abused its' discretion by failing to resolve all his constitutional claims for relief.

2) Whether the district court is in error, where it claimed that the Eleventh Circuit Court of Appeals ruled on Mr. Riggs's appeal that was not properly before the court.

Statement of the Case

1) The case which Mr. Riggs is appealing from began with an amended motion to vacate, set aside, or correct his sentence under 28 D.S.C. §2255. App-12.

2) On March 2, 2018, the district court ordered the government to appear and show cause.

3) On March 9, 2018, Mr. Riggs filed for the appointment of counsel.

4) On March 20, 2018, the government filed its response.

5) On April 23, 2018, Mr. Riggs filed his final reply.

6) On April 24, 2018, the court issued an order regarding summary disposition.

7) On May 2, 2018, the court issued its final order to deny Mr. Riggs's §2255 and its 'memorandum opinion.' App-39.

8) On May 3, 2018, Mr. Riggs filed his objection and opposition to the court's order regarding summary disposition.

9) Mr. Riggs filed a timely notice of appeal, and this court assigned appeal number 18-12111-F.

10) Mr. Riggs paid the filing fee for this appeal through the district court clerk in the Northern District of Alabama. (see minute entry, May 31, 2018).

11) On June 6, 2018, Mr. Riggs filed his Certificate of Interested Persons and Corporate Disclosure Statement along with his "Motion for Issuance of a Certificate of Appealability," with the clerk of the Eleventh Circuit Court of Appeals. (Dionne S. Young, F). The clerk of the Court of Appeals entered the filing into the record on June 15, 2018 [8485964-1].

12) On February 21, 2019, Mr. Riggs filed a petition for a writ of mandamus in the Supreme Court of the United States seeking an order requiring the Eleventh Circuit to issue an order regarding his motion for a Certificate of Appealability.

13) On February 27, 2019, the Eleventh Circuit clerk, Dionne S. Young, F, issued a letter stating that the appeal had been closed.

14) On March 18, 2019, Mr. Riggs filed a motion requesting service of any order that may have dissolved his appeal. (Case No.: 18-12111-F).

15) On March 26, 2019, clerk Dionne S. Young, F, refused to provide the order and returned the motion unfiled.

16) On April 1, 2019, Mr. Riggs filed for relief from final judgment under Rule 60(b). In his motion, Mr. Riggs seeks resolution of all outstanding claims in his §2255. App-2.

17) On April 11, 2019, the district court denies the motion alleging the Eleventh Circuit Court of Appeals denied his previous appeal (appeal no.: 18-12111-F) on the merits: "… when the Eleventh Circuit denied Mr. Riggs's motion for a certificate of appealability, it had before it this same issue and denied Mr. Riggs any relief." App-8.

18) Again, on April 30, 2019, Mr. Riggs appealed from the district court's abuse of its discretion. App-10.

19) On May 20, 2019, Eleventh Circuit Court clerk, Michaela Dolhoncyk, G, issued a letter giving notice of a new appeal number (19-11778-G) and requiring the filing of a Certificate of Interested Persons and Corporate Disclosure statement, allowing 14 days.

20) On May 23, 2019, Eleventh Circuit Court clerk, Michaela Dolhoncyk, G, issued a second letter advising Mr. Riggs that his filing of his Certificate of Interested Persons and Disclosure statement was delinquent because he had "... not completed the below required filings ... ."

21) On May 30, 2019, Mr. Riggs filed his C.I.P. and a "Motion for Disclosure Order" specifically requesting the local rules that the clerk was using for pro se litigants that allowed only 3 days to file the C.I.P.

22) On June 11, 2019, the clerk of this court, Michaela Dolhancyk, G, issued a letter and returning Mr. Riggs's motion, refusing to allow him access to the court.

23) On June 12, 2019, the clerk of this court issues a letter giving Mr. Riggs notice that he has thirty (30) days to file motion with the Eleventh Circuit Court of Appeals seeking to proceed In Forma Pauperis.

24) Mr. Riggs now presents for filing his application for issuance of a Certificate of Appealability. Mr. Riggs also asks this court to expedite the impending judgment so he may move on to seek a writ of certiorari.

Standard of Review

The appeal of a rule 60(b) motion is limited to a determination of whether the district court abused its discretion in denying the motion, and our review shall not extend to the validity of the underlying judgment. *Rice v. Ford Motor Co.*, 88 F. 3d 914, 918-919 (11th Cir. 1996). Under an abuse-of-discretion standard, this court ordinarily leaves a district courts' ruling undisturbed unless it finds that "the district court has made a clear error of judgment or has applied the wrong legal standard." *Arthur v. Thomas*, 739 F. 3d 611, 628 (11th Cir. 2014).

Federal Rule of Civil Procedure 60(b) allows a party to seek relief or reopen his case based upon the following limited circumstances: 1) mistake or excusable neglect; 2) newly discovered evidence; 3) fraud; 4) the judgment is void; 5) the judgment has been discharged; or 6) any other reason that justifies relief. Fed. R. Civ. P. 60(b). Although a Rule 60(b) motion may not be used to attack the district courts previous resolution of a claim on the merits, it may be used to challenge a defect in the integrity of the federal habeas proceeding. *Gonzalez v. Crosby*, 545 U.S. 524, 532, 125 S.Ct. 2641, 162 L. Ed. 2d 480 (2005) (involving a Rule 60(b) motion filed in a 28 U.S.C. §2255 proceeding).

When a district court fails to address the claims presented in a §2254 habeas petition, we vacate without prejudice and remand the case for consideration of all the remaining claims. *Clisby v. Jones*, 960 F. 2d 925, 936 (11th Cir. 1992) (en banc).

In *Clisby v. Jones*, this court held that if a district court fails to address each claim raised in a habeas petition, it "will vacate the district courts' judgment without prejudice and remand the case for consideration of all remaining claims," 960 F. 2d at 938; see also *Rhode v. United States*, 583 F. 3d 1289, 1291 (11th Cir. 2009) (per curiam) (applying *Clisby* to §2255 motions). Under *Clisby*, this court's only role is to determine whether a district court failed to address a claim; it does not address whether the underlying claim is meritorious. See *Dupree v. Warden*, 715 F. 3d 1295, 1299 (11th Cir. 2013). Also see *Carver v. United States*, 722 Fed. Appx. 906 (11th Cir. 2018).

<u>ISSUE ONE</u>

Mr. Riggs asks if the district court abused its discretion by failing to resolve all his Constitutional claims for relief.

According to the precedential rulings of the Eleventh Circuit, the district court has abused its discretion in Mr. Riggs case because it has failed to resolve all claims for relief that were raised in his §2255 proceeding.

UNRESOLVED CLAIMS

1) In Mr. Riggs's §2255, ground three, paragraph ten, he raised the claim that a defense counsel, Brett M. Bloomston, failed to amend and/or clarify his (Mr. Riggs's) motion to withdraw his guilty plea. App-30.

In Mr. Riggs's criminal case, his defense counsel, Glennon F. Threatt, Jr., illegally obtained Mr. Riggs's guilty plea under a threat of harm to Mr. Riggs's family. Mr. Threatt took advantage of two inmates (Mr. Riggs and Alvin Ray Johnson, Jr.) to cultivate a fear in Mr. Riggs. Mr. Threatt had Mr. Riggs report the incident to the U.S. Marshals service and then later advised Mr. Riggs that the only way to get protection was to plead guilty. Mr. Threatt also advised that he would have Mr. Riggs's case overturned in appeal. Mr. Riggs, believing Mr. Threatt, entered a plea of guilty.

Once Mr. Riggs discovered that Mr. Threatt had lied to him about the threat and the expected appeal, Mr. Riggs moved to withdraw his guilty plea. Mr. Riggs filed in pro se to the best of his ability, a motion he had written in his own hand on blank paper.

Mr. Riggs was granted a hearing and new counsel was appointed. Later, Mr. Brett M. Bloomston appeared as counsel but refused to amend or clarify Mr. Riggs's pro se motion. Thus, Mr. Bloomston failed to provide the service that is expected from professional lawyers. Mr. Bloomston's failure to provide his expertise in Mr. Riggs's case constitutes either a constructive denial of counselor the ineffective assistance of trial counsel at a critical stage of the trial process.

The merit of this claim is not properly before this court. Thus, it cannot consider claims that the district court has not resolved in the first instance. See *Clisby*, 960 F. 2d at 935. Therefore Mr. Riggs

173

moves this court to "vacate the district court's judgment without prejudice and remand the case for consideration of all remaining claims." *Id.* at 938.

2) In Mr. Riggs §2255, ground three, paragraph nine, he raised the claim that he was deprived of the assistance of counsel at a second conflict of interest hearing. Unlike the first, Mr. Riggs was completely alone at the defense table and speaking on his own behalf. In that hearing, held on October 18, 2013, Mr. Threatt and Mr. Butler from the Federal Public Defender's office were seated separately from Mr. Riggs and representing their own interests. That hearing was called on Mr. Riggs's pro se motion he filed after he discovered that the Federal Public Defender's office made a meaningful effort to have him murdered in a Clay County Jail cell. App.-30.

The merit of this claim is not properly before this court. Thus, it cannot consider claims that the district court has not resolved in the first instance. See *Clisby*, 960 F. 2d at 935. Therefore Mr. Riggs moves this court to "vacate the district court's judgment without prejudice and remand the case for consideration of all remaining claims." *Id.* at 938.

3) In Mr. Riggs's §2255, ground three, paragraph seven, he raised the claim that the Federal Public Defender's Office, through its employee Sabra M. Barnett, attempted to murder Mr. Riggs in a jail cell. Ms. Barnett never represented Mr. Riggs in any way, thus Mr. Riggs has no claim of ineffective assistance against her. Mr. Riggs, however, inartfully pleaded, claimed in his §2255 motion that she and Glennon F. Threatt, Jr., attempted to murder Mr. Riggs by providing information to foreign nationals concerning his testimony against them. Ms. Barnett, in a letter, later admitted to having a conversation with a foreign national concerning Mr. Riggs and particularized her conspiracy with Glennon Threatt, Jr. See App. 59.

The merit of this claim is not properly before this court. Thus, it cannot consider claims that the district court has not resolved in the first instance. See *Clisby*, 960 F. 2d at 935. Therefore, Mr. Riggs

POST-CONVICTION RELIEF: SECOND LAST CHANCE

moves this court to "vacate the district court's judgment without prejudice and remand the case for consideration of all remaining claims." *Id.* at 938.

4) In Mr. Riggs's §2255, ground three, paragraph eleven, he also raised the claim that he was abandoned by counsel, Brett Bloomston, when counsel decided to withdraw from Mr. Riggs's direct appeal. Mr. Riggs filed his notice of appeal based on a challenge to the validity of the statutes, 18 U.S.C. §2422(b) and §1470. Mr. Bloomston, however, waited until Mr. Riggs was committed to prison and then proceeded to withdraw from Mr. Riggs's appeal based on his appeal waiver.

In *Garza v. Idaho*, 586 U.S. ___, 139 S.Ct. ___, 203 L. Ed. 2d 77 (2019), the Supreme Court held that: "Under *Strickland v. Washington*, 466 U.S. 668, 104 S.Ct. 2052, 80 L. Ed. 2d 674, a defendant who claims ineffective assistance of counsel must prove (1) 'that counsel's representation fell below an objective standard of reasonableness.' *Id.* at 687-688, 104 S.Ct. 2052, 80 L. Ed. 2d 674, and (2) that any such deficiency was 'prejudicial to the defense.' *Id.*, at 692, 104 S.Ct. 2052, 80 L. Ed. 2d 674. However, 'prejudice is presumed' in 'certain Sixth Amendment contexts,' *ibid*, such as 'when counsel's constitutionally deficient performance deprived a defendant of an appeal that he otherwise would have taken.' *Flores-Ortega*, 528 U.S., at 484, 120 S.Ct. 1029, 145 L. Ed. 2d 985. Pp. ___ - ___, 203 L. Ed. 2d, at 85."

Additionally, the court held that, "no appeal waiver serves an absolute bar to all appellate claims. Because a plea agreement is essentially a contract, it does not bar claims outside its scope. And, like any contract, the language of appeal waivers can vary widely, leaving many types of claims unwaived. A waived appellate claim may also proceed if the prosecution forfeits or waives or if the government breaches the agreement. Separately, some claims are treated as unwaivable. Most, fundamentally, courts agree that defendants retain the right to challenge whether the waiver itself was knowing and voluntary," such as Mr. Riggs was forced to raise in his own appeal brief filed in Pro se.

In considering the Supreme Court's ruling in *Garza*, it is clear that the district court in Mr. Riggs's §2255, and his 60(b) motion, abused its discretion, by failing to reach the underlying merit of Mr. Riggs's constitutional claim.

The merit of this claim is not properly before this court. Thus, it cannot consider claims that the district court has not resolved in the first instance. See *Clisby*, 960 F. 2d at 935. Therefore, Mr. Riggs moves this court to "vacate the district court's judgment without prejudice and remand the case for consideration of all remaining claims." *Id.* at 938.

ISSUE TWO

Mr. Riggs asks whether the district court is in error, where it claimed that the Eleventh Circuit Court of Appeals ruled on Hr. Riggs's appeal that was not properly before the court.

Mr. Riggs filed a motion under Federal Rules of Civil Procedure, Rule 60(b), based on the aforementioned *Clisby* errors. The district court denied the motion based on this court's denial of his motion for a certificate of appealability in appeal no.: 18-12111-F.

Reviewing this court's docket in appeal no. 18-12111-F, it shows that:

A) On June 6, 2018, the clerk of this court issued a "notice of C.I.P. filing deficiency," to Mr. Riggs.

B) On June 15, 2018, Mr. Riggs filed his motion for a Certificate of Appealability.

C) On June 22, 2018, the clerk of this court issued a "notice of C.I.P. filing deficiency, to the U. S. Attorney.

D) On June 25, 2018, the U.S. Attorney filed its Certificate of Interested Persons, along with a notice of appearance from Michael Billingsley.

E) On July 20, 2018, the clerk of this court issued an order denying Mr. Riggs motion for a Certificate of Appealability. It is easy to determine from the record that this court never had before it "this same issue" as the district court suggests. Because this court's record reflects that Mr. Riggs failed to file his Certificate of Interested Persons, the clerk was "not authorized to submit to the court any … motion" that Mr. Riggs filed, including his motion for a Certificate of Appealability. See Cir. R. 26. 1-5. Failure to submit a C.I.P. or complete the web based C.I.P.

The district court's error concerning this issue is properly before this court and Mr. Riggs asks that the district court's judgment be vacated.

Wherefore, Mr. Riggs moves this court to vacate the district court's judgment and remand this case for resolution on all remaining claims.

Submitted on July 10, 2019, by:

Kelly Patrick Riggs, Pro se
Reg. #
Federal Correctional Institution
P.O. Box 9000
Seagoville, TX 75159

CERTIFICATE OF SERVICE

I certify that on July 1, 2019, I served a copy of the foregoing motion for issuance of a Certificate of Appealability with the clerk of this court by placing it in the prison legal mailing system, properly addressed and first-class postage pre-paid.

Identical service was provided to:

Michael B. Billingsley
1801 4th Avenue N.
Birmingham, AI. 35203

Submitted on July 10, 2019, by:

Kelly Patrick Riggs, Pro se
Reg. #
Federal Correctional Institution
Seagoville, TX 75159

CHAPTER SEVEN

COMPASSIONATE RELEASE

This is the last chapter of what is likely to be the last book I will write from prison. Don't get me wrongs I'll still finish this series of books by writing "Post-Conviction Relief: The Advocate," but I'll be writing it from home. Also know that I did not intend to include this information in this book.

Before now, Compassionate Release has always been nothing more than a bad joke. Compassionate Release has been around for decades. It is a commonly known fact that Congress granted the authority to the director of the Federal Bureau of Prisons, to move for the release of a prisoner under the Compassionate Release Statute. Federal law provides that a court may reduce a prisoner's term of imprisonment under specific circumstances, see 18 U. S.C. §3582(c) (1). This law is commonly known as the "Compassionate Release" Statute.

This law, however, was seldom used because the court could only grant Compassionate Release upon the filing of a motion by the director of the Bureau of Prisons. This gave the Bureau of Prisons sole gatekeeping power over whether to grant release to an inmate. When considering the "Cost of Incarceration Fee," that pays the prisons for each federal prisoner (currently $102.60 per day), it is easy to understand why prison wardens do not move for Compassionate Release even for prisoners who they know are dying.

This authority changed on December 21, 2018, when the First Step Act was enacted into law. The First Step Act gave individual prisoners the right to petition the United States District Courts directly for Compassionate Release. The law now provides that:

> "the Court, upon motion of the Director of the Bureau of Prisons, or upon motion of the defendant after the defendant has fully exhausted all administrative rights to appeal a failure of the Bureau of Prisons to bring a motion on the defendant's behalf or the lapse of 30 days from the receipt of such a request ... whichever is earlier ..." See 18 U.S.C. §3582(c)(1)(A).

This change to the Compassionate Release Statute means that a prisoner can take control of filing a motion for Compassionate Release after being denied or not answered by the Warden where they are imprisoned.

> *Author's Note: Please pay special attention to this portion of the statute. You can file your motion after you "fully exhaust all administrative rights ..." that means if you are denied you must file, and be denied by the Warden, not the central office in a BP-231 "Or" you may file a motion after "the lapse of 30 days from the receipt of such a request by the warden ...." This means that you may petition the court after the thirty (30) day window, regardless of if your request goes unanswered or is denied by the Warden, not your unit team, or the central office.*

The next issue of concern, and the reason I did not take Compassionate Release too seriously after the passing of the First Step Act, is that the term "Extraordinary Circumstances" was still undefined in the law. But in the year that followed, the courts started to broaden their thinking. Even after the clarification of 18 U.S.C. §924(c) and the Supreme Court's decision in *Davis* that invalidated §924(c)'s residual clause, the Courts were still moving slowly to establish a clear meaning of what "extraordinary" and "compelling" really means.

It took a national emergency, the Covid-19 pandemic, to move the Courts and U.S. District Judges to find the compassion in their hearts to release a few prisoners who would otherwise die at their hands. If this sounds like they are really human after all, don't kid yourself. The reason that the district judges are granting relief is because the whole world is watching them and the largest human trafficking scheme (U.S. federal prison system) that the world has ever known. The facts and statistics will show that the horrors of the American Criminal Justice System are second only to the atrocities that occurred in Nazi Germany. So please pay close attention as we move through the steps for filing for Compassionate Release.

STEP ONE

Send the Warden of your facility an electronic "Request to Staff." In your request you must specifically ask that the Warden "file a motion for Compassionate Release" on your behalf. Keep in mind that prison staff love to play word games like "go through your unit team" and other similar statements. Also, don't try using a BP-229. The "BP-9" as they are called must be preceded by a request to staff, which will cause you to wait longer as you navigate your way through unnecessary prison procedures. Send your electronic "Cop Out" to the warden. Thirty (30) days later you can file a motion in the court.

STEP TWO

Make sure you mark your electronic "Cop Out" for printing. After eight years of dealing with BOP staff, at seven different facilities, I can guarantee you that they will lie. They will claim that you never asked the Warden to file a motion if you can't prove it. Remember the Warden's motivation, the $102.60 per day Cost of Incarceration Fee. If the prison can stall your motion by thirty (30) days they will be paid an extra $3078.00. *Make sure you print out the request and save it.*

Those of you who are unable to file a request with the warden – like anyone who may be locked down for one reason or another – may have your request filed by a friend or a family member from outside.

The process, just as if a prisoner was filing, starts with a letter to the Warden of the prisoner's facility. The letter should include:

- The prisoner's name and register number;

- The specific relationship between the prisoner and the author of the letter, even if only a friend;

- An explanation, in the letter's first paragraph, that the author is seeking "Compassionate Release" on behalf of the prisoner.

- An explanation of what makes the prisoner's circumstances extraordinary and compelling (whether the reasons are medical, a national pandemic, or actual innocence, coupled with an increased threat of death);

- A complete and thorough home plan. Be very specific about all needs – employment, address, education, medical, income, etc.; and

- The full name, return address, telephone number, email address, and any other contact information so the Warden can contact the letter's author.

The letter should be dated. A copy should be made and kept in a file for later use. The letter must be sent via certified mail so a record of its receipt, by the Warden, is made.

Once the request for Compassionate Release is received by the Warden, the Warden has thirty (30) days to grant or deny the request. In some cases, a Warden may send the request on to the BOP's Central Office for a final decision whether or not to move forward (by filing a motion on the prisoner's behalf). No matter how the Bureau of Prisons handles the request, the date of the letter's receipt will officially

179

start the thirty-day clock. Again, *certified mail* – the BOP will test anyone who does not know how they operate by claiming the letter was "lost in the mail."

STEP THREE

File a motion for the appointment of counsel with the clerk of the district court that prosecuted your criminal case. This motion does not need to be fancy. If you remember what I said about not trying to sound like a lawyer, in "Post-Conviction Relief: Advancing Your Claim," this is a good time to prove it.

A motion to appoint counsel is not required. Because it is not required, its submission to the court is not governed by rule or law. I file the motion for counsel as soon as possible after I make my request to the Warden.

STEP FOUR

Here we are, the nuts and bolts of writing a motion for Compassionate Release under 18 U.S.C. §3582(c)(1)(A). Just as with any other motion filed in pro se, or without the assistance of counsel, a §3582 motion should be heavy on facts. I mean your own personal facts. It should make clear what you want in the first paragraph, explain the Court's jurisdiction to hear the motion, and only then explain the Court's authority to reduce the sentence.

Although there exists enough information out there to turn this chapter into a long and useless academic exercise, I'm going to skip all that and provide you with a number of examples that have worked in the past. These "example motions" are divided up by a few Roman numerals to keep it simple.

You can use these examples by listing the parts of each that apply to your own situation, but they must be personalized. As you can see, my own motion is the very first.

You can also see that the very first words in the first paragraph are "Mr. Riggs moves." So, as I've explained before, nothing in this book will serve as an all-encompassing "Magic Motion."

Also know that each section must also match your specific circumstances. In other words, you wouldn't want to list the Covid-19 pandemic as a contributing factor after it is over. You wouldn't want to claim to be a living kidney donor if you are not. Nor would you want to claim to be over 65 years of age if you are only 30.

Ok, that is the end of the "do nots". I do, however, strongly suggest that you file your motion as quickly as you possibly can. I say this because if you don't, the government will use any perceived delay against you. What I usually do is start on the elements of my motion as soon as I drop my counsel motion in the mail. If you have paid close attention to my personal motion, you will discover that this one time I did not follow my own advice. That gave me absolutely no tactical advantage. What I was doing was preparing requests and counsel motions for twenty other people. If you find it in your heart to do something similar, be sure not to go over a month past your first opportunity to file. I say this because of the example we find in the *McQuiggin v. Perkins*, 569 U.S. 383, case. In that case the Courts decided that because McQuiggin sat on his newly discovered evidence of actual innocence, he did not deserve any type of relief. So, again, don't waste any time.

Just so you know, many of you out there will not be granted the appointment of counsel. As a matter of fact, my own Judge, Karon Owen Bowdre, refused to appoint counsel in my case for two reasons. One, she is deliberately indifferent to the needs and welfare of prisoners; and two, she is once again punishing me for being successful in changing my own future. In her April 2020 order you will discover her words of contempt for law and justice. So, no matter what happens, make sure your request for Compassionate Release is filed. See the examples in the remainder of this chapter.

UNITED STATES DISTRICT COURT
NORTHERN DISTRICT OF ALABAMA
SOUTHERN DIVISION

Kelly Patrick Riggs

Case No.:

v.

2:12-CR-297-KOB-JEO

United States of America

MOTION FOR THE APPOINTMENT OF
COUNSEL PURSUANT TO 18 U.S.C. § 3006A

Mr. Riggs moves this court to appoint counsel, to help him with filing a petition for Compassionate Release. Mr. Riggs wishes to file for Compassionate Release in an effort to escape from the additional, and unnecessary risk to his health and life caused by the likely infection of the Coronavirus, while in a prison environment.

Mr. Riggs's circumstances are extraordinary because:

1) he is unable to provide self-care within a prison environment because of the growing Covid-19 pandemic; and

2) prisoners are unable to practice effective social distancing and hygiene to minimize risk of exposure; and

3) he has less than sixty (60) days left until he is eligible for release; and

4) he is less likely to survive an infection than the average person because he has undergone surgery to donate a kidney to a fellow veteran; and

5) he would have been released two months ago had the Bureau of Prisons allowed him to apply his earned Time Credits to additional halfway house, see The First Step Act.

Wherefore, Mr. Riggs moves this court to appoint counsel to better articulate his claim. It is clear that the circumstances that he faces in a prison system during this highly contagious, and proven deadly, global pandemic are unprecedented. Thus, Mr. Riggs's circumstances are extraordinary and compelling.

Submitted on April 5, 2020, by:

Kelly Patrick Riggs, pro se
Reg. #
Federal Correctional Institution
P.O. Box 9000
Seagoville, TX 75159

CERTIFICATE OF SERVICE

I certify .that on April 5, 2020, I served the clerk of this court with this motion, for service to all parties who are registered CM/ECF system users, via U.S. mail, properly addressed, first class postage prepaid, by placing a copy in the remaining mailing system currently available at the prison in which I am confined.

Kelly Patrick Riggs
Reg. #

UNITED STATES DISTRICT COURT
NORTHERN DISTRICT OF ALABAMA
SOUTHERN DIVISION

Kelly Patrick Riggs

    v.

United States of America

Case No.:

2:12-CR-297-KOB-JEO

MOTION FOR SENTENCE REDUCTION PURSUANT TO
18 U.S.C. §3582 (c)(1)(A)(i)

Mr. Riggs moves this court to reduce his sentence to time served based on the Bureau of Prisons inability to provide medical care to all prisoners who continue to become infected with the Coronavirus; his inability to protect himself in a prison setting during the global pandemic; his qualification for immediate release under the First Step Act, had the Bureau of Prisons properly applied his earned time credits; and because he now has less than sixty (60) days left to complete his original sentence, with his current halfway house date applied. Mr. Riggs's circumstances satisfy the "extraordinary and compelling reasons" standard set out in both 18 U.S.C. §3582 (c) (1) (A) (i) and U.S.S.G. §1B1.13. In light of the factors in 18 U.S.C. §3553 (a), Mr. Riggs moves this court to reduce his sentence to time served.

I

JURISDICTION

On December 21, 2018, the President of the United States signed the First Step Act of 2018 into law. The newly enacted law amended 18 U.S.C. §3582 (c)(1) (A) to give the sentencing judge jurisdiction to consider a defendant's motion for a sentence reduction based on extraordinary and compelling reasons. The Court has jurisdiction whenever "the defendant has fully exhausted all administrative rights to appeal a failure of the Bureau of Prisons to bring a motion on the defendant's

behalf," or after "the lapse of 30 days from the receipt of such a request by the Warden of the

defendant's facility, whichever is earlier." See the First Step Act of 2018, §603(b), Pub. L. 115-391, 132

Stat. 5194, 5239 (Dec. 21, 2018). Mr. Riggs has attempted to exhaust his administrative remedies within

the Bureau of Prisons ("BOP"). The Warden at FCI Seagoville recharacterized Mr. Riggs's March 11,

2020, request and forwarded it to his unit team; his request was denied on March 17, 2020. See

attached. Mr. Riggs refiled his request as an appeal to the denial on April 4, 2020. The Bureau of

Prisons ("BOP") has not responded because a lack of staff has caused a breakdown in the administrative

relief process. Even if Mr. Riggs could pursue additional appeals within the administrative processes of

the BOP, a period of over 30 days has elapsed since the Warden's receipt of Mr. Riggs's request for

Compassionate Relief. This gives the Court jurisdiction. See 18 U.S.C. §3582 (c)(l)(A).

II

Authority to Reduce a Sentence Under
18 U.S.C. § 3582 (c)(l)(A)(i)

This Court "may reduce the term of imprisonment , after considering the factors set forth in [18 U.S.C.

§] 3553 (a) to the extent they are applicable, if it finds that ... extraordinary and compelling reasons

warrant such a reduction ... [,] and that such a reduction is consistent with applicable policy statements

issued by the Sentencing Commission." See 18 U.S.C. §3582 (c)(l)(A)(i). In 28 U.S.C. §994(t),

Congress delegated to the Sentencing Commission the authority to "describe what should be considered

extraordinary and compelling reasons for sentence reduction, including the criteria to be applied and a

list of specific examples." Here, the examples of "extraordinary and compelling reasons" include:

(A) Medical Condition of the Defendant
   (ii) The defendant is –
   (I)   suffering from a serious physical or medical condition,
   (II)   suffering from a serious functional or cognitive impairment, or
   (III)   experiencing deteriorating physical or mental health because of the aging
           process, that substantially diminishes the ability of the defendant to provide self-

184

        care within the environment of a correctional facility and from which he or she is not expected to recover.

(B) Age of the Defendant – The defendant

    (i)   is at least 65 years old;

    (ii)   is experiencing a serious deterioration in physical or mental health because of the aging process; and

    (iii)   has served at least 10 years or 75 of his or her term of imprisonment, whichever is less. See Application Note 1 to D.S.S.G. §1B1.13.

The Sentencing Commission's standard has parallels under the BOP program statement on Compassionate Release, P.S. 5050.50, Compassionate Release/Reduction in Sentence: Procedures for Implementation of 18 D.S.C. §§ 3582 and 4205 (g) (Jan. 17, 2019) (providing Compassionate Release consideration for elderly inmates with medical conditions). The BOP's program statement remains relevant only if its criteria are broader than the standards set by the Sentencing Commission. See Application Note 1(D) to D.S.S.G. §1B1.13 (recognizing that the Director of the BOP can designate additional "extraordinary and compelling reasons other than, or in combination with, the reasons described in" the commentary). For example, the BOP provides for a reduction in sentence for:

Elderly inmates with Medical Conditions. Inmates who fit the following criteria:

- Age 65 and older.

- Suffer from chronic or serious medical conditions related to the aging process.

- Experiencing deteriorating mental or physical health that substantially diminishes their ability to function in a correctional facility.

- Conventional treatment promises no substantial improvement to their mental or physical condition.

- Have served at least 50% of their sentence.

BOP Program Statement 5050.50 4. b.

III

Relevant Facts and Procedural History

The indictment in Case #2:12-CR-297-KOB-JEO charged Mr. Riggs with one (1) count under 18 U.S.C. §2422(b) and one (1) count under 18 U.S.C. §1470. Mr. Riggs entered into a binding plea agreement on both counts. On April 22, 2014, Mr. Riggs was sentenced to 120 months on counts one and two, to be served concurrently. At the time of sentencing, Mr. Riggs was 45 years old; he had no significant ailment and had donated his left kidney to a fellow veteran just two years prior.

Mr. Riggs is currently 51 years old. He has been in federal custody since his arrest on May 26, 2012, nearly 8 years of actual incarceration or 79.8% of his total term of imprisonment (as of April, 2020). The BOP has Mr. Riggs listed as a "chronic care" inmate.

IV

Argument

A. **Mr. Riggs Has Established Extraordinary and Compelling Reasons That Warrant a Sentence Reduction.**

There are extraordinary and compelling reasons, as defined in Application Note 1 (A) and (B) to U.S.S.G. §1B1.13, to reduce Mr. Riggs's sentence to time served. Mr. Riggs has only one remaining kidney and is at a higher risk of death from any serious foreign infection. He is currently incarcerated in close proximity with 190 other prisoners from which he cannot distance himself. Thus, Mr. Riggs is subject to a discernable threat even as the BOP's death toll rises. Although Mr. Riggs is not 75 years of age, he is subject to a medical emergency that the BOP cannot reasonably control; his physical health has deteriorated due to aging, and he has served over 75% of his sentence.

Under the current statutory regime, the existence of extraordinary and compelling circumstances confers on this court the authority to consider the 18 U.S.C. §3553 factors and determine whether the circumstances warrant a sentence reduction.

This Court should not give value to the BOP's denial of Compassionate Release due to its recharacterization of Mr. Riggs's request. The BOP has failed to reasonably consider Mr. Riggs's request based on its merit. Due to the BOP's lack of diligence, Mr. Riggs is still waiting for a meaningful response from the Warden of his facility. The statutory responsibility to decide whether to grant a motion to reduce a sentence falls to this court, not the BOP. Decisions about sentencing "[should] not be left to employees of the same Department of Justice that conducts the prosecution." *Setser v. United States*, 566 U.S. 231, 242 (2012); see also *Id.* at 240 ([T]he Bureau is not charged with applying §3553(a).") Under 18 U.S.C. §3582 (c) (1) (A) (L) and U.S.S.G. §1B1.13, it is the Court, not the BOP, that is charged with considering the "extraordinary and compelling reasons," then evaluating whether the sentencing factors under 18 U.S.C. §3553 (a) warrant a reduction in sentence.

The First Step Act's amendment to 18 U.S.C. §3582(c)(1)(A) reflects the Congressional intent to diminish the BOP's control over Compassionate Release by permitting defendants to file sentence reduction motions directly with the sentencing court. The BOP's administration of the Compassionate Release Program has long been the subject of criticism. The Department of Justice's Office of Inspector General has repeatedly found that the program results in needless and expensive incarceration and is administered ineffectively. Department of Justice, Office of the Inspector General, the Federal Bureau of Prison's Compassionate Release Program, at page 11 (April 2013) ("the BOP does not properly manage the Compassionate Release Program, resulting in inmates who may be eligible candidates for release not being considered."); Department of Justice, Office of the Inspector General, The Impact of an Aging Inmate Population on the Federal Bureau of Prisons, at page 51 (May 2015) ("Although the BOP has revised its Compassionate Release policy to expand consideration for early release to aging inmates, which could help mitigate the effects of a growing aging inmate population, few aging inmates have been released under it."). Prisoner advocates have also documented the human cost of the BOP's stinting view of Compassionate Release. See Human Rights Watch; Families Against Mandatory

Minimums, *The Answer is No: Too Little Compassionate Release* in U.S. Federal Prisons (Nov. 2012); and Kelly Patrick Riggs's Post-Conviction Relief book series (2017-2020).

The First Step Act shifts the authority to this Court to decide whether Mr. Riggs's extraordinary and compelling reasons warrant a sentence reduction without deference to any administrative agency.

B) After Considering the 18 U.S.C. §3553 (a) Factors, Mr. Riggs's Nearly 8 Years of Incarceration Constitutes a Sentence Sufficient But Not Greater Than Necessary, to Accomplish the Goals of Sentencing.

Under the circumstances, the 8 years of incarceration that Mr. Riggs has served satisfies the purpose of sentencing. Under *Pepper v. United States*, 562 U.S. 476, 490-93 (2011), the Court can, and must, consider post-offense developments under 18 U.S.C. §3553(a), which provides "the most up-to-date picture" of the defendant's history and characteristics and "sheds light on the likelihood that [Mr. Riggs] will engage in future criminal conduct." ld. at 492. The Warden did not identify any disciplinary violations received by Mr. Riggs as a reason for not granting Compassionate Release. Here, the overriding factor under 18 U.S.C. §3553(a) that was not present at the time of sentencing, is Mr. Riggs's potentially deadly exposure to the Covid-19 virus while incarcerated. Although the circumstances of the present offenses and Mr. Riggs's criminal history qualified him for the imposed sentence this Court originally imposed, Mr. Riggs's potential exposure to a deadly disease at the time of sentencing provided no indication that he was likely to face a life-threating illness because of his incarceration. The current trend shows that the number of positive Covid-19 cases in the BOP is growing daily. The CDC has identified certain classes of people who are unusually susceptible to be overcome by the Coronavirus. As a general class of people, not withstanding Mr. Riggs having only one kidney, consists of those who cannot practice social distancing and good personal hygiene. The World's health communities also advise people to wash regularly with alcohol-based hand sanitizer – an unauthorized commodity to all people in prison.

- Mr. Riggs's Post Incarceration Activities and Educational Efforts Have Greatly Reduced the Probability of Recidivism.

Prior to prison, Mr. Riggs had reached the pinnacle of his professional career. During his 8 years of incarceration, he has dedicated himself to diligent and intense study of Sociology, literature, philosophy, and American Jurisprudence. He has risen from among the ranks of his peers and has become one of the most successful jailhouse lawyers America has ever known. He has written a growing collection of books that have helped thousands of prisoners understand the laws and the Constitution of the United States. He is a founding member of Release of Innocent Prisoners Effort, Inc., a 501(c)(3) non-profit corporation. Mr. Riggs also serves as a volunteer for Fair Shake, which assists ex-felons understand re-entry resources, and recently joined forces with The California Innocence Project.

Mr. Riggs has engaged in rehabilitative programs offered by the Bureau of Prisons such as:

- The non-residential drug abuse program
- Creative writing, I and II
- Legal Research I, II, and III
- Criminal Justice Law I and II

Mr. Riggs has also served as a trusted inmate worker, 1st grade, in a prison laundry. His duties included equipment maintenance, labor management, inventory, and scheduling. Mr. Riggs served as the instructor of Advanced Habeas corpus Law at Oakdale FCI. He also has mentored several other inmates in their pursuit of writing and publishing their own books.

In summary, Mr. Riggs is now 51 years old, has experienced a deep-seated personal change, has developed a love for helping his fellow man achieve their goals, and as such does not pose a danger to any other person or the community. Mr. Riggs has secured employment with Freebird Publishers and they both currently await the moment when Mr. Riggs will be released and will set forth on the path that leads to his greatest potential.

CONCLUSION

Wherefore, Mr. Riggs moves this Court to reduce his total sentence, in Case No.: 2:12-CR-297-

KOB-JEO, to time served, and for all other relief to which he may be entitled.

Submitted on April 13, 2020, by:

_____

Kelly Patrick Riggs, pro se
Reg. #
Federal Correctional Institution
P.O. Box 9000
Seagoville, TX 75159

CERTIFICATE OF SERVICE

I certify that on April 13, 2020, I filed the foregoing motion with the Clerk of the Court, so that service

may be completed to all parties by entering it into the CM/ECF system, via U.S. Mail, properly

addressed, and First Class postage prepaid and affixed thereto, by placing it in the only remaining

mailing system that is available to inmates in the national lock-down triggered by the Covid-19

pandemic.

_____

Kelly Patrick Riggs
Reg. #

UNITED STATES DISTRICT COURT
WESTERN DISTRICT OF PENNSYLVANIA

United States of America	Case No.:
v.	2:11-CR-133-DWA
Edward Leonard Finley Hilts	

MOTION FOR SENTENCE REDUCTION
PURSUANT TO 18 U.S.C. § 3582 (c)(1)(A)(i)

Mr. Hilts moves the Court to reduce his sentence to time served based on the Bureau of Prison's inability to provide medical care to all prisoners who continue to become infected with the Coronavirus and his inability to protect himself in a prison setting during the global pandemic. Mr. Hilts's circumstances satisfy the "extraordinary and compelling reasons" standard set out in both .18 U.S.C. § 3582 (c) (1) (A) (i) and U.S.S.G. § 1B1.13. In light of the factors in 18 U.S.C. § 3553 (a), Mr. Hilts moves this court to reduce his sentence to time served.

I

JURISDICTION

On December 21, 2018, the President of the United States signed the First Step Act of 2018 into law. The newly enacted law amended 18 U.S.C. § 3582 (c)(1)(A) to give the sentencing judge jurisdiction to consider a defendant's motion for a sentence reduction based on extraordinary and compelling reasons. The Court has jurisdiction whenever "the defendant has fully exhausted all administrative rights to appeal a failure of the Bureau of Prisons to bring a motion on the defendant's behalf," or after "the lapse of 30 days from the receipt of such a request by the Warden of the defendant's facility, whichever is earlier." See the First Step Act of 2018, §603(b), Pub. L. 115-391, 132 stat. 5194, 5239, (Dec. 21, 2018).

191

Mr. Hilts has attempted to exhaust his administrative remedies within the Bureau of Prisons

("BOP"). The Warden at FCI Seagoville received Mr. Hilts's request for relief on April 1, 2020. His

request is still unanswered as of May 5, 2020. Although Mr. Hilts could pursue additional appeals

within the administrative processes of the BOP, a period of over 30 days has elapsed since the Warden's

receipt of Mr. Hilts's request for Compassionate Release. This gives the Court jurisdiction. See 18

U.S.C. § 3582 (c)(l)(A).

II

COURT'S AUTHORITY TO REDUCE A SENTENCE
UNDER 18 D.S.C. § 3582 (c)(I)(A)(I)

This Court "may reduce the term of imprisonment, after considering the factors set forth in [18

U.S.C. §J 3553(a) to the extent they are applicable, if it finds that … extraordinary and compelling

reasons warrant such a reduction … [,] and that such a reduction is consistent with applicable policy

statements issued by the Sentencing Commission." See 18 U.S.C. § 3582 (c)(1) (A) (i). In 28 U.S.C.

§994(t), Congress delegated to the sentencing Commission the authority to "describe what should be

considered extraordinary and compelling reasons for sentence reduction, including the criteria to be

applied and a list specific examples." Here, the examples of "extraordinary and compelling reasons"

include:

(A) Medical Condition of the Defendant
(ii) The defendant is –
  (I) suffering from a serious physical or medical condition,
  (II) suffering from a serious functional or cognitive impairment, or
  (III) experiencing deteriorating physical or mental health because of the aging process, that substantially diminishes the ability of the defendant to provide self-care within the environment of a correctional facility and from which he or she is not expected to recover.

(B) Age of the Defendant – The Defendant
  (i) is at least 65 years old;
  (ii) is experiencing a serious deterioration in physical or mental health because of the aging process; and
  (iii) has served at least 10 years or 75 of his or her term of imprisonment, whichever is less. See Application Note 1 to U.S.S.G. §1B1.13.

The Sentencing Commission's standard has parallels under the BOP program statement on Compassionate Release, P.S. 5050.50, Compassionate Release/Reduction in Sentence: Procedures for Implementation of 18 U.S.C. §§ 3582 and 4205(g) (Jan. 17, 2019) (providing Compassionate Release consideration for elderly inmates with medical conditions). The BOP's program statement remains relevant only if its criteria are broader than the standards set by the Sentencing Commission. See Application Note 1(D) to U.S.S.G. §1B1.13 (recognizing that the Director of the BOP can designate additional "extraordinary and compelling reasons other than, or in combination with, the reasons described in" the commentary). For example, the BOP provides for a reduction in sentence for:

(B) **Elderly Inmates with Medical Conditions**. Inmates who fit the following criteria:
- Age 65 and older.
- Suffer from chronic or serious medical conditions related to the aging process.
- Experiencing deteriorating mental or physical health that substantially diminishes their ability to function in a correctional facility.
- Conventional treatment promises no substantial improvement to their mental or physical condition.
- Have served at least 50 percent of their sentence.

BOP Program Statement 5050.50 4. b.

III

Relevant Facts and Procedural History

The indictment in Case No. 2:11-CR-133-DWA charged Mr. Hilts with one (1) count under 18 U.S.C. § 2422(b), one (1) count under 18 U.S.C. § 2423(b), one (1) count under 18 U.S.C. § 2252A (1), and one count under 18 U.S.C. § 2252A (4) (B). Mr. Hilts proceeded to trial on June 13, 2014 and was found guilty on all charges.

On December 10, 2014, Mr. Hilts was sentenced to 324 months on all counts, to be served concurrently. At the time of sentencing, Mr. Hilts was 69 years old.

Mr. Hilts is currently 74 years old. He was arrested on October 1, 2009 and was on bond until May 25, 2011. He has served nearly 9 years of actual incarceration, or 33.3% of his total term of imprisonment (as of April, 2020). The BOP has Mr. Hilts listed as a "Chronic Care" inmate.

IV

Argument

A. Mr. Hilts Has Established Extraordinary and Compelling Reasons That Warrant a Sentence Reduction.

There are extraordinary and compelling reasons, as defined in Application Note 1 (A) and (B) to U.S.S.G. §1B1.13, to reduce Mr. Hilts' sentence to time served. Mr. Hilts has a compromised immune system and chronic bronchitis along with other respiratory issues. He is at a high risk of death from any serious foreign infection. He is currently incarcerated in close proximity with 190 other prisoners from which he cannot distance himself, on a prison compound that has an active case of Covid-19 in its medical isolation unit. Thus, Mr. Hilts is subject to a discernable threat even as the BOP's death toll rises. Mr. Hilts is 74 years of age and he is subject to medical emergencies that the BOP cannot reasonably control; his physical health has deteriorated due to aging, and he has served almost 9 years of his sentence.

Under the current statutory regime, the existence of extraordinary and compelling circumstances confers on this Court the authority to consider the 18 D.S.C. § 3553 factors and determine whether the circumstances warrant a sentence reduction.

This Court should not give value to the BOP's failure to seek Compassionate Release. The BOP has failed to reasonably consider Mr. Hilts's request based on its merit. Due to the BOP's lack of diligence, Mr. Hilts is still waiting for a response to his administrative appeal. The statutory responsibility to decide whether to grant a motion to reduce a sentence falls to this Court not the BOP. Decisions about sentencing "[should] not be left to employees of the same Department of Justice that conducts the prosecution." *Setser v. United States*, 566 U.S. 231, 242 (2012); See also Ed. at 240 ("[T]he Bureau is not charged with applying § 3553(a).") Under 18 U.S.C. § 3582(c)(1) (A)(i) and U.S.S.G. §1B1.13, it is the Court, not the BOP, that is charged with considering the "extraordinary and compelling reasons," then evaluating whether the sentencing factors under 18 U.S.C. § 3553(a) warrant a reduction in sentence.

The First Step Act's amendment to 18 U.S.C. § 3582(c)(1)(A) reflects the Congressional intent to diminish the BOP's control over Compassionate Release by permitting defendants to file sentence reduction motions directly with the sentencing count. The BOP's administration of the Compassionate Release Program has long been the subject of criticism. The Department of Justice's Office of the Inspector General has repeatedly found that the program results in needless and expensive incarceration and is administered ineffectively. Department of Justice, Office of the Inspector General, The Federal Bureau of Prison's Compassionate Release Program, at page 11 (April 2013) ("the BOP does not properly manage the Compassionate Release Program, resulting in inmates who may be eligible candidates for release not being considered."); Department of Justice, Office of the Inspector General, The Impact of an Aging Inmate Population on the Federal Bureau of Prisons, at page 51 (May 2015) ("Although the BOP has revised its Compassionate Release policy to expand consideration for early release to aging inmates, which could help mitigate the effects of a growing aging inmate population, few aging inmates have been released under it."). Prisoner advocates have also documented the human cost of the BOP's stinting view of Compassionate Release. See Human Rights Watch; Families Against Mandatory Minimums, *The Answer is No: Too Little Compassionate Release in U.S. Federal Prisons* (Nov. 2012); and Kelly Patrick Riggs's Post-Conviction Relief book series (2017-2020).

The First Step Act shifts the authority to this Court to decide whether Mr. Hilts's extraordinary and compelling reasons warrant a sentence reduction without deference to any administrative agency.

B. After Considering the 18 U.S.C. § 3553(a) Factors, Mr. Hilts's Nearly 9 Years of Incarceration Constitutes a Sentence Sufficient But Not Greater Than Necessary, to Accomplish the Goals of Sentencing.

Under the circumstances, the 9 years of incarceration that Mr. Hilts has served satisfies the purpose of sentencing. Under *Pepper v. United States*, 562 U.S. 476, 490-93 (2011), the Court can, and must, consider post-offense developments under 18 U.S.C. § 3553(a), which provides ''the most up-to-date picture'' of the defendant's history and characteristics and "sheds light on the likelihood that [Mr. Hilts] will or will not engage in future criminal conduct." *Id.* at 492. The Warden did not identify any disciplinary violations received by Mr. Hilts as a reason for not granting Compassionate Release. Here, the overriding factor under 18 U.S.C. § 3553(a) that was not present at the time of sentencing, is Mr. Hilts's potentially deadly exposure to the Covid-19 virus while incarcerated. Although the circumstances of the present offenses and Mr. Hilts's criminal history qualified him for the imposed sentence this Court originally imposed, Mr. Hilts's potential exposure to a deadly disease at the time of sentencing provided no indication that he was likely to face a life-threatening illness because of his incarceration. The current trend shows that the number of positive Covid-19 cases in the BOP is growing daily. The CDC has identified certain classes of people who are unusually susceptible to be overcome by the Coronavirus. As a general class of people, not withstanding Hilts's immune system and respiratory problems, consists of those who cannot practice social distancing and good personal hygiene. The world's health communities also advised people to wash regularly with alcohol-based hand sanitizer – an unauthorized commodity to all 'people' in prison.

C. Subsequent To His Incarceration, Mr. Hilts Became The Only Family Member Who Can Provide Necessary care To His Disabled Wife.

Mr. Hilts's wife, Barbara Hilts, has been diagnosed under Wisconsin statute § 55.08(1) as follows: "The individual needs protective placement and meets the standards ... (3) as a result of a degenerative brain disorder, the individual is so totally incapable of providing for her own care or custody as to create a substantial risk of serious harm to herself or others. Serious harm may be evidenced by overt acts or acts of omission."

She has been under the care and custody of a hospital:

Door County Medical Center
323 South 18th Avenue
Sturgeon Bay, Wi. 54235
920-743-5566

The County Social Worker in the Department of Health and Human Services, Kim Kramer, filed a petition for (1) temporary and (2) permanent guardianship due to incompetency. This filing is done prior to transfer of the individual from a hospital to a nursing facility or community-based residential facility (Wis. Stats. § 50.06).

Barbara's only remaining family, her brother and sister, signed the petition, indicating no interest in providing for her as a guardian, nor taking any powers of attorney. Her powers of attorney for health care and guardianship, held by Gene Lanney, are no longer going to be effective, as he is no longer willing to serve in those roles.

The social worker states, "Ms. Hilts has probably (sic) dementia with paranoid and delusional thinking; she is extremely confused and disoriented and unable to make her own decisions or provide for her own care or custody."

The Circuit Court Judge, D. Todd Ehlers, on August 8, 2019, found probable cause that the individual needs protective placement. He ordered a hearing for permanent protective placement on September 4, 2019. The Court's contact information is:

Hon. D. Todd Ehlers
1209 South Duluth Avenue
Justice Center
Sturgeon Bay, Wi. 54235

The Court ordered: "A copy of the physician or psychologist's report shall be filed with the Court and Provided by the petitioner to the guardian AD LITEM and the attorney for the proposed ward at least 96 hours before the time of the hearing.

The Court ordered the appointment of a guardian AD LITEM:

Matt Pribyl
30 North 18th Avenue #10A
Sturgeon Bay, WI. 54235
920-743-8485

On September 6, 2019, Judge Ehlers issued his incompetency rulings regarding Ms. Hilts.

Corporate Guardians of Northeast Wisconsin was appointed as her guardian, effective 9/06/2019. The

Guardian's contact information is:

Corporate Guardians of NEW
P.O. Box 117
Two Rivers, WI. 54241
920-553-8780

D. Mr. Hilts' Post Incarceration Activities and Educational Efforts Have Greatly Reduced the Probability of Recidivism.

Prior to prison, Mr. Hilts had reached the pinnacle of his professional career. During his 9 years of

incarceration, he has dedicated himself to diligent and intense study of finance, history, philosophy, and

American jurisprudence. He has worked with his peers on financial and occupational strategies, helped

multiple inmates with their legal issues, and helped inmates edit and publish their own books. He

assisted the founders of Release of Innocent Prisoners Effort, Inc., a 501(c)(3) non-profit corporation,

with strategies and to implement a sound fund-raising campaign. Mr. Hilts also assists ex-felons

understand re-entry resources and has written business plans for several companies founded by

releasing inmates.

Mr. Hilts has engaged in programs offered by the Bureau of Prisons. Mr. Hilts has engaged in over

20 programs offered by the Bureau of Prisons and has 5 years as a valued employee of UNICOR, the

prison products corporation.

In summary, Mr. Hilts is now 74 years old and has re-established his "roots" as a community-

focused organizer. Mr. Hilts founded the Mid-City Community Clinic in 1973 to provide medical care to less fortunate people. Now he has a new group of people to assist, and as such is a positive asset to his community.

At 74 years of age, Mr. Hilts' age places him in the class of prisoners least likely to recidivate. United States Sentencing Commission, The Effects of Aging on Recidivism Among Federal Offenders (Dec. 2017). Having served a long period of incarceration and experiencing deteriorating physical health, Mr. Hilts does not pose a danger to any other person or to the community.

In the Sentencing Commission's policy statement on physical condition, extraordinary impairments provide reason for downward departure for "seriously infirm" defendants, including to have detention at initial sentencing because home detention "may be as efficient as, and less costly than, imprisonment." U.S.S.G. §5H1.4; see also 18 U.S.C. § 3553(a)(2)(D) (consideration of providing needed medical care in the most effective manner). Clearly, the BOP has proven that they are unable to effectively treat elderly prisoners, like Mr. Hilts, in the likely event they are infected with the Coronavirus.

The Court should consider that the nearly 9 years that Mr. Hilts has served, coupled with his health, and the current global threat, will meet the purpose of sentencing, considering Mr. Hilts's deteriorating physical health caused by the aging process.

CONCLUSION

For the foregoing reasons, Mr. Hilts respectfully requests that the Court reduce his total sentence to time served, and all other relief he may be due.

Respectfully submitted on May 6, 2020, by:

Edward Leonard Finley Hilts, pro se
Reg. #
Federal Correctional Institution
P.O. Box 9000
Seagoville, TX 75159

199

KELLY PATRICK RIGGS

CERTIFICATE OF SERVICE

I certify that on May 6, 2020, I served a copy of this motion on the Clerk of the Court, via U.S.

Mail, properly addressed, with prepaid first-class postage affixed thereto.

Respectfully submitted on May 6, 2020, by:

Edward Leonard Finley Hilts, pro se
Reg. #

UNITED STATES DISTRICT COURT
NORTHERN DISTRICT OF TEXAS
LUBBOCK DIVISION

United States of America	Case No.:
v.	5:18-CR-55-C-01
Dustin Leonard	

**MOTION FOR SENTENCE REDUCTION PURSUANT TO
18 U.S.C. § 3582 (c)(1)(A)(i)**

Mr. Leonard moves this Court to reduce his sentence to time served based on the Bureau of Prison's inability to provide medical care to the large and growing number of prisoners who continue to become infected with the Coronavirus; his inability to protect himself in a prison setting during the deadly global pandemic; acute asthma; his proof that he is actually innocent; and the fact that he was not sentenced in such a way that he should have to fear being exposed to a long and painful death instead of the ten years that this Court imposed. Mr. Leonard's circumstances satisfy the "extraordinary and compelling reason" standard set out in 18 U.S.C. § 3582 (c)(1)(A)(i). In light of the factors in 18 U.S.C. § 3553 (a), Mr. Leonard moves this Court to reduce his sentence to time served.

I

JURISDICTION

On December 21, 2018, the President of the United States signed the First Step Act of 2018 into law. The newly enacted law amended 18 U.S.C. § 3582 (c) (1)(A) to give the sentencing judge jurisdiction to consider a defendant's motion for a sentence reduction based on extraordinary and compelling reasons. The Court has jurisdiction whenever "the defendant has fully exhausted all administrative rights to appeal a failure of the Bureau of Prisons to bring a motion on the defendant's behalf," or after "the lapse of 30 days from the receipt of such a request by the Warden of the defendant's facility, whichever is earlier." See the First Step Act of 2018, § 603 (b), Pub. L. 115-391, 132 stat. 5194, 5239 (Dec. 21, 2018).

Mr. Leonard has attempted to exhaust his administrative remedies within the Bureau of Prisons ("BOP"). The Warden received Mr. Leonard's request on April 13, 2020; his request was denied on April 23, 2020; and he filed his appeal to the Regional Office on April 23, 2020. The Bureau of Prisons has not responded because of a lack of staff that has made it impossible for them to answer Mr. Leonard's appeal within 30 days. Even if Mr. Leonard could pursue an additional avenue for appeal within the administrative processes of the BOP, a period of over 30 days has elapsed since the Warden's receipt of Mr. Leonard's request for Compassionate Relief. This gives the sentencing Court jurisdiction to reduce Mr. Leonard's sentence for extraordinary and compelling reasons. See 18 U.S.C. § 3582 (c)(l)(A)(i).

II

RECHARACTERIZATION

This motion is a request for a sentence reduction for extraordinary and compelling reasons. One of Mr. Leonard's reasons is that the facts and laws in his criminal case show that he is actually innocent. Therefore, Mr. Leonard's motion may not be recharacterized, as an initial 28 U.S.C. § 2255 motion to vacate his sentence, because an actual innocence claim is not cognizable in a § 2255 proceeding. This Court has the authority to "reduce the term of [Mr. Leonard's] imprisonment, after considering the factors set forth in [18 U.S.C. §] 3553 (a) to the extent they are applicable, if it finds that ... extraordinary and compelling reasons warrant such a reduction ... [,] and that such a reduction is consistent with applicable policy statements issued by the Sentencing Commission." See 18 U.S.C. § 3582 (c)(1)(A). In 28 U.S.C. § 994 (t), Congress delegated to the Sentencing Commission the Authority to "describe what should be considered extraordinary and compelling reasons for sentence reduction, including the criteria to be applied and a list of specific examples." Mr. Leonard's claim of actual innocence and his health concerns in the wake of the Covid-19 pandemic are not listed as extraordinary and compelling reasons by the Sentencing Commission. The list that was made by the Commission is years old and predates even the enactment of the latest changes to 18 U.S.C. § 3582. The Sentencing Commission's list should not be viewed as a limitation to bar all other claims outside of its text. But should be considered only as some examples of "extraordinary and compelling reasons."

III

RELEVANT FACTS AND PROCEDURAL HISTORY

Mr. Leonard was working at Slaton High School as a senior level history teacher and a coach. He also spent his seventh period of school time tutoring students who needed a little extra instruction. During his seventh period Mr. Leonard was approached by a senior high school student who was not in any of his classes but requested extra instruction from Mr. Leonard none-the-less.

Mr. Leonard agreed to help and added her to his seventh period tutoring list. She (the female student) visited the seventh period class almost daily. When alone she expressed a personal desire for Mr. Leonard, which he deftly deflected. She continued to visit the class almost daily, often becoming aggressively flirtatious. Over several weeks, Mr. Leonard often subdued her advances causing her to become even more aggressive.

After coming back to the school from a basketball game late in the season, on a cold Friday night, Mr. Leonard stayed in his office until nearly 3 a.m. watching game footage and making Saturday practice plans. When leaving his office, Mr. Leonard found the 17-year-old female student on the hood of his car, freezing and shivering, dressed only in her cheerleader outfit. She claimed to have no way home and Mr. Leonard agreed to drive her.

When Mr. Leonard stopped outside of the student's home, she made it clear that she wanted a relationship with him. She knew that Mr. Leonard was leaving his teaching position at the end of the year and claimed that they could have a legal relationship, yet still intending to keep it "under the radar." The student then asked to borrow Mr. Leonard's phone, to which she quickly downloaded the "snapchat" app and added herself as a contact.

Mr. Leonard and the female student interacted for seven months on many levels. Their relationship grew more personal and by April 18, 2018, Mr. Leonard decided it was time to resign his position as an employee at the high school. Mr. Leonard's resignation listed personal reasons and was later accepted by Superintendent Julie Becker.

As the relationship between Mr. Leonard and the former student grew, they began to speak of moving in together and marriage. On or around May 21st, 2018, Mr. Leonard's estranged wife searched his social media and found some current messages between Mr. Leonard and his new love. The former Mrs. Leonard turned the messages over to the authorities and claimed that an inappropriate relationship existed prior to Mr. Leonard's resignation. Mrs. Leonard's statements were untrue but, blinded by jealousy, she found her revenge for Mr. Leonard's happiness.

The indictment in Case No.: 5:18-CR-55-C-01 charged Mr. Leonard with one (1) count under 18 U.S.C. §2422(b). Later, Mr. Leonard pleaded guilty unknowingly, on November 16, 2018, Mr. Leonard was sentenced to 120 months on count one to be served in the Federal Bureau of Prisons. At the time of sentencing, Mr. Leonard was 28 years old and suffering from acute asthma. Mr. Leonard is now 30 years old. He has been in custody since his arrest on May 22, 2018, nearly two years ago. The BOP currently has Mr. Leonard listed as under care for asthma.

IV

ARGUMENT

1)   Mr. Leonard Has Established Extraordinary and Compelling Reasons That Warrant a Sentence Reduction.

There are extraordinary and compelling reasons, as defined in Application Note 1 (A) and (B) in U.S.S.G §1B1.13, to reduce Mr. Leonard's sentence to time served.

Mr. Leonard has been diagnosed with Acute Asthma and is at a higher risk of death from any serious foreign infection. He is currently incarcerated in close proximity with 190 other prisoners from which he cannot distance himself. Thus, Mr. Leonard is subject to a discernable threat as the BOP's death toll rises. Although Mr. Leonard is not 65 years of age, he is none-the-less subject to a medical emergency that the BOP cannot reasonably control; his physical health is in danger because of asthma; and he now faces a potential sentence of death for conduct that is not criminal under any statute.

Under the current statutory regime, the existence of extraordinary and compelling circumstances confers on this Court the authority to consider the 18 U.S.C. §3553 factors and determine whether the circumstances warrant a sentence reduction.

This Court should not give value to the BOP's denial of Compassionate Release. The BOP has failed to reasonably consider Mr. Leonard's request based on its merit. Due to the BOP's lack of diligence, Mr. Leonard is still waiting for a meaningful response from the appeal from the Warden's decision. The statutory responsibility to decide whether to grant a motion to reduce a sentence falls to this Court, not the BOP. Decisions about sentencing "[should] not be left to employees of the same Department of Justice that conducts the prosecution." *Setser v. United States*, 566 U.S. 231, 242 (2012); See also *Id.* at 240 ([T]he Bureau is not charged with applying §3553(a).") Under 18 U.S.C. §3582(c)(1)(A)(i) and U.S.S.G. §1B1.13, it is the Court, not the BOP, that is charged with considering the "extraordinary and compelling reasons," then evaluating whether the sentencing factors under, 18 U.S.C. §3553(a) warrant a reduction in sentence.

The First Step Act's amendment to 18 U.S.C. §3582(c)(1)(A) reflects the Congressional intent to diminish the BOP's control over Compassionate Release by permitting defendants to file sentence reduction motions directly with the sentencing Court. The BOP's administration of the Compassionate Release Program has long been the subject of criticism. The Department of Justice's Office of Inspector General has repeatedly found that the Program results in needless and expensive incarceration and is administered ineffectively. Department of Justice, Office of the Inspector General, the Federal Bureau of Prisons Compassionate Release Program, at page 11 (April 2013) ("the BOP does not properly manage the Compassionate Release Program, resulting in inmates who may be eligible candidates for release not being considered.") Prisoner advocates have also documented the human cost of the BOP's stinting view of Compassionate Release. See Human Rights Watch; Families Against Mandatory Minimums, *The Answer is No: Too Little Compassionate Release in U.S. Federal Prisons* (Nov. 2012); and Kelly Patrick Riggs's Post-Conviction Relief book series (2017-2020).

The First Step Act shifts the authority to this Court to decide whether Mr. Leonard's extraordinary and compelling reasons warrant a sentence reduction without deference to any administrative agency.

2)   After Considering the 18 U.S.C. §3553(a) Factors, Mr. Leonard's Two Years of Incarceration Constitutes a Sentence Sufficient But Not Greater Than Necessary, to Accomplish the Goals of Sentencing.

Under the circumstances, the 2 years of incarceration that Mr. Leonard has served satisfies the purpose of sentencing. Under *Pepper v. United States*, 562 U.S. 476, 490-93 (2011), the Court can, and must, consider post offense developments under 18 U.S.C. §3553(a), which provides "the most up-to-date picture" of the defendant's history and characteristics and "sheds light on the likelihood that [Mr. Leonard] will engage in future criminal conduct." *Id.* at 492. The Warden did not identify any disciplinary violations received by Mr. Leonard as a reason for not granting Compassionate Release. Here, the overriding factor under 18 U.S.C. §3553(a) that was not present at the time of sentencing, is Mr. Leonard's potentially deadly exposure to the Covid-19 virus while incarcerated. Although the circumstances of the present offenses and Mr. Leonard's criminal history qualified him for the sentence this Court originally imposed, Mr. Leonard's potential exposure to a deadly disease at the time of sentencing provided no indication that he was likely to face a life-threatening illness because of his incarceration. The current trend shows that the number of positive Covid-19 cases in the BOP is growing daily. The CDC has identified certain classes of people who are unusually susceptible to be overcome by the Coronavirus. As a general class of people, who are at risk, are those who cannot practice social distancing and good personal hygiene. The World's health communities also advise people to wash regularly with alcohol-based hand sanitizer – an unauthorized commodity to all people in prison.

Wherefore, Mr. Leonard moves this Court to grant this motion and reduce his sentence to time served based on extraordinary and compelling reasons.

Respectfully submitted on May 13th, 2020, by:

Dustin Leonard, pro se
Reg. #
Federal Correctional Institution
P.O. Box 9000
Seagoville, TX 75159

CERTIFICATE OF SERVICE

I certify that on May-13, 2020, I filed the foregoing motion with the Clerk of the Court, so that service may be perfected to all parties by entering it into the CM/ECF system, via U.S. Mail, properly addressed, first class postage prepaid and affixed thereto, by placing it in the only remaining mailing system that is available to inmates during the national lock-down triggered by the Covid-19 pandemic.

Dustin Leonard, pro se
Reg. #

UNITED STATES DISTRICT COURT
NORTHERN DISTRICT OF TEXAS
FORT WORTH DIVISION

United States of America	Case No.:
v.	4:93-cr-20-A
Michael D. Davis	

MOTION FOR SENTENCE REDUCTION PURSUANT
TO 18 U.S.C. § 3582 (c)(1)(A)

Mr. Davis moves this Court to grant him a sentence reduction based on extraordinary and compelling circumstances brought about by the outbreak of the Coronavirus. Good Cause is shown based on the following:

1) That 18 U.S.C. § 3582 (c)(l)(A)(i) states in the relevant part that this Court is empowered to reduce a defendant's sentence when "extraordinary and compelling reasons warrant such reduction."

2) That under the First Step Act, Congress revised 18 U.S.C. § 3582 (c)(l)(A) to empower the District Court – rather than the Director of the Federal Bureau of Prisons – to determine what circumstances constitute "extraordinary and compelling reasons" for a sentence reduction, in conjunction with the factors set forth in 18 U.S.C. § 3553 (a).

3) That 28 U.S.C. § 944 (t) delegates authority to the United States Sentencing Commission to promulgate general policy statements regarding sentence modification provisions in § 3582 (c) (1) (A), describing what "should be considered extraordinary and compelling reasons for sentencing reduction, including the criteria to be applied and a list of specific examples."

4) That the Sentencing Commission complied with this directive in drafting U.S.S.G. §1B1.13 and its commentary.

5) That §1B1.13 states in relevant part that upon motion of the Director of the BOP, under 18 U.S.C. § 3582 (c)(l)(A), the Court may reduce a defendant's sentence if, after considering 18 U.S.C. § 3553 (a)'s factors, the Court determines that – "(I) (A) extraordinary and compelling reasons warrant the reduction …"

6) That the commentary to §1B1.13 then gives four categories of "reasons" which would meet the extraordinary and compelling standard, those being:

    a. Medical condition of the defendant;

    b. Age of 65 years or over;

    c. Family circumstances; and

    d. As determined by the Director of the BOP, there exists in the defendant's case an extraordinary and compelling reason other than, or in combination with, the reasons in subdivision (a) through (c)."

7) That subdivision (d) hereinabove is a "catch-all provision" and it is this subdivision upon which defendant bases this motion. §1B1.13's commentary is outdated and does not track the revisions Congress made to §3582 under the First Step Act.

8) That it was the clear intent of Congress to empower the district courts to make determinations as to what constituted "extraordinary and compelling" under the so-called "catch-all provision," and specifically to remove this determination from the BOP's purview. The commentary is outdated and in need of revision, but since the Sentencing Commission cannot now even convene a quorum due to the failure to appoint new members, it is within the province of the district court to effectuate the will of Congress, particularly where said intent is clear and unambiguous.

9) That a request to modify and reduce Mr. Davis's sentence pursuant to 18 U.S.C. § 3582 (c)(l)(A) was filed electronically with Warden K. Zook and was received by her on or about April 2, 2020.

10) That Warden Zook denied Mr. Davis's request on April 10, 2020, a copy of which is attached.

11) That Mr. Davis followed the express instructions of Warden Zook, by filing an appeal from her decision on a BP-9, a copy of which is attached.

12) That extraordinary and compelling reasons exist to warrant a reduction in Mr. Davis's sentence to time served, and he sets forth these reasons herein below.

13) That the current pandemic is putting prisoners with poor health like Mr. Davis at high risk of infection and death. Infection rates in prison are astronomically higher than in the general populace; thus, it is imperative that this Court rule on Mr. Davis's motion with all due haste.

14) Mr. Davis has several health conditions which may materially affect his ability to survive an infection by the Coronavirus:

    a. Mr. Davis suffers from arthritis, high blood pressure, heel spurs, a history of heart disease, allergies, other respiratory issues, and also some gastric issues.

    b. Mr. Davis has been prescribed a strict regimen of several medications which, combined, cause his immune system to be compromised. Prescribed medications include the following:

- Losartan Potassium;
- Hydrochlorothiazide;
- Omeprazole;
- Indomethacin; and
- Chlorpheniramine Maleate.

15) That Mr. Davis is serving an unusually long sentence, based on the stacking of 18 U.S.C. §924(c) convictions in a single indictment, that would be unlawful and unconstitutional to impose by today's standards.

16) That in December of 2018, Congress enacted the First Step Act of 2018, Pub. L. No. 115-291, 132 Stat. 5194 ("the First Step Act"). Under the First Step Act, the mandatory minimum sentence for

convictions under 18 U.S.C. §924(c) was reduced for sentences imposed after the passage of the First Step Act. Had Mr. Davis been sentenced under these reduced penalties, he would have received a sentence of 217 months as opposed to 457 months with respect to his two §924(c) convictions. The First Step Act also authorized courts, without the Bureau of Prison's motion, as previously required, to reduce sentences for "extraordinary and compelling reasons" once a defendant exhausts his administrative appeals to the Bureau of Prisons ("BOP"). As stated herein, Mr. Davis applied to the Warden of his facility for a sentence reduction based on extraordinary and compelling circumstances; and he has exhausted his administrative remedies receiving no answer from his latest appeal, as required under the First Step Act.

17) That in assessing whether Mr. Davis has presented extraordinary and compelling reasons, the Court should initially and centrally consider the sentence he received relative to the sentence he would now receive for the same offense, whether and to what extent there is a disparity between the two sentences, and why that disparity exists. The Court should also consider Pre-Booker sentences like Mr. Davis's and how different they are from sentences of today. Had Mr. Davis been sentenced since December 21, 2018, his sentence would be **20 years less**. See *Dean v. United States*, 137 S.Ct. 1170, 1177 (2017) (holding that, post-Booker, "nothing in [§924(c)] prevents a sentencing Court from considering a mandatory minimum under §924(c) when calculating an appropriate sentence for the predicate offense, which can justify a below-guidelines sentence).

18) That Mr. Davis asks the Court to exercise its discretion by considering all applicable 18 U.S.C. § 3553 (a) factors, along with the Court's obligation to avoid sentencing disparities between defendants who are similarly situated. Recently, courts around the country, to include the Southern District of Texas, have taken the length of a defendant's sentence into consideration while evaluating what constitutes "extraordinary and compelling reasons," for the purpose of deciding 18 U.S.C. §3582 (c)(l)(A) sentence reductions. See *United States v. Maumau*, 08-CR-758, Lexis

28392, District of Utah (2/18/20); *Cantu-Rivera*, 1:05-CR-458-1, 2019 WL 2498923 at *2 (S.D.

Tex. June 17, 2019); *Brown*, 4:05-CR-227-1, 2019 WL 4942051 at *3 (S.D. Iowa Oct. 8, 2019);

and *Ukrevich*, 8:03-CR-37, 2019 WL 6037391, where the district court determined that a sentence

modification based on the First Step Act's changes to 924 (c) sentencing was appropriate.

Wherefore, Defendant Michael D. Davis prays that this Court grant the requested relief, reducing

his sentence to time served, and for all other relief just and proper on the premises.

Submitted on May 3, 2020, by:

_____
Michael D. Davis, pro se
Reg. #
Federal Correctional Institution
P.O. Box 9000
Seagoville, TX 75159

CERTIFICATE OF SERVICE

I hereby certify that on May 3, 2020, I filed the foregoing motion with the Clerk of the Court in the

Northern District of Texas, so that service may be completed to all parties by entering it into the

CMjECF system, in our time of national emergency.

Respectfully submitted on May 3, 2020, by:

_____
Michael D. Davis, pro se
Reg. #

APPENDIX

<u>18 U.S.C. § 3553</u>
IMPOSITION OF A SENTENCE

(a) **Factors to be considered in imposing a sentence**. The Court shall impose a sentence sufficient, but not greater than necessary, to comply with the purpose set forth in paragraph (2) of this subsection. The Court, in determining the particular sentence to be imposed, shall consider –

(1) the nature and circumstances of the offense and the history and characteristics of the defendant;

(2) the need for the sentence imposed –

    (A) to reflect the seriousness of the offense, to promote respect for the law, and to provide just punishment for the offense;

    (B) to afford adequate deterrence to criminal conduct;

    (C) to protect the public from further crimes of the defendant; and

    (D) to provide the defendant with needed educational or vocational training, medical care, or other correctional treatment in the most effective manner;

(3) the kinds of sentences available;

(4) the kinds of sentences and the sentencing range established for –

    (A) the applicable category of offense committed by the applicable category of defendant as set forth in the guidelines –

        (i) issued by the Sentencing Commission pursuant to Section 994(a)(1) of title 28, United States Code, subject to any amendments made to such guidelines by act of Congress (regardless of whether such amendments have yet to be incorporated by the Sentencing Commission into amendments issued under Section 994 (p) of title 28); and

        (ii) that, except as provided in Section 3742(g) [18 U.S.C.S. § 3742(g)], are in effect on the date the defendant is sentenced; or

    (B) in the case of a violation of probation or supervised release, the applicable guidelines or policy statements issued by the Sentencing Commission pursuant to Section 994(a)(3) of title 28, United States Code, taking into account any amendments made to such guidelines or policy statements by an act of Congress (regardless of whether such amendments have yet to be incorporated by the Sentencing Commission into amendments issued under Section 994(p) of title 28);

(5) any pertinent policy statements –

    (A) issued by the Sentencing Commission pursuant to Section 994(a)(2) of title 28, United States Code, subject to any amendments made to such policy statement by act of Congress (regardless of whether such amendments have yet to be incorporated by the Sentencing Commission into amendments issued under Section 994(p) of title 28); and

(B)   that, except as provided in Section 3742(g) [18 U.S,C.S. § 3742(g)], is in effect on the date the defendant is sentenced. [;]

(6)   the need to avoid unwarranted sentence disparities among defendants with similar records who have been found guilty of similar conduct; and

(7)   the need to provide restitution to any victims of the offense.

(b)   application of guidelines in imposing a sentence.

(1)   In general [Caution: In United States *v.* Booker (2005) 543 U.S.220, 160 L. Ed. 2d 621, 125 S.Ct. 738, the Supreme Court held that 18 U.S.C.S. §3553(b) (1), which makes the Federal Sentencing Guidelines mandatory, is incompatible with the requirements of the Sixth Amendment and therefore must be severed and excised from the Sentencing Reform Act of 1984.] Except as provided in paragraph (2), the Court shall impose a sentence of the kind, and within the range, referred to ,in Subsection (a)(4) unless the Court finds that there exists an aggravating or mitigating circumstance of a kind, or to a degree, not adequately taken into consideration by the Sentencing Commission in formulating the guidelines that should result in a sentence different from that described. In determining whether a circumstance was adequately taken into consideration, the Court shall consider only the sentence guidelines, policy statements, and official commentary of the Sentencing Commission. In the absence of an applicable sentencing guideline, the Court shall impose an appropriate sentence, having due regard for the purposes set forth in subsection (a)(2). In the Absence of an applicable sentencing guideline in the case of an offense other than a petty offense, the Court shall also have due regard for the relationship of the sentence imposed to sentences prescribed by guidelines applicable to similar offenses and offenders, and to the applicable policy statements of the Sentencing Commission.

(2)   Child crimes and sexual offenses.
[(A)] Sentencing. In sentencing a defendant convicted of an offense under Section 1201 [18 U.S.C.S. §1201] involving a minor victim, an offense under Section 1591 [18 U.S.C.S. §1591], or an offense under Chapter 71, 109A, 110, or 117 [18 U.S.C.S. §§1460 et. seq., 2241 et. seq., 2251 et. seq., or 2421 et. seq.], the Court shall impose a sentence of the kind, and within the range, referred to in subsection (a)(4) unless –

(i)   the Court finds that there exists an aggravating circumstance of a kind, or to a degree, not adequately taken into consideration by the Sentencing Commission in formulating the guidelines that should result in a sentencing greater than that described;

(ii)   the Court finds that there exists a mitigating circumstance of a kind or to a degree, that –

(I)   has been affirmatively and specifically identified as a permissible ground of downward departure in the sentencing guidelines or policy statements issued under Section 994(a) of title 28, taking account of any amendments to such sentencing guidelines or policy statements by Congress;

(II)   has not been taken into consideration by the Sentencing Commission in formulating the guidelines; and

(III)   should result in a sentence different from that described; or

215

(iii) the Court finds, on motion of the Government, that the defendant has provided substantial assistance in the investigation or prosecution of another person who has committed an offense and that this assistance established a mitigating circumstance of a kind, or to a degree, not adequately taken into consideration by the Sentencing Commission in formulating the guidelines that should result in a sentence lower than that described. In determining whether a circumstance was adequately taken into consideration, the Court shall consider only the sentencing guidelines, policy statements, and official commentary of the Sentencing Commission, together with any amendments thereto by act of Congress. In the absence of an applicable sentencing guideline, the Court shall impose an appropriate sentence, having due regard for the purposes set forth in Subsection (a)(2). In the absence of an applicable sentencing guideline in the case of an offense other than a petty offense, the Court shall also have due regard for the relationship of the sentence imposed to sentences prescribed by guidelines applicable to similar offenses and offenders, and to the applicable policy statements of the Sentencing Commission, together with any amendments to such guidelines or policy statements by acts of Congress.

(c) **Statement of reasons for imposing a sentence.** The Court, at the time of sentencing, shall state in open Court the reasons for its imposition of the particular sentence, and, if the sentence –

(1) is of the kind, and within the range, described in Subsection (a)(4), and that range exceeds 24 months, the reason for imposing a sentence at a particular point within the range; or

(2) is not of the kind, or is outside the range, described in Subsection (a)(4), the specific reason for the imposition of a sentence different from that described, which reasons must also be stated with specificity in a statement of reasons form issued under Section 994(w)(1)(B) of title 28 [28 U.S.C.S. §994(w)(1)(B)], except to the extent that the Court relies upon statements received in Camera in accordance with Federal Rule of Criminal Procedure 32. In the event that the Court relies upon statements received in Camera in accordance with Federal Rule of Criminal Procedure 32, the Court shall state that such statements were so received and that it relied upon the content of such statements.
If the Court does not order restitution, or orders only partial restitution, the Court shall include in the statement the reason therefor. The Court shall provide a transcription or other appropriate public record of the Court's statement of reasons, together with the order of judgment and commitment, to the Probation System and to the Sentencing Commission, [,J and, if the sentence includes a term of imprisonment, to the Bureau of Prisons.

(d) **Presentence procedure for an order of notice**. Prior to imposing an order of notice pursuant to Section 3555 [18 U.S.C.S. §3555J, the Court shall give notice to the defendant and the Government that it is considering imposing such an order. Upon motion of the defendant or the Government, or on its own motion, the Court shall –

(1) permit the defendant and the Government to submit affidavits and written memoranda addressing matters relevant to the imposition of such an order;

(2) afford counsel an opportunity in open Court to address orally the appropriateness of the imposition of such an order; and

(3) include in its statement of reasons pursuant to Subsection (c) specific reasons underlying its determinations regarding the nature of such an order. Upon motion of the defendant or the

Government, or on its own motion, the Court may in its discretion employ any additional procedures that it concludes will not unduly complicate or prolong the sentencing process.

(e) **Limited authority to impose a sentence below a statutory minimum**. Upon motion of the Government, the Court shall have the authority to impose a sentence below a level established by statute as a minimum sentence so as to reflect a defendant's substantial assistance in the investigation or prosecution of another person who has committed on offense. Such sentence shall be imposed in accordance with the guidelines and policy statements issued by the Sentencing Commission pursuant to Section 994 of title 28, United States Code.

(f) Limitation on applicability of statutory minimums in certain cases. Notwithstanding any other provision of law, in the case of an offense under Section 401, 404,or 406 of the Controlled Substance Act (21 U.S.C. 841, 844, 846), Section 1010 or 1013 of the Controlled Substance Import and Export Act (21 U.S.C. 960, 963), or Section 70503 or 70506 of title 46, the Court shall impose a sentence pursuant to guidelines promulgated by the United States Sentencing Commission under Section 994 of title 28 without regard to any statutory minimum sentence, if the Court finds at sentencing, after the Government has been afforded the opportunity to make a recommendation, that –

   (1) the defendant does not have –

      (A) more than 4 criminal history points, excluding any criminal history points resulting from a 1-point offense, as determined under the sentencing guidelines;

      (B) a prior 3-point offense, as determined under the sentencing guidelines; and

      (C) a prior 2-point violent offense, as determined under the sentencing guidelines; Information disclosed by a defendant under this subsection may not be used to enhance the sentence of the defendant unless the information relates to a violent offense.

   (2) the defendant did not use violence or credible threats of violence or possess a firearm or other dangerous weapon (or induce another participant to do so) in connection with the offense;

   (3) the offense did not result in death or serious bodily injury to any person;

   (4) the defendant was not an organizer, leader, manager, or supervisor of others in the offense, as determined under the sentencing guidelines and was not engaged in a continuing criminal enterprise, as defined in Section 408 of the Controlled Substance Act [21 U.S.C.S. §848]; and

   (5) not later than the time of the sentencing hearing, the defendant has truthfully provided to the Government all information and evidence the defendant has concerning the offense or offenses that were part of the same course of conduct or of a common scheme or plan, but the fact that the defendant has no relevant or useful other information to provide or that the Government is already aware of the information shall not preclude a determination by the Court that the defendant has complied with this requirement.

(g) **Definition of violent offense**. As used in this section, the term "violent offense" means a crime of violence, as defined in Section 16 [18 U.S.C.S. §16], that is punishable by imprisonment.

18 U.S.C. § 3582
IMPOSITION OF A SENTENCE OF IMPRISONMENT

(a) **Factors to be considered in imposing a term of imprisonment.** The court, in determining whether to impose a term of imprisonment, and, if a term of imprisonment is to be imposed, in determining the length of the term, shall consider the factors set forth in section 3553(a)[18 USCS § 3553(a)] to the extent that they are applicable, recognizing that imprisonment is not an appropriate means of promoting correction and rehabilitation. In determining whether to make a recommendation concerning the type of prison facility appropriate fo~ the defendant, the court shall consider any pertinent policy statements issued by the Sentencing Commission pursuant to 28 U.S.C. 994(a)(2).

(b) **Effect of finality of judgment.** Notwithstanding the fact that a sentence to imprisonment can subsequently be –

    (1) modified pursuant to the provisions of subsection (c);

    (2) corrected pursuant to the provisions of Rule 35 of the Federal Rules of Criminal Procedure and section 3742 [18 USCS § 3742]: or

    (3) appealed and modified, if outside the guideline range, pursuant to the provisions of section 3742 [18 USCS § 3742];

a judgment of conviction that includes such a sentence constitutes a final judgment for all other purposes.

(c) Modification of an imposed term of imprisonment. The court may not modify a term of imprisonment once it has been imposed except that –

    (1) in any case –

        (A) the court, upon motion of the Director of the Bureau of Prisons, or upon motion of the defendant after the defendant has fully exhausted all administrative rights to appeal a failure of the Bureau of Prisons to bring a motion on the defendant's behalf or the lapse of 30 days from the receipt of such a request by the warden of the defendant's facility, whichever is earlier, may reduce the term of imprisonment (and may impose a term of probation or supervised release with or without conditions that does not exceed the unserved portion of the original term of imprisonment), after considering the factors set forth in section 3553(a)[18 USCS§3553(a)] to the extent that they are applicable, if it finds that –

            (i) extraordinary and compelling reasons warrant such a reduction; or

            (ii) the defendant is at least 70 years of age, has served at least 30 years in prison, pursuant to a sentence imposed under section 3559(c)[18 USCS § 3959 (c)], for the offense or offenses for which the defendant is currently imprisoned, and a determination has been made by the Director of the Bureau of Prisons that the defendant is not a danger to the safety of any other person or the community, as provided under section 3142(g)[18'USCS §3142];

    and that such a reduction is consistent with applicable policy statements issued by the Sentencing Commission; and (B) the court may modify an imposed term of imprisonment to the extent otherwise expressly permitted by statute or by Rule 35 of the Federal Rules of Criminal Procedure; and

(2) in the case of a defendant who has been sentenced to a term of imprisonment based on a sentencing range that has subsequently been lowered by the Sentencing Commission pursuant to 28 U.S.C.994(o), upon motion of the defendant or the Director of the Bureau of Prisons, or on its own motion, the court may reduce the term of imprisonment, after considering the factors set forth in section 3553(a) [18 USCS §3553(a)] to the extent that they are applicable, if such a reduction is consistent with applicable policy statements issued by the Sentencing Commission.

(d) Notification requirements

(1) Terminal illness defined. In this subsection, the term "terminal illness" means a disease or condition with an end-life trajectory.

(2) Notification. The Bureau of Prisons shall, subject to any applicable confidentiality requirements –

   (A) in the case of a defendant diagnosed with a terminal illness –

   (i) not later than 72 hours after the diagnosis notify the defendant's attorney, partner, and family members of the defendant's condition and inform the defendant's attorney, partner, and family members that they may prepare and submit on the defendant's behalf a request for a sentence reduction pursuant to subsection (c)(l)(A);

   (ii) not later than 7 days after the diagnosis, provide the defendant's partner and family members (including extended family) with an opportunity to visit the defendant in person;

   (iii) upon request from the defendant or his attorney, partner, or a family member, ensure that Bureau of Prisons employees assist the defendant in the preparation, drafting, and submission of a 'request for a sentence reduction pursuant to subsection (c)(l)(A); and

   (iv) not later than 14 days of receipt of a request for a sentence reduction submitted on the defendant's behalf by the defendant or the defendant's attorney, partner, or family member, process the request;

   (B) in the case of a defendant who is physically or mentally unable to submit a request for a sentence reduction pursuant to subsection (c)(l)(A) –

   (i) inform the defendant's attorney, partner, and family members that they may prepare and submit on the defendant's behalf a request for a sentence reduction pursuant to subsection (c)(l)(A);

   (ii) accept and process a request for a sentence reduction that has been prepared and submitted on the defendant's behalf by the defendant's attorney, partner, or family member under clause (i); and

   (iii) upon request from the defendant or his attorney, partner, or family member, ensure that Bureau of Prisons employees assist the defendant in the preparation, drafting, and submission of a request for a sentence reduction pursuant to subsection (c)(I)(A); and

(C) ensure that all Bureau of Prisons facilities regularly and visibly post, including in prisoner handbooks, staff training materials, and facility law libraries and medical and hospice facilities, and make available to prisoners upon demand, notice of –

   (i) a defendant's ability to request a sentence reduction pursuant to subsection (c)(I)(A);

   (ii) the procedures and timelines for initiating and resolving requests described in clause (i); and

   (iii) the right to appeal a denial of a request described in clause (i) after all administrative rights to appeal within the Bureau of Prisons have been exhausted.

(3) Annual report. Not later than I year after the date of enactment of this subsection, and once every year thereafter, the Director of the Bureau of Prisons shall submit to the Committee on the Judiciary of the Senate and the Committee on the Judiciary of the House of Representatives a report on requests pursuant to subsection (c)(I)(A), which shall include a description of, for the previous year –

   (A) the number of prisoners granted and denied sentence reductions, categorized by the criteria relied on as grounds for a reduction in sentence;

   (B) the number of requests initiated by or on behalf of prisoners, categorized by the criteria relied on a grounds for a reduction in sentence;

   (C) the number of requests that Bureau of Prisons employees assisted prisoners in drafting, preparing, or submitting, categorized by the criteria relied on as grounds for a reduction in sentence, and the final decision made in each request;

   (D) the number of requests that attorneys, partners, or family members submitted on a defendant's behalf, categorized by the criteria relied on as grounds for a reduction in sentence, and the final decision made in each request;

   (E) the number of requests approved by the Director of the Bureau of Prisons, categorized by the criteria relied on as grounds for a reduction in sentence;

   (F) the number of requests denied by the Director of the Bureau of Prisons and the reasons given for each denial, categorized by the criteria relied on as grounds for a reduction in sentence;

   (G) (G) for each request, the time elapsed between the date the request was received by the warden and the final decision, categorized by the criteria relied on as grounds for a reduction in sentence.

   (H) for each request, the number of prisoners who died while their request was pending and, for each, the amount of time that had elapsed between the date the request was received by the Bureau of Prisons, categorized by the criteria relied on as grounds for a reduction in sentence;

   (I) the number of Bureau of Prisons notifications to attorneys, partners, and family members of their right to visit a terminally ill defendant as required under paragraph (2)(A)(ii) and, for each, whether a visit occurred and how much time elapsed between the notification and the visit;

(J)   the number of visits to terminally ill prisoners that were denied by the Bureau of Prisons due to security or other concerns, and the reasons given for each denial: and

(K)   the number of motions filed by defendants with the court after all administrative rights to appeal a denial of a sentence reduction had been exhausted, the outcome of motion, and the time that had elapsed between the date the request was first received by the Bureau of Prisons and the date the defendant filed the motion with the court.

(e) **Inclusion of an order to limit criminal association of organized crime and drug offenders**. The court, in imposing a sentence to a term of imprisonment upon a defendant convicted of a felony set forth in chapter 95 [18 USCS §§ 1951 et seq.] (racketeering) or 96 [18 USCS §§ 1961 et seq.] (racketeer influenced and corrupt organizations) of this title or in the Comprehensive Drug Abuse Prevention and Control Act of 1970 (21 U.S.C. 801 et seq.), or at any time thereafter upon motion by the Director of the Bureau of Prisons or a United States attorney, may include as a part of the sentence an order that requires that the defendant not associate or communicate with a specified person, other than his attorney, upon showing of probable cause to believe that association or communication with such person is for the purpose of enabling the defendant to control, manage, direct, finance, or otherwise participate in an illegal enterprise.

28 D.S.C. § 994
DUTIES OF THE COMMISSION

(a) The Commission, by affirmative vote of at least four members of the Commission, and pursuant to its rules and regulations and consistent with all pertinent provisions of any Federal statute shall promulgate and distribute to all Courts of the United States and to the United States Probation System –

    (1) guidelines, as described in this section, for use of a Sentencing Court in determining the sentence to be imposed in a criminal case, including –

        (A) a determination whether to impose a sentence to probation, a fine, or a term of imprisonment;

        (B) a determination as to the appropriate amount of a fine or the appropriate length of a term of probation or a term of imprisonment;

        (C) a determination whether a sentence to a term of imprisonment should include a requirement that the defendant be placed on a term of supervised release after imprisonment, and, if so, the appropriate length of such a term;

        (D) a determination whether multiple sentences to terms of imprisonment should be ordered to run concurrently or consecutively; and

        (E) a determination under paragraphs (6) and (11) of Section 3563(b) of title 18;

    (2) general policy statements regarding application of the guidelines or any other aspect of sentencing or sentence implementation that in the view of the Commission would further the purpose set forth in Section 3553(a)(2) of title 18, United States Code, including the appropriate use of –

        (A) The sanctions set forth in Section 3554, 3555, and 3556 of title 18;

        (B) the conditions of probation and supervised release set forth in Section 3563(b) and 3583(d) of title 18;

        (C) the sentence modification provisions set forth in Section 3563(c), 3564, 3573, and 3582(c) of title 18;

        (D) the fine imposition provision set forth in Section 3572 of title 18;

        (E) the authority granted under rule 11(e)(2) of the Federal Rules of Criminal Procedure to accept or reject a plea agreement entered into pursuant to rule 11(e)(1); and

        (F) the temporary release provision set forth in Section 3622 of title 18, and the pre-release custody provision set forth in Section 3624(c) of title 18; and

    (3) guidelines or general policy statements regarding the appropriate use of the provisions for revocation of probation set forth in Section 3565 of title 18, and the provisions for modification of the term or conditions of supervised release and revocation of supervised release set forth in Section 3583(e) of title 18.

(b)

    (1) The Commission, in the guidelines promulgated pursuant to Subsection (a)(l), shall, for each category of offense involving each cats gory of defendant, establish a sentencing range that is consistent with all pertinent provisions of title 18, United States Code.

    (2) If a sentence specified by the guidelines includes a term of imprisonment, the maximum of the range established for such a term shall not exceed the minimum of that range by more than the greater of 25 percent or 6 months, except that, if the minimum term of the range is 30 years or more, the maximum may be life imprisonment.

(c) The Commission, in establishing categories of offenses for use in the guidelines and policy statements governing the imposition of sentences of probation, a fine, or imprisonment, governing the imposition of other authorized sanctions, governing the size of a fine or the length of a term of probation, imprisonment, or supervised release, and governing the conditions of probation, supervised release, or imprisonment, shall consider whether the following matters, among others, have any relevance to the nature, extent, place of service, or other incidents [incidence] of an appropriate sentence, and shall take them into account only to the extent that they do have relevance –

    (1) the grade of the offense;

    (2) the circumstances under which the offense was committed which mitigate or aggravate the seriousness of the offense;

    (3) the nature and degree of the harm caused by the offense, including whether it involved property, irreplaceable property, a person, a number of persons, or a breach of public trust;

    (4) the community view of the gravity of the offense;

    (5) the public concern generated by the offense;

    (6) the deterrent effect a particular sentence may have on the commission of the offense by others; and

    (7) the current incidence of the offense in the community and in the Nation as a whole.

(d) The Commission in establishing categories of defendants for use in the guidelines and policy statements governing the imposition of sentences of probation, a fine, or imprisonment, governing the imposition of other authorized sanctions, governing the size of a fine or the length of a term of probation, imprisonment, or supervised release, and governing the conditions of probation, supervised release, or imprisonment, shall consider whether the following matters, among others, with respect to a defendant, have any relevance to the nature, extent, place of service, or other incidents [incidence] of an appropriate sentence, and shall take them into account only to the extent that they do have relevance –

    (1) age;

    (2) education;

    (3) vocational skills;

    (4) mental and emotional condition to the extent that such condition mitigates the defendant's culpability or to the extent that such condition is otherwise plainly relevant;

(5) physical condition, including drug dependence;

(6) previous employment record;

(7) family ties and responsibilities;

(8) community ties;

(9) role in the offense;

(10) criminal history; and

(11) degree of dependence upon criminal activity for a livelihood.

The Commission shall assure that the guidelines and policy statements are entirely neutral as to the race, sex, national origin, creed, and socioeconomic status of offenders.

(e) The Commission shall assure that the guidelines and policy statements, in recommending a term of imprisonment or length of a term of imprisonment, reflect the general inappropriateness of considering the education, vocational skills, employment record, family ties and responsibilities, and community ties of the defendant.

(f) The Commission, in promulgating guidelines pursuant to subsection (a)(l), shall promote the purposes set forth in section 99l(b)(1) [28 U.S.C.S. §99l(b)(l)J, with particular attention to the requirements of subsection 99l(b)(1)(B) for providing certainty and fairness in sentencing and reducing unwarranted sentence disparities.

(g) The Commission, in promulgating guidelines pursuant to subsection (a)(l) to meet the purposes of sentencing as set forth in section 3553(a)(2) of title 18, United States Code, shall take into account the nature and capacity of the penal, correctional, and other facilities and services available, and shall make recommendations concerning any change or expansion in the nature or capacity of such facilities and services that might become necessary as a result of the guidelines promulgated pursuant to the provisions of this chapter [28 U.S.C.S. §§ 991 et. Seq.]. The sentencing guidelines prescribed under this chapter [28 U.S.C.S. §§ 991 et. Seq.] shall be formulated to minimize the likelihood that the Federal prison population will exceed the capacity of the Federal prisons, as determined by the Commission.

(h) The Commission shall assure that the guideline9 specify a sentence to a term of imprisonment at or near the maximum term authorized for categories of defendants in which the defendant is eighteen years old or older and –

(1) has been convicted of a felony that is –

(A) a crime of violence; or

(B) on offense described in Section 401 of the Controlled Substance Act (21 U.S.C. 841), Sections 1002(a), 1005, and 1009 of the Controlled Substance Import and Export Act (21 U.S.C. 952(a), 955, and 959), and chapter 705 of title 46 [46 U.S.C.S. §§ 70501 et. Seq.]; and

(2) has previously been convicted of two or more prior felonies, each of which is –

(A) a crime of violence; or

    (B) an offense described in Section 401 of the Controlled Substance Act (21 D.S.C. 841), Sections 1002(a), 1005, and 1009 of the Controlled Substance Import and Export Act (21 D.S.C. 952(a), 955, and 959), and chapter 705 of title 46 [46 U.S.C.S. §§ 70501 et. Seq.].

(i) The Commission shall assure that the guidelines specify a sentence to a substantial term of imprisonment for categories of defendants in which the defendant –

    (1) has a history of two or more prior Federal, State, or local felony convictions for offenses committed on different occasions;

    (2) committed the offense as part of a pattern of criminal conduct from which the defendant derived a substantial portion of the defendant's income;

    (3) committed the offense in furtherance of a conspiracy with three or more persons engaging in a pattern of racketeering activity in which the defendant participated in a managerial or supervisory capacity;

    (4) committed a crime of violence that constitutes a felony while on release pending trial, sentence, or appeal from a Federal, State, or local felony for which he was ultimately convicted; or

    (5) committed a felony that is set forth in Section 401 or 1010 of the Comprehensive Drug Abuse Prevention and Control Act of 1970 (21 D.S.C. 841 and 960), and that involved trafficking in a substantial quality of a controlled substance.

(j) The Commission shall insure that the guidelines reflect the general appropriateness of imposing a sentence other than imprisonment in cases in which the defendant is a first offender who has not been convicted of a crime of violence or an otherwise serious offense, and the general appropriateness of imposing a term of imprisonment on a person convicted of a crime of violence that results in serious bodily injury.

(k) The commission shall insure that the guidelines reflect the inappropriateness of imposing a sentence to a term of imprisonment for the purpose of rehabilitating the defendant or providing the defendant with needed education or vocational training, medical care, or other correctional treatment.

(l) The Commission shall insure that guidelines promulgated pursuant to Subsection (a)(l) reflect –

    (1) The appropriateness of imposing an incremental penalty for each offense in a case in which a defendant is convicted of –

        (A) Multiple offenses committed in the same course of conduct that result in the exercise of ancillary jurisdiction over one or more of the offenses; and

        (B) Multiple offenses committed at different times, including those cases in which the subsequent offense is a violation of Section 3147 [28 U.S.C.S. § 3147] (penalty for failure to appear) or is committed while the person is released pursuant to the provisions of Section 3147 [28 U.S.C.S. § 3147J (penalty for an offense committed while on release) of title 18; and

    (2) the general inappropriateness of imposing consecutive terms of imprisonment for an offense of conspiring to commit an offense or soliciting commission of an offense and for an offense that was the sole object of the conspiracy or solicitation.

(m) The Commission shall insure that the guidelines reflect the fact that, in many cases, current sentences do not accurately reflect the seriousness of the offense. This will require that, as a starting point in its development of the initial sets of guidelines for particular categories of cases, the Commission ascertain the average sentences imposed in such categories of cases prior to the creation of the Commission, and in cases involving sentences to terms of imprisonment, the length of such terms actually served. The Commission shall not be bound by such average sentences and shall independently develop a sentencing range that is consistent with the purpose of sentencing described in Section 3553(a)(2) of title 18, United States Code.

(n) The Commission shall assure that the guidelines reflect the general appropriateness of imposing a lower sentence than would otherwise be imposed, including a sentence that is lower than that established by statute as a minimum sentence, to take into account a defendant's substantial assistance in the investigation or prosecution of another person who has committed an offense.

(o) The Commission periodically shall review and revise, in consideration of comments and data coming to its attention, the guidelines promulgated pursuant to the provisions of this section. In fulfilling its duties and in exercising its powers, the Commission shall consult with authorities on, and individuals and institutional representatives of, various aspects of the Federal criminal justice system, the United States Probation System, the Bureau of Prisons, the Judicial Conference of the United States, the Criminal Division of the United States Department of Justice, and a representative of the Federal Public Defenders shall submit to the Commission any observations, comments, or questions pertinent to the work of the Commission whenever they believe such communication would be useful, and shall, at least annually, submit to the Commission a written report commenting on the operation of the Commission's guidelines suggesting changes in the guidelines that appear to be warranted, and otherwise assessing the Commission's work.

(p) The Commission, at or after the beginning of a regular session of Congress, but not later than the first day of May, may promulgate under subsection (a) of this section and submit to Congress amendments to the guidelines and modifications to previously submitted amendments that have not taken effect, including modifications to the effective dates of such amendments. Such an amendment or modification shall be accompanied by a statement of the reasons therefor and shall take effect on a date specified by the Commission, which shall be no earlier than 180 days after being so submitted and no later than the first day of November of the calendar year in which the amendment or modification is submitted, except to the extent that the effective date is revised or the amendment is otherwise modified or disapproved by Act of Congress.

(q) The Commission and the Bureau of Prisons shall submit to Congress an analysis and recommendations concerning maximum utilization of resources to deal effectively with the Federal prison population. Such report shall be based upon consideration of a variety of alternatives, including –

(1) modernization of existing facilities;

(2) inmate classification and periodic review of such classification for use in placing inmates in the least restrictive facility necessary to ensure adequate security; and

(3) use of existing Federal facilities, such as those currently within military jurisdiction.

(r) The Commission, not later than two years after the initial set of sentencing guidelines promulgated under Subsection (a) goes into effect, and thereafter whenever it finds it advisable, shall recommend to the Congress that it raise or lower the grades, or otherwise modify the maximum penalties, of those offenses for which such an adjustment appears appropriate.

(s) The Commission shall give due consideration to any petition filed by a defendant requesting modification of the guidelines utilized in the sentencing of such defendant, on the basis of changed circumstances unrelated to the defendant, including changes in –

(1) the community view of the gravity of the offense;

(2) the public concern generated by the offense; and

(3) the deterrent effect particular sentences may have on the Commission of the offense by others.

(t) The Commission, in promulgating general policy statements regarding the sentencing modification provision in Section 3582(c)(1)(A) of title 18, shall describe what should be considered extraordinary and compelling reasons for sentence reduction, including the criteria to be applied and a list of specific examples. Rehabilitation of the Defendant alone shall not be considered an extraordinary and compelling reason.

(u) If the Commission reduces the term of imprisonment recommended in the guidelines applicable to a particular offense or category of offenses, it shall specify in what circumstances and by what amount the sentences of prisoners serving terms of imprisonment for the offense may be reduced.

(v) The Commission shall ensure that the general policy statements promulgated pursuant to Subsection (a)(2) include a policy limiting consecutive terms of imprisonment for an offense involving a violation of a general prohibition and for an offense involving a violation of a specific prohibition encompassed within the general prohibition.

(w)

(1) The Chief Judge of each district court shall ensure that, within 30 days following entry of judgment in every criminal case. The sentencing court submits to the Commission, in a format approved and required by the Commission, a written report of the sentence, the offense for which it is imposed, the age, race, sex of the offender, and information regarding factors made relevant by the guidelines. The report shall also include –

(A) the judgment and commitment order;

(B) the written statement of reasons for the sentence imposed (which shall include the reason for any departure from the otherwise applicable guideline range and which shall be stated on the written statement of reasons form issued by the Judicial Conference and approved by the United States Sentencing Commission);

(C) any plea agreement

(D) the indictment or other charging document;

(E) the presentence report; and

(F) any other information as the Commission finds appropriate. The information referred to in subparagraphs (A) through (F) shall be submitted by the Sentencing Court in a format approved and required by the Commission.

(2) The commission shall, upon request, make available to the House and Senate Committees and the Judiciary, the written reports and all underlying records accompanying those reports described in this section, as well as other records received from the courts.

(3) The Commission shall submit to Congress at least annually an analysis of these documents, any recommendations for legislation that the Commission concludes is warranted by that analysis, and an accounting of those districts that the Commission believes have not submitted the appropriate information and documents required by this section.

(4) The Commission shall make available to the Attorney General, upon request, such data files as the Commission itself may assemble or maintain in electronic form as a result of the information submitted under paragraph (1). Such data files shall be made available in electronic form and shall include all data fields requested, including the identity of the sentencing judge.

(x) The provisions of section 553 of title 5, relating to publication in the Federal Register and public hearing procedure, shall apply to the promulgation of guidelines pursuant to this section.

(y) The Commission, in promulgating guidelines pursuant to Subsection (a) (I), may include, as a component of a fine, the expected cost of the Government of any imprisonment, supervised release, or probation sentence that is ordered.

28 U.S.C. § 2244
FINALITY OF DETERMINATION

(a) No circuit or district judge shall be required to entertain an application for a writ of habeas corpus to inquire into the detention of a person pursuant to a judgment of a court of the United States if it appears that the legality of such detention has been determined by a judge or court of the United States on a prior application for a writ of habeas corpus, except as provided in section 2255 [28 USCS § 2255].

(b)

    (1) A claim presented in a second or successive habeas corpus application under section 2254 [28 USCS § 2254] that was presented in a prior application shall be dismissed.

    (2) A claim presented in a second or successive habeas corpus application under section 2254 [28 USCS § 2254] that was not presented in a prior application shall be dismissed unless –

        (A) the applicant shows that the claim relies on a new rule of constitutional law, made retroactive to cases on collateral review by the Supreme Court, that was previously unavailable; or

        (B)

            (i) the factual predicate for the claim could not have been discovered previously through the exercise of due diligence; and

            (ii) the facts underlying the claim, if proven and viewed in light of the evidence as a whole, would be sufficient to establish by clear and convincing evidence that, but for constitutional error, no reasonable factfinder would have found the applicant guilty of the underlying offense.

    (3)

        (A) Before a second or successive application permitted by this section is filed in the district court, the applicant shall move in the appropriate court of appeals for an order authorizing the district court to consider the application.

        (B) A motion in the court of appeals for an order authorizing the district court to consider a second or successive application shall be determined by a three-judge panel of the court of appeals.

        (C) The court of appeals may authorize the filing of a second or successive application only if it determines that the application makes prima facie showing that the application satisfies the requirements of this subsection.

        (D) The court of appeals shall grant or deny the authorization to file a second or successive application not later than 30 days after the filing of the motion.

        (E) The grant or denial of an authorization by a court of appeals to file a second or successive application shall not be appealable and shall not be the subject of a petition for rehearing or for a writ of certiorari.

    (4) A district court shall dismiss any claim presented in a second or successive application that the court of appeals has authorized to be filed unless the applicant shows that the claim satisfies the requirements of this section.

(c) In a habeas corpus proceeding brought in behalf of a person in custody pursuant to the judgment of a State court, a prior judgment of the Supreme Court of the United States on an appeal or review by a writ of certiorari at the instance of the prisoner of the decision of such State court, shall be conclusive as to all issues of fact or law with respect to an asserted denial of a Federal right which constitutes ground for discharge in a habeas corpus proceeding, actually adjudicated by the Supreme Court therein, unless the applicant for the writ of habeas corpus shall plead and the court shall find the existence of a material and controlling fact which did not appear in the record of the proceeding in the Supreme Court and the court shall further find that the applicant for the writ of habeas corpus could not have caused such fact to appear in such record by exercise of reasonable diligence.

(d)

(1) A 1-year period of limitation shall apply to an application for a writ of habeas corpus by a person in custody pursuant to the judgment of a State court. The limitation period shall run from the latest of –

(A) the date on which the judgment became final by the conclusion of direct review or the expiration of the time for seeking such review;

(B) the date on which the impediment to filing an application created by State action in violation of the Constitution or laws of the United States is removed, if the applicant was prevented from filing by such State action;

(C) the date on which the constitutional right asserted was initially recognized by the Supreme Court, if the right has been newly recognized by the Supreme Court and made retroactively applicable to cases on collateral review; or

(D) the date on which the factual predicate of the claim or claims presented could have been discovered through the exercise of due diligence.

(2) The time during which a properly filed application for State post-conviction or other collateral review with respect to the pertinent judgment or claim is pending shall not be counted toward any period of limitation under this subsection.

28 U.S.C. § 2255
FEDERAL CUSTODY; REMEDIES ON MOTION ATTACKING SENTENCE

(a) A prisoner in custody under sentence of a court established by Act of Congress claiming the right to be released upon the ground that the sentence was imposed in violation of the Constitution or laws of the United States, or that the court was without jurisdiction to impose such sentence, or that the sentence was in excess of the maximum authorized by law, or is otherwise subject to collateral attack, may move the court which imposed the sentence to vacate, set aside or correct the sentence.

(b) Unless the motion and the files and records of the case conclusively show that the prisoner is entitled to no relief, the court shall cause notice thereof to be served upon the united States attorney, grant a prompt hearing thereon, determine the issues and make findings of the fact and conclusions of law with respect thereto. If the court finds that the judgment was rendered without jurisdiction, or that the sentence imposed was not authorized by law or otherwise open to collateral attack, or that there has been such a denial or infringement of the constitutional rights of the prisoner as to render the judgment vulnerable to collateral attack, the court shall vacate and set the judgment aside and shall discharge the prisoner or resentence him or grant a new trial or correct the sentence as may appear appropriate.

(c) A court may entertain and determine such motion without the production of the prisoner at the hearing.

(d) An appeal may be taken to the court of appeals from the order entered on the motion as from the final judgment on application for a writ of habeas corpus.

(e) An application for a writ of habeas corpus in behalf of a prisoner who is authorized to apply for relief by motion pursuant to this section, shall not be entertained if it appears that the applicant has failed to apply for relief, by motion, to the court which sentenced him, or that such court has denied him relief, unless it also appears that the remedy by motion is inadequate or ineffective to test the legality of his detention.

(f) A 1-year period of limitation shall apply to a motion under this section. The limitation period shall run from the latest of –

   (1) the date on which the judgment of conviction becomes final.

   (2) the date on which the impediment to making a motion created by governmental action in violation of the Constitution or the laws of the United States is removed, if the movant was prevented from making a motion by such governmental action;

   (3) the date on which the right asserted was initially recognized by the Supreme Court and made retroactively applicable to cases on collateral review: or

   (4) the date on which the facts supporting the claim or claims presented could have been discovered through the exercise of due diligence.

(g) Except as provided in section 408 of the Controlled Substances Act [21 USCS § 848], in all proceedings brought under this section, and any subsequent proceedings on review, the court may appoint counsel, except as provided by the rule promulgated by the Supreme Court pursuant to statutory authority. Appointment of counsel under this section shall be governed by section 3006A of title 18.

(h) A second or successive motion must be certified as provided in section 2244 [28 USCS § 2244] by a panel of the appropriate court of appeals to contain –

   (1) Newly discovered evidence that, if proven and viewed in light of the evidence as a whole, would be sufficient to establish by clear and convincing evidence that no reasonable factfinder would have found the movant guilty of the offense; or (2) a new rule of constitutional law, made retroactive to cases on collateral review by the Supreme Court, that was previously unavailable.

Rules Governing
Section 2255 Proceedings

Rule 1. Scope

These rules govern a motion filed in a United States district court under 28 U.S.C. § 2255 by:

(a) a person in custody under a judgment of that court who seeks a determination that:

    (1) the judgment violates the Constitution or laws of the United States;

    (2) the court lacked jurisdiction to enter the judgment;

    (3) the sentence exceeded the maximum allowed by law; or

    (4) the judgment or sentence is otherwise subject to collateral review; and

(b) a person in custody under a judgment of a state court or another federal court, and subject to future custody under a judgment of the district court, who seeks a determination that:

    (1) future custody under a judgment of the district court would violate the Constitution or laws of the United States;

    (2) the district court lacked jurisdiction to enter the judgment;

    (3) the district court's sentence exceeded the maximum allowed by law; or

    (4) the district court's judgment or sentence is otherwise subject to collateral review.

Rule 2. The Motion

(a) **Applying for relief**. The application must be in form of a motion to vacate, set aside, or correct the sentence.

(b) **Form**. The motion must:

    (1) specify all the grounds for relief available to the moving party;

    (2) state the facts supporting each ground;

    (3) state the relief requested;

    (4) be printed, typewritten, or legibly handwritten; and

    (5) be signed under penalty of perjury by the movant or by a person authorized to sign it for the movant.

(c) **Standard form**. The motion must substantially follow either the form appended to these rules or a form prescribed by a local district-court rule. The clerk must make forms available to moving parties without charge.

(d) **Separate motions for separate judgments**. A moving party who seeks relief from more than one judgment must file a separate motion covering each judgment.

Rule 3. Filing the Motion; Inmate Filing

(a) **Where to file; copies**. An original and two copies of the motion must be filed with the clerk.

(b) **Filing and service**. The clerk must file the motion and enter it on the criminal docket of the case in which the challenged judgment was entered. The clerk must then deliver or serve a copy of the motion on the United States attorney in that district, together with a notice of its filing.

(c) **Time to file**. The time for filing a motion is governed by 28 U.S.C. § 2255 para. 6.

(d) **Innate filing**. A paper filed by an inmate confined in an institution is timely if deposited in the institution's internal mailing system on or before the last day for filing. If an institution has a system designed for legal mail, the inmate must use that system to receive the benefit of this rule. Timely filing may be shown by a declaration in compliance with 28 U.S.C. § 1746 or by a notarized statement, either of which must set forth the date of deposit and state that first-class postage has been prepaid.

Rule 4. Preliminary Review

(a) **Referral to a judge**. The clerk must promptly forward the motion to the judge who conducted the trial and imposed sentence or, if the judge who imposed sentence was not the trial judge, to the judge who conducted the proceedings being challenged. If the appropriate judge is not available, the clerk must forward the motion to a judge under the court's assignment procedure.

(b) **Initial consideration by the judge**. The judge who receives the motion must promptly examine it. If it plainly appears from the motion, any attached exhibits, and the record of prior proceedings that the moving party is not entitled to relief, the judge must dismiss the motion and direct the clerk to notify the moving party. If the motion is not dismissed, the judge must order the United States attorney to file an answer, motion, or other response within a fixed time, or to take other action the judge may order.

Rule 5. The Answer and the Reply [Effective until, December 1, 2019]

(a) **When required**. The respondent is not required to answer the motion unless a judge so orders.

(b) **Contents**. The answer must address the allegations in the motion. In addition, it must state whether the moving party has used any other federal remedies, including any prior post-conviction motions under these rules or any previous rules, and whether the moving party received an evidentiary hearing.

(c) **Records of prior proceedings**. If the answer refers to briefs or transcripts of the prior proceedings that are not available in the court's records, the judge must order the government to furnish them within a reasonable time that will not unduly delay the proceedings.

(d) **Reply**. The moving party may file a reply to the respondent's answer or other pleading. The judge must set the time to file unless the time is already set by local rule.

Rule 6. Discovery

(a) **Leave of court required**. A judge may, for good cause, authorize a party to conduct discovery under the Federal Rules of Criminal Procedure or Civil Procedure, or in accordance with the practices and principles of law. If necessary, for effective discovery, the judge must appoint an attorney for a moving party who qualifies to have counsel appointed under 18 U.S.C. § 3006A.

(b) **Requesting discovery**. A party requesting discovery must provide reasons for the request. The request must also include any proposed interrogatories and requests for admission and must specify any requested documents.

(c) **Deposition expenses**. If the government is granted leave to take a deposition, the judge may require the government to pay the travel expenses, subsistence expenses, and fees of the moving party's attorney to attend the deposition.

Rule 7. Expanding the Record

(a) **In general**. If the motion is not dismissed, the judge may direct the parties to expand the record by submitting additional materials relating to the motion. The judge may require that these materials be authenticated.

(b) **Types of materials**. The materials that may be required include letters predating the filing of the motion, documents, exhibits, and answers under oath to written interrogatories propounded by the judge. Affidavits also may be submitted and considered as part of the record.

(c) **Review by the opposing party**. The judge must give the party against whom the additional materials are offered an opportunity to admit or deny their correctness.

Rule 8. Evidentiary Hearing

(a) **Determining whether to hold a hearing**. If the motion is not dismissed, the judge must review the answer, any transcripts and records of prior proceedings, and any materials submitted under Rule 7 to determine whether an evidentiary hearing is warranted.

(b) **Reference to a magistrate judge**. A judge may, under 28 U.S.C. § 636(b), refer the motion to a magistrate judge to conduct hearings and to file proposed findings of fact and recommendations for disposition. When they are filed, the clerk must promptly serve copies of the proposed findings and recommendations on all parties. Within 14 days after being served, a party may file objections as provided by local court rule. The judge must determine de novo any proposed finding or recommendations to which objection is made. 'The judge may accept, reject, or modify any proposed finding or recommendation.

(c) **Appointing counsel**. time of hearing. If an evidentiary hearing is warranted, the judge must appoint an attorney to represent a moving party who qualifies to have counsel appointed under 18 U .S.C. § 3006A. The judge must conduct the hearing as soon as practicable after giving the attorneys adequate time to investigate and prepare. These rules do not limit the appointment of counsel under § 3006A at any stage of the proceeding.

(d) **Producing a statement**. Federal Rule of Criminal Procedure 26.2(a)-(d) and (f) applies at a hearing under this rule. If a party does not comply with a Rule 26.2(a) order to produce a witness's statement, the court must not consider that witness's testimony.

Rule 9. Second or Successive Motions

Before presenting a second or successive motion, the moving party must obtain an order from the appropriate court of appeals authorizing the district court to consider the motion, as required by 28 U.S.C. § 2255, para. 8.

Rule 10. Powers of a Magistrate Judge

A magistrate judge may perform the duties of a district judge under these rules, as authorized by 28 U.S.C. § 636.

Rule 11. Certificate of Appealability; Time to Appeal

(a) **Certificate of appealability**. The district court must issue or deny a certificate of appealability when it enters a. final order adverse to the applicant. Before entering the final order, the court may direct the parties to submit arguments on whether a certificate should issue. If the court issues a certificate, the court must state the specific issue or issues that satisfy the showing required by 28 U.S.C. § 2253(c)(2). If the court denies a certificate, a party may not appeal the denial but may seek a certificate from the court of appeals under Federal Rule of Appellate Procedure 22. A motion to reconsider a denial does not extend the time to appeal.

(b) **Time to appeal**. Federal Rule of Appellate Procedure 4(a) governs the time to appeal an order entered under these rules. A timely notice of appeal must be filed even if the district court issues a certificate of appealability. These rules do not extend the time to appeal the original judgment of conviction.

Rule 12. Applicability of the Federal Rules of Civil Procedure and the Federal Rules of Criminal Procedure

The Federal Rules of Civil Procedure and the Federal Rules of Criminal Procedure, to the extent that they are not inconsistent with any statutory provisions or these rules, may be applied to a proceeding under these rules.

FEDERAL RULES OF
CIVIL PROCEDURE

Rule 59. New Trial; Altering or Amending a Judgment

(a) **In General**.

  (1) **Grounds for New Trial**. The court may, on motion, grant a new trial on all or some of the issues – and to any party – as follows:

   (A) after a jury trial, for any reason for which a new trial has heretofore been granted in an action at law in federal court; or

   (B) after a nonjury trial, for any reason for which a rehearing has heretofore been granted in a suit in equity in federal court.\

  (2) **Further Action After a Nonjury Trial**. After a nonjury trial, the court may, on motion for a new trial, open the judgment if one has been entered, take additional testimony, amend findings of fact and conclusions of law or make new ones, and direct the entry of a new judgment.

(b) **Time to File a Motion for a New Trial**. A motion for a new trial must be filed no later than 28 days after the entry of judgment.

(c) **Time to Serve Affidavits**. When a motion for a new trial is based on affidavits, they must be filed with the motion. The opposing party has 14 days after being served to file opposing affidavits. The court may permit reply affidavits.

(d) **New Trial on the Court's Initiative or for Reasons Not in the Motion**. No later than 28 days after the entry of judgment, the court, on its own, may order a new trial for any reason that would justify granting one on a party's motion. After giving the parties notice and an opportunity to be heard, the court may grant a timely motion for a new trial for a reason not stated in the motion. In either event, the court must specify the reasons in its order.

(e) **Motion to Alter or Amend a Judgment**. A motion to alter or amend a judgment must be filed no later than 28 days after the entry of the judgment.

FEDERAL RULES OF
CIVIL PROCEDURE

Rule 60. Relief from a Judgment or Order

(a) **Corrections Based on Clerical Mistakes: Oversights and Omissions**. The court may correct a clerical mistake or a mistake arising from oversight or omission whenever one is found in a judgment, order, or other part of the record. The court may do so on motion or on its own, with or without notice. But after an appeal has been docketed in the appellate court and while it is pending, such a mistake may be corrected only with the appellate court's leave.

(b) **Grounds for Relief from a Final Judgment, Order, or Proceeding**. On motion and just terms, the court may relieve a party or its legal representative from a final judgment, order, or proceeding for the following reasons:

  (1) mistake, inadvertence, surprise, or excusable neglect;

  (2) newly discovered evidence that, with reasonable diligence, could not have been discovered in time to move for a new trial under Rule 59(b);

  (3) fraud (whether previously called intrinsic or extrinsic), misrepresentation, or misconduct by an opposing party:

  (4) the judgment is void;

  (5) the judgment has been satisfied, released, or discharged; it is based on an earlier judgment that has been reversed or vacated; or applying it prospectively is no longer equitable; or

  (6) any other reason that justifies relief.

(c) **Timing and effect of the Motion**.

  (1) **Timing**. A motion under Rule 60(b) must be made within a reasonable time and for reason (1), (2), and (3) no more than a year after the entry of the judgment or order or the date of the proceeding.

  (2) **Effect on Finality**. The motion does not affect the judgment's finality or suspend its operation.

(d) **Other Powers to Grant Relief**. This rule does not limit a court's power to:

  (1) entertain an independent action to relieve a party from a judgment, order, or proceeding;

  (2) grant relief under 28 D.S.C. § 1655 to a defendant who was not personally notified of the action; or

  (3) set aside a judgment for fraud on the court.

(e) Bills and writs Abolished. The following are abolished; bills of review, bills in the nature of bills of review, and writs of *coram nobis*, *coram vobis*, and *audita querela*.

ABOUT THE AUTHOR

Kelly Patrick Riggs is best known as the author of *The Post-Conviction Relief Series*. He is a former prisoner who discovered his life's passion while serving a prison sentence for a crime he did not commit. Since his release he has pledged himself to serve the people who need him the most, the American prisoners who need something better out of life.

KELLY PATRICK RIGGS

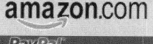

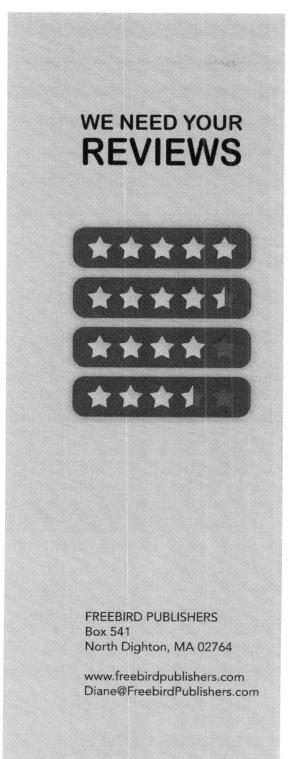

Thanks for your interest in
Freebird Publishers!

We value our customers and would love to hear from you! Reviews are an important part in bringing you quality publications. We love hearing from our readers-rather it's good or bad (though we strive for the best)!

If you could take the time to review/rate any publication you've purchased with Freebird Publishers we would appreciate it!

If your loved one uses Amazon, have them post your review on the books you've read. This will help us tremendously, in providing future publications that are even more useful to our readers and growing our business.

Amazon works off of a 5 star rating system. When having your loved one rate us be sure to give them your chosen star number as well as a written review. Though written reviews aren't required, we truly appreciate hearing from you.

⭐⭐⭐⭐⭐ **Everything a prisoner needs is available in this book.**
January 30, 201 June 7, 2018
Format: Paperback

A necessary reference book for anyone in prison today. This book has everything an inmate needs to keep in touch with the outside world on their own from inside their prison cell. Inmate Shopper's business directory provides complete contact information on hundreds of resources for inmate services and rates the companies listed too! The book has even more to offer, contains numerous sections that have everything from educational, criminal justice, reentry, LGBT, entertainment, sports schedules and more. The best thing is each issue has all new content and updates to keep the inmate informed on todays changes. We recommend everybody that knows anyone in prison to send them a copy, they will thank you.

* No purchase neccessary. Reviews are not required for drawing entry. Void where prohibited.
  Contest date runs July 1 - June 30, 2019.

Federal Reference Pocket Guides

Federal Rules of Evidence

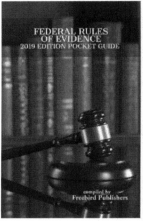

First adopted in 1975, the Federal Rules of Evidence codify the evidence law that applies in United States federal courts. In addition, many states in the United States have either adopted the Federal Rules of Evidence, with or without local variations, or have revised their own evidence rules or codes to at least partially follow the federal rules.

In general, the purpose of rules of evidence is to regulate the evidence that the jury may use to reach a verdict. Historically, the rules of evidence reflected a marked distrust of jurors. The Federal Rules of Evidence strive to eliminate this distrust and encourage admitting evidence in close cases. Even so, there are some rules that perpetuate the historical mistrust of jurors, expressly limiting the kind of evidence they may receive or the purpose for which they may consider it.

At the same time, the Rules center on a few basic ideas – relevance, unfair surprise, efficiency, reliability, and overall fairness of the adversary process. The Rules grant trial judges broad discretion to admit evidence in the face of competing arguments from the parties. This ensures that the jury has a broad spectrum of evidence before it, but not so much evidence that is repetitive, inflammatory, or unnecessarily confusing. The Rules define relevance broadly and relax the common-law prohibitions on witnesses' competence to testify. Hearsay standards are similarly relaxed, as are the standards for authenticating written documents. At the same time, the judge retains power to exclude evidence that has too great a danger for unfair prejudice to a party due to its inflammatory, repetitive, or confusing nature or its propensity to waste the court's time.

Federal Rules of Criminal Procedure

The Federal Rules of Criminal Procedure are the procedural rules that govern how federal criminal prosecutions are conducted in United States district courts and the general trial courts of the U.S. government. They are the companion to the Federal Rules of Civil Procedure. The admissibility and use of evidence in criminal proceedings (as well as civil) is governed by the separate Federal Rules of Evidence.

The rules are promulgated by the Supreme Court of the United States, pursuant to its statutory authority under the Rules Enabling Act The Supreme Court must transmit a copy of its rules to the United States Congress no later than May 1 of the year in which they are to go into effect, and the new rule can then become effective no earlier than December 1 of that year.

Congress retains the power to reject the Court's proposed rules or amendments, to modify them, or to enact rules or amendments itself. Congress has rarely rejected the Court's proposed amendments, though it has frequently passed its own.

The rules are initially drafted by an Advisory Committee of the Judicial Conference of the United States, which consists of appointed judges, U.S. Department of Justice representatives, practicing lawyers, and legal scholars. After public comment, the draft rules are submitted to the Standing Committee on Rules of Practice and Procedure, which in turn submits them to the Judicial Conference, which finally recommends them to the Supreme Court for approval. The explanatory notes of the drafting Advisory Committee are published with the final adopted rules and are frequently used as an authority on their interpretation.

Under the Sumners Courts Act, the U.S. Attorney General was given the responsibility of transmitting amendments of the rules to Congress, though this was amended in 1949 to give that duty to the Chief Justice. The turn-around period for the rules becoming effective was originally one full congressional session. This was amended in 1950 to impose the May 1 deadline, but with a 90-day delay in effectiveness. In 1988, authorization for the Rules was incorporated under the Rules Enabling Act, and codified at 28 U.S.C. §§ 2072, 2074.

Each Book
2019 Editions
Current Laws
Pocket Guides

Only $10.99each
plus $5 S/H with tracking
SOFTCOVER, 5" x 8", 58 pages

Only $10.99each
plus $5 S/H with tracking
SOFTCOVER, 5" x 8", 128 pages

NEW FULL COLOR CATALOG 80-pages filled with books, gifts and services.

CATALOG ONLY $4 - SHIPS BY FIRST CLASS MAIL

We have created four different versions of our new catalog A:Complete B:No Pen Pal Content C:No Sexy Photo Content D:No Pen Pal and Sexy Content. Available in full Color or B&W (please specify), please make sure you order the correct catalog based on your prison mail room regulations. We are not responsible for rejected or lost in the mail catalogs. Send SASE for payment by stamp options.
ADDITIONAL OPTION: add $4 for Shipping with Tracking

NO ORDER FORM NEEDED CLEARLY WRITE ON PAPER & SEND PAYMENT TO:
FREEBIRD PUBLISHERS Box 541, North Dighton, MA 02764
www.FreebirdPublishers.com Diane@FreebirdPublishers.com Text/Phone: 774-406-8682

Made in the USA
Columbia, SC
19 September 2024

42600133R00143